Advanced
Origami Animals

Marc Kirschenbaum

Fit to Print Publishing, Inc.
New York, NY

Advanced Origami Animals

Copyright © 2020
Fit To Print Publishing, Inc.

All rights reserved. No part of this publication may be reproduced, stored in a retrieval system or transmitted in any form or by any means, electronic, mechanical, photocopying, recording or otherwise, without the permission of the copyright holder.

ISBN 978-1-951146-11-5 (Paperback Edition)
ISBN 978-1-951146-12-2 (Hardcover Edition)

The diagrams in this book were produced with Macromedia's Freehand, and image processing was done with Adobe Photoshop. The Backtalk family of typefaces was used for the body text and the cover and headers use Akzidenz Grotesk. Ellen Cohen assisted with the cover design and provided valuable artistic assistance.

Contents

Introduction	5
Symbols and Terminology	6
Bunny	10
Cutie Cat	17
Elephant	26
En Route to the Observatory	36
Giant Panda	46
Giraffe	58
Koala	67
Peacock	73
Penguin	78
Raccoon	87
Reindeer	95
Skunk	107
Spectacled Bear	116
Swan	124
Toucan	127
Turtle	132

Introduction

Animals have long been a popular subject in origami. There is plenty of room to be expressive, and people relate well with art that has a personality to it. This collection of origami animals strives to facilitate more artistry by not holding back on the folding techniques employed. Simply put, many of the sequences found here are on the advanced end of the folding spectrum. There are plenty of challenges to be found for even the most seasoned origami aficionado.

The extra folding complexity contained here often serves to simplify how neatly the models collapse and offer the opportunity to realize the forms in ways that would be unlikely with only simpler folds. Ultimately, elegance is achieved through intricacy. Much of the extra folds are concealed with decidedly streamlined forms. Attention to proportions and contours takes precedence over anatomical accuracy and excessive details.

For all the serious folding going on, most of the models belie their complexity with a whimsical appearance. A few of them are loosely based on playful icons of popular culture. Even the most casual moviegoer will know the giant gorilla depicted in *En Route to the Observatory* and soft drink fans will recognize the *Spectacled Bear*. Devotees of Japanese merchandising will appreciate the *Cutie Cat*.

Not all the models have lengthy sets of directions. Their inclusion is warranted by key steps employing some unusual folds. The *Bunny* contains an unusual crimp fold and the *Swan* features a novel sink that gets stretched into position.

Given that the level of difficulty is roughly equal amongst this collection, the contents are ordered alphabetically. Some folders might find pieces like the *Koala*, *Peacock* and *Toucan* to be a bit more accessible than the other pieces, so they can serve as a good starting point. Information on the materials and methods used can be found at *sakuraorigami.com* within the *articles* menu. All these pieces follow the one square no cuts philosophy, ensuring for some interesting and sometimes challenging folding sequences. Many hours of folding fun are to be found here. Enjoy!

Symbols and Terminology

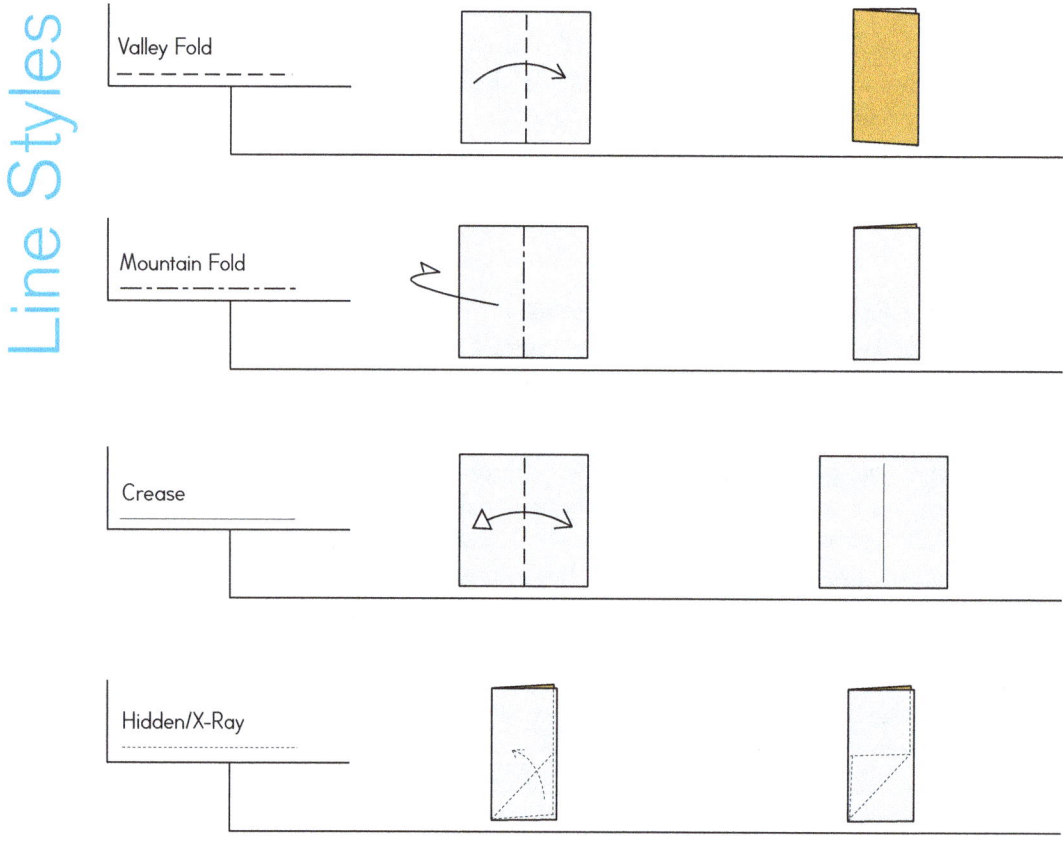

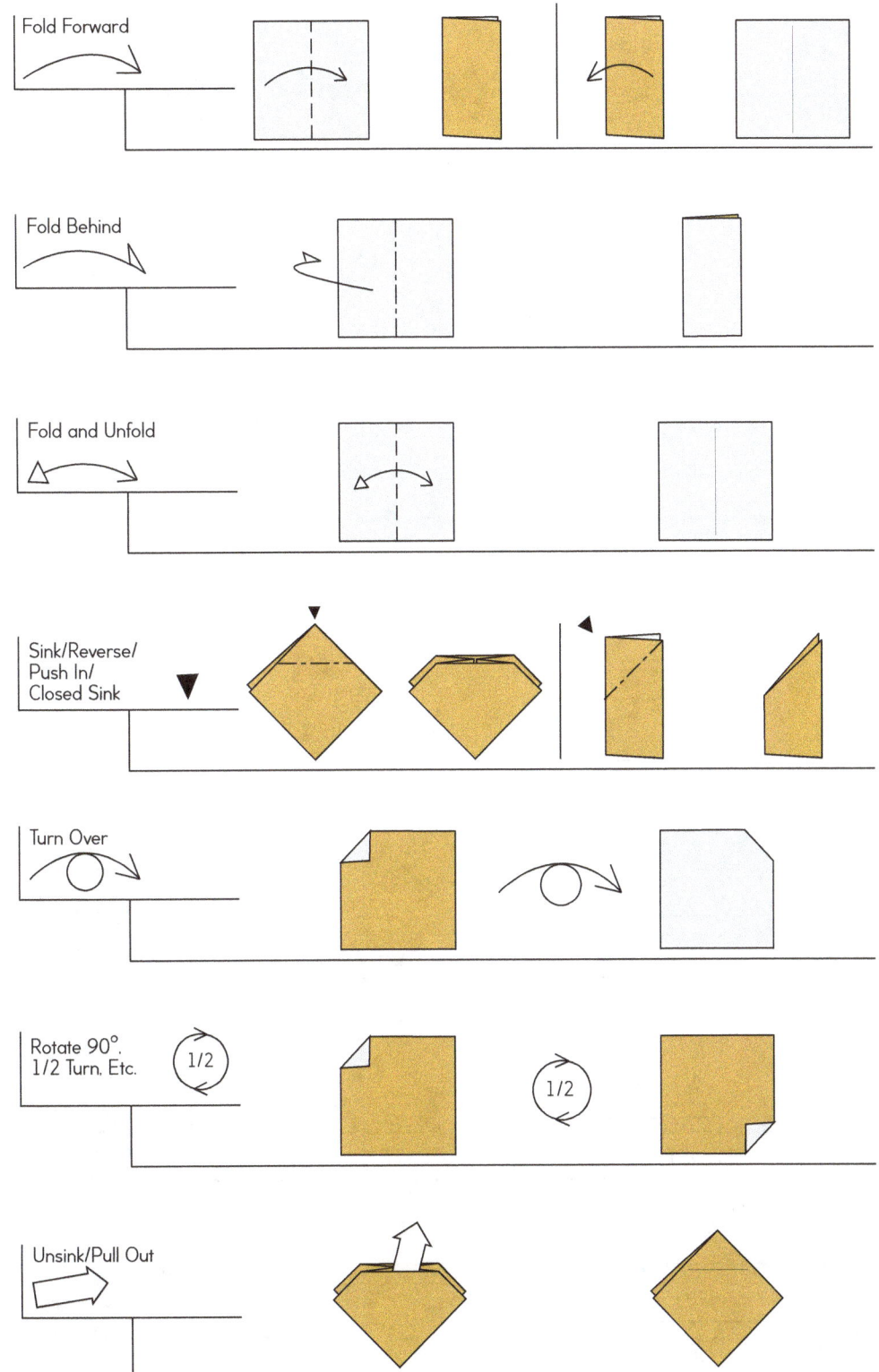

Maneuvers

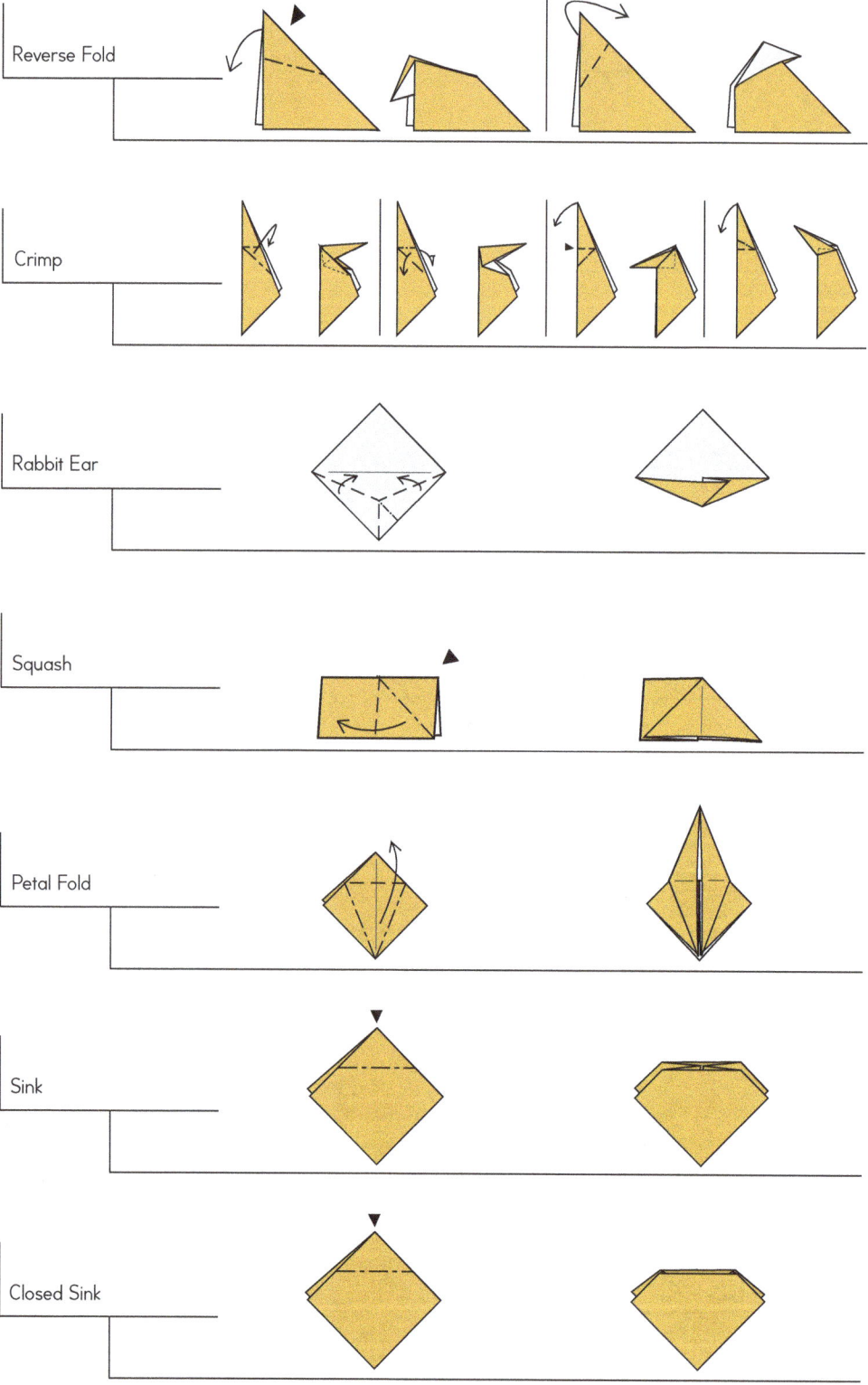

Sink Triangularly

Pleat

Swivel

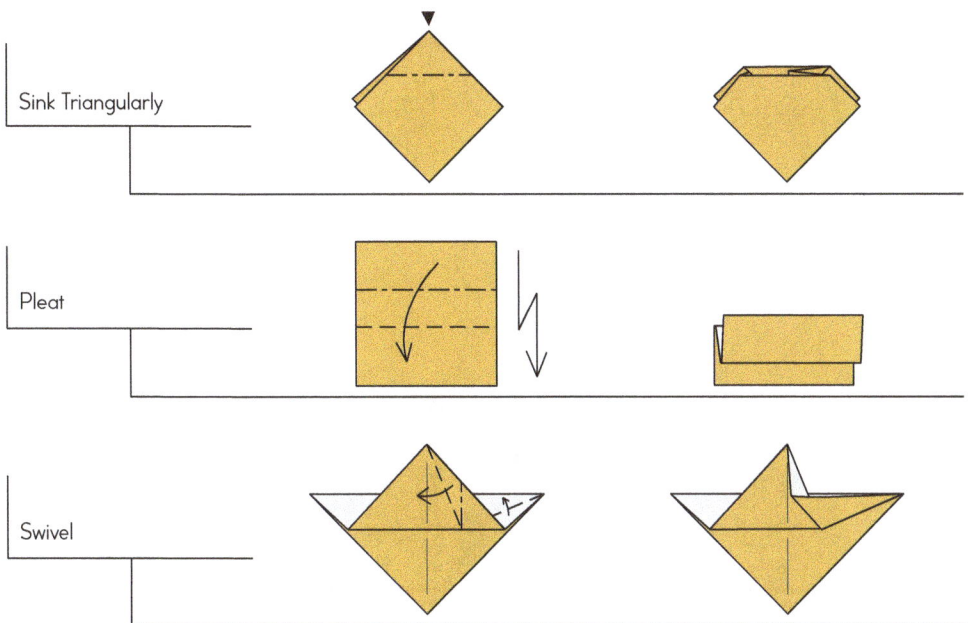

Bunny

Maxim Magazine needed some rabbits folded to add a visual for their article on the growth of money. As it turned out, they needed them folded from hundred-dollar bills in a fornicating pose. This *Bunny* model was slightly modified by puffing it out a bit to allow for this suggestive stance. Accordingly, the bills were cut down into squares so it could be folded without additional changes (and later taped back together so they could resume their role as legal tender). Despite the sink fold and unusual crimps, this is one of the easier pieces to fold of this collection.

bunny

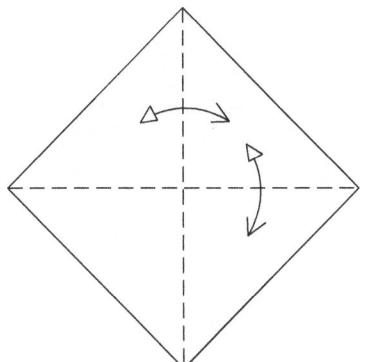

1. Precrease along both diagonals.

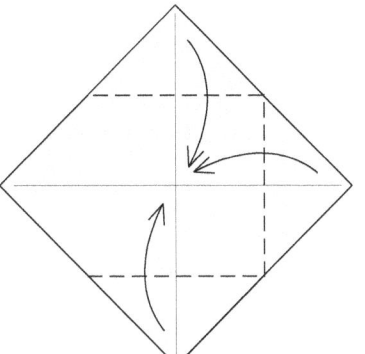

2. Valley fold three of the corners to the center.

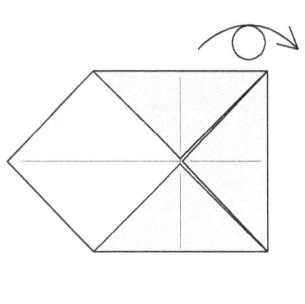

3. Turn over.

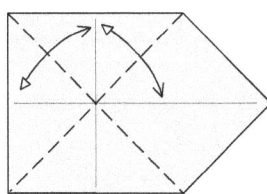

4. Precrease along the diagonals.

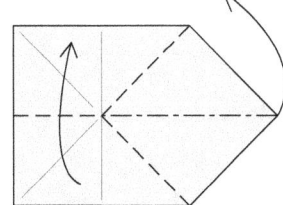

5. Fold in half while reverse folding.

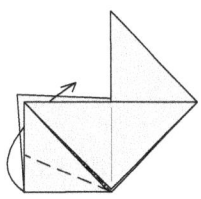

6. Crimp the corner into the model.

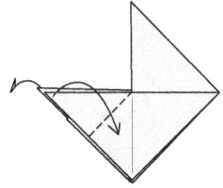

7. Valley fold the sides down, allowing squash folds to form.

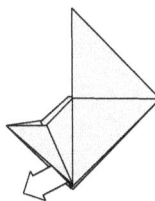

8. Pull out the original corner.

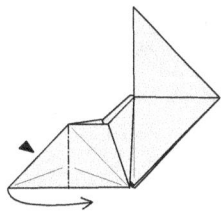

9. Reverse fold.

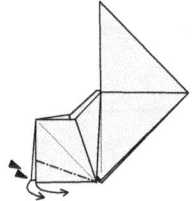

10. Reverse fold the two flaps.

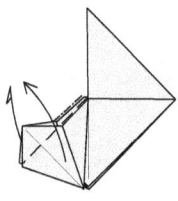

11. Swing the two flaps up.

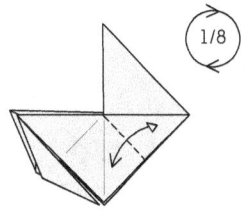

12. Precrease the top layer. Repeat behind, and rotate the model.

11

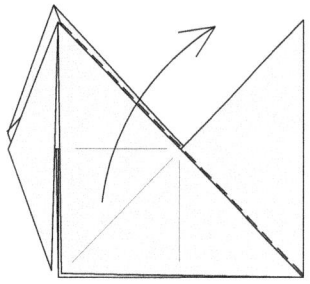

13. Swing up the top layer.

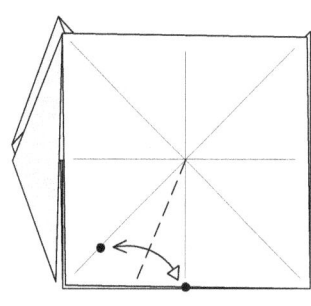

14. Precrease along the angle bisector.

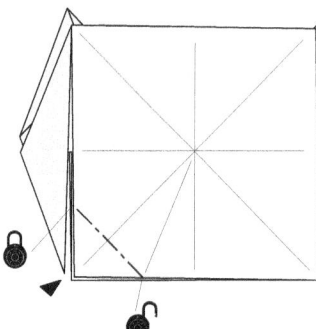

15. Sink the corner (open at the bottom, and closed at the side).

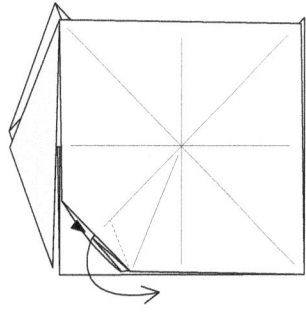

16. Reverse fold the hidden flap along the angle bisector.

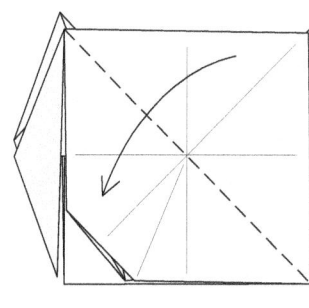

17. Valley fold the flap back down.

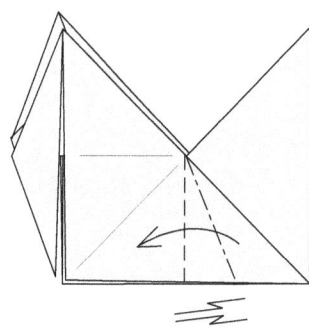

18. Crimp the right side downward.

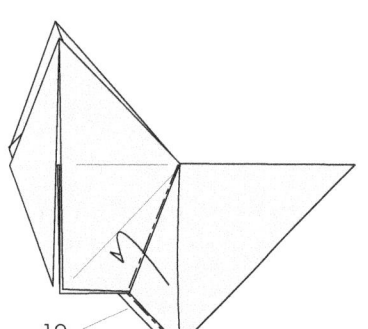

19. Wrap around a single layer. Repeat behind.

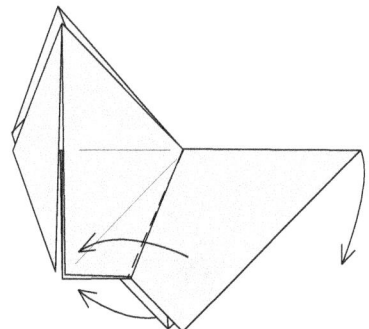

20. Pull the side flaps towards the left.

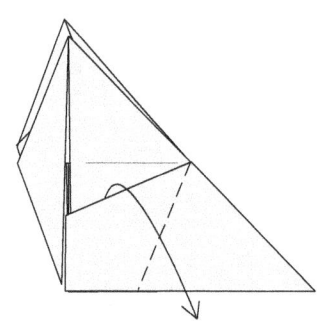

21. Lightly swing the top flap down.

bunny

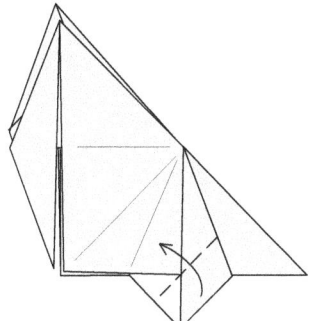

22. Valley fold up.

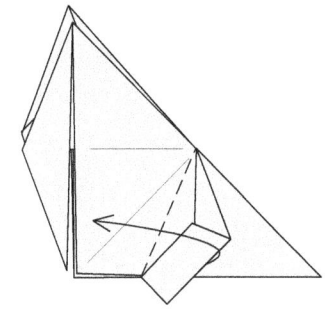

23. Swing the flap back over.

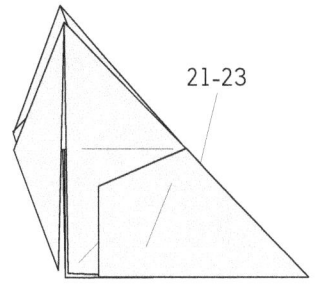

24. Repeat steps 21-23 behind.

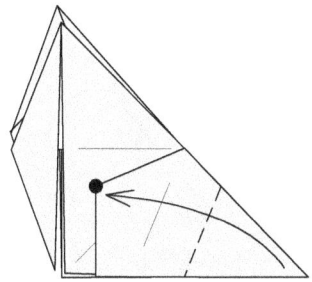

25. Valley fold over to the dotted corner.

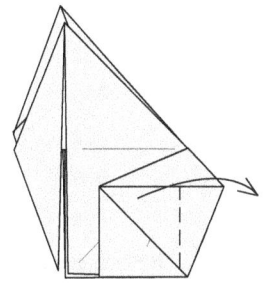

26. Valley fold over, noting the fold does not start at the bottom corner.

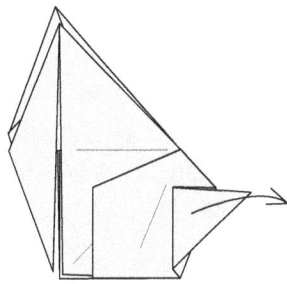

27. Unfold the pleat.

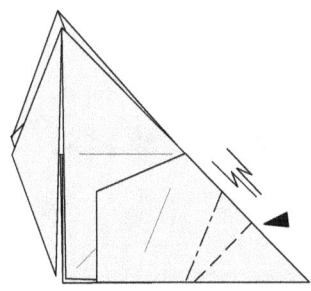

28. Crimp the flap along the existing creases.

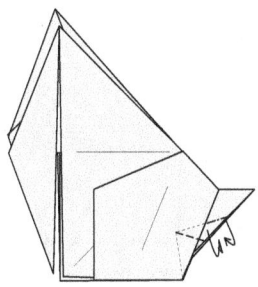

29. Swivel in the lower edges.

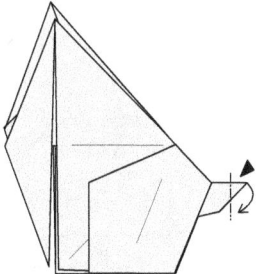

30. Reverse fold the tip of the flap.

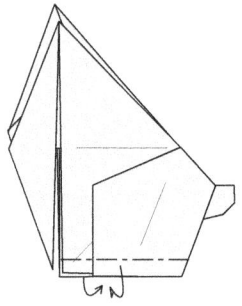

31. Mountain fold in the bottom edges as far as possible.

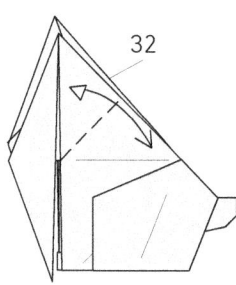

32. Precrease the top flap. Repeat behind.

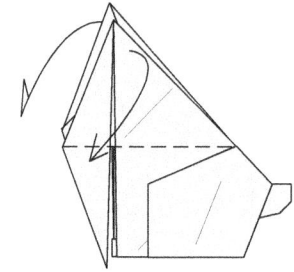

33. Swing the top flaps down.

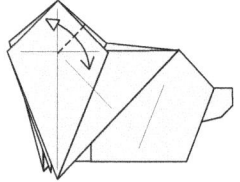

34. Precrease the top flap.

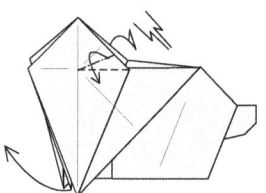

35. Crimp the top point, allowing the bottom flaps to swing outwards. The model will not lie flat.

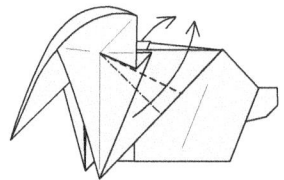

36. Pleat the side flaps upwards.

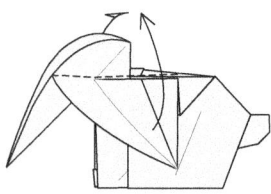

37. Swing the side flaps up to flatten.

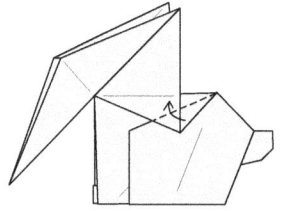

38. Valley fold along the angle bisector.

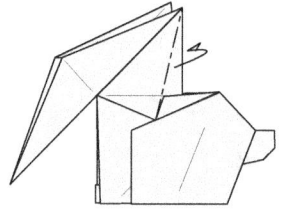

39. Mountain fold the side edge inwards, swiveling at the bottom.

bunny

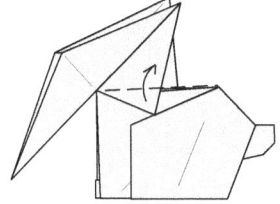

40. Valley fold the flap up.

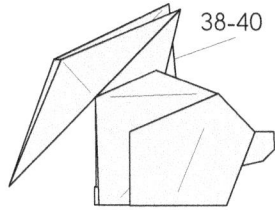

41. Repeat steps 38-40 behind.

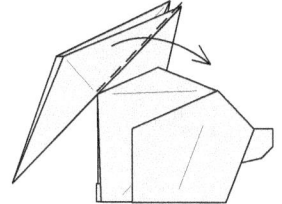

42. Swing down one flap.

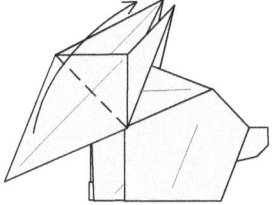

43. Valley fold the flap up.

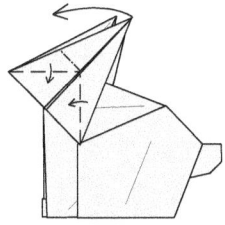

44. Rabbit ear the flap, aligning the folds with the edges underneath.

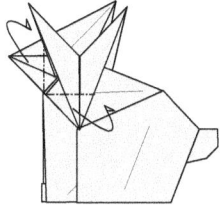

45. Mountain fold the side corners.

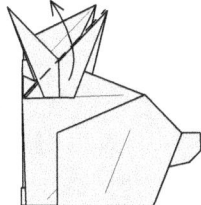

46. Swing the flap back up.

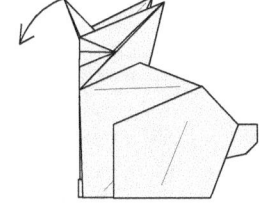

47. Pull out the center flap, undoing a crimp in the process.

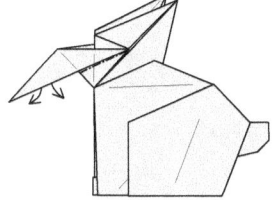

48. Pull out the single layers from inside the flap as far as possible.

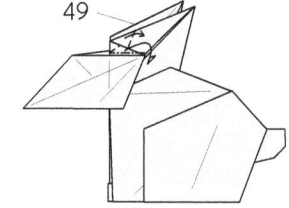 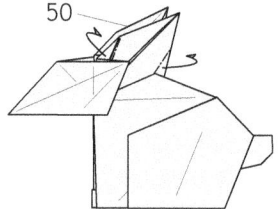 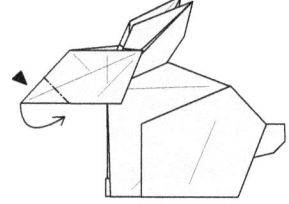

49. Swivel fold the ear. Repeat behind.

50. Mountain fold the sides of the ear. Repeat behind.

51. Reverse fold the corner.

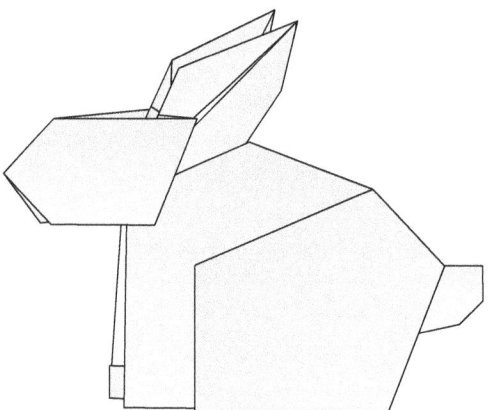

52. Completed *Bunny*.

Cutie Cat

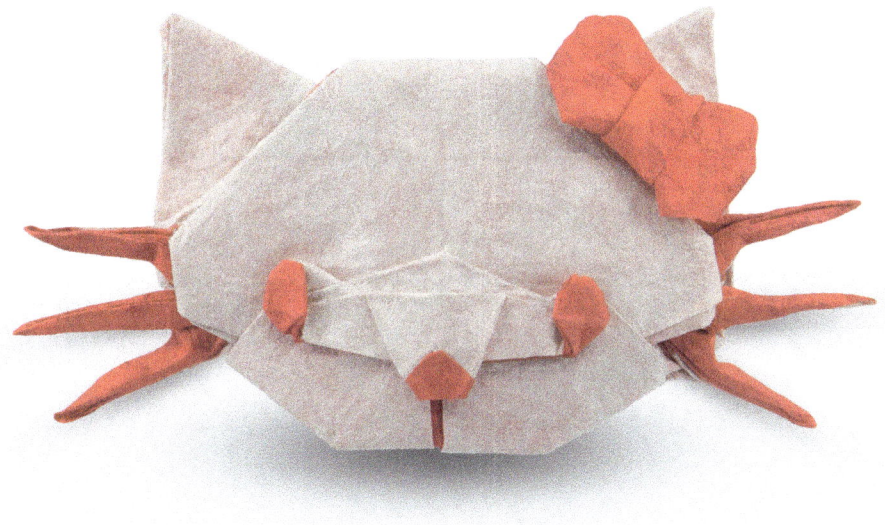

The Japanese are masters of developing cute icons, and even better at harnessing their trademarks for merchandising. They developed an anthropomorphic feline with babyish features, pronounced whiskers and a distinctive bow. This *Cutie Cat* approximates these salient features by inverting some of the flaps to create a distinctive facial; color pattern. The illusion of asymmetry is achieved by swinging a center flap to one side to form the bow.

cutie cat

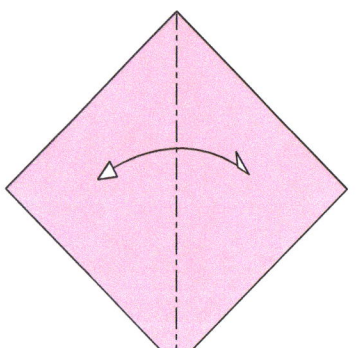

1. Precrease lightly with a mountain fold.

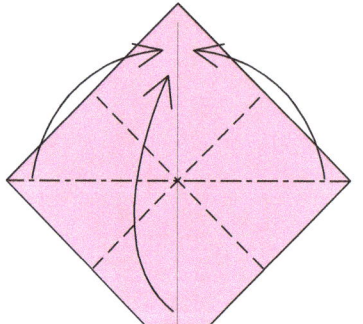

2. Collapse upwards.

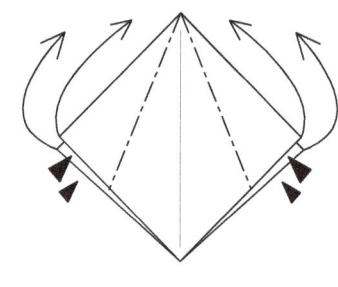

3. Reverse fold all four sides.

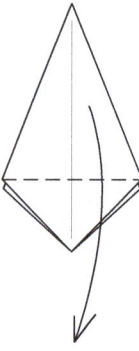

4. Valley fold down.

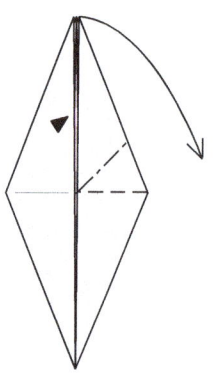

5. Squash fold.

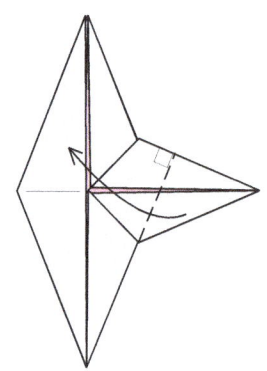

6. Valley fold, keeping the upper edges aligned.

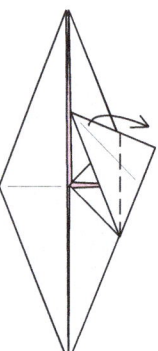

7. Valley fold.

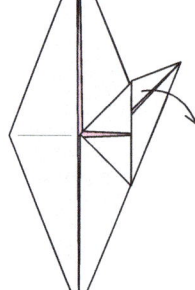

8. Unfold the pleat.

9. Repeat steps 6-8 in the opposite direction.

cutie cat

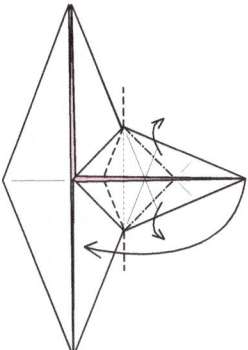

10. Spread apart the sides and squash flat.

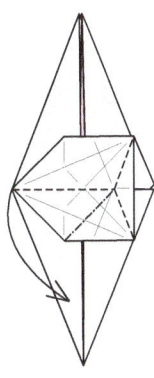

11. Rabbit ear the flap down.

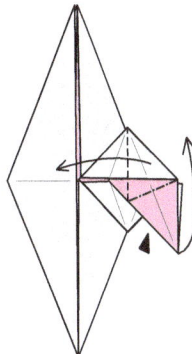

12. Squash fold.

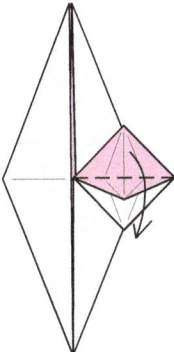

13. Valley fold down.

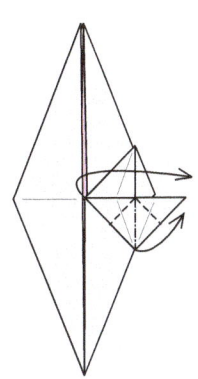

14. Valley fold over while incorporating a reverse fold.

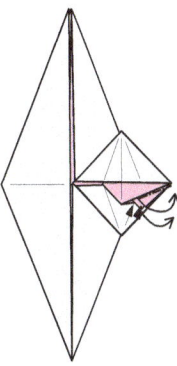

15. Reverse fold the two corners.

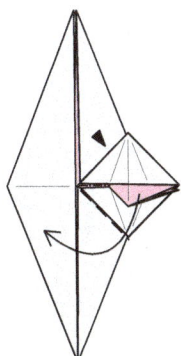

16. Pull the cluster of flaps down, allowing the square region to flatten.

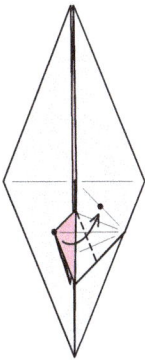

17. Valley fold, such that the corner hits the crease.

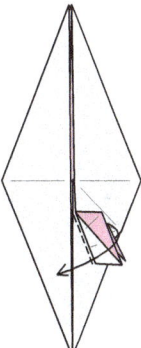

18. Unfold.

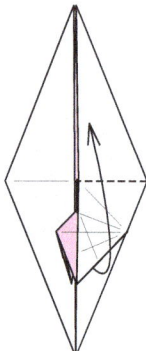

19. Valley fold the cluster of flaps up.

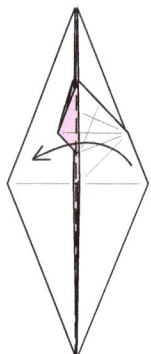

20. Valley fold one flap over.

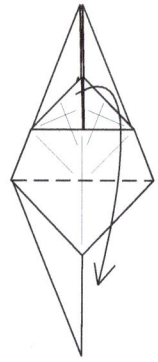

21. Valley fold down.

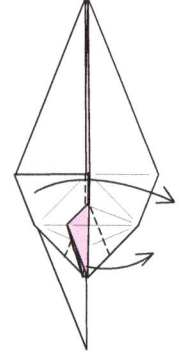

22. Valley fold over while incorporating a reverse fold along existing creases.

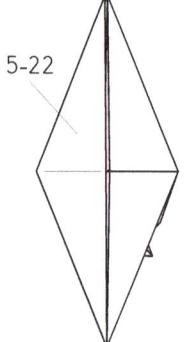

23. Repeat steps 5-22 in mirror image.

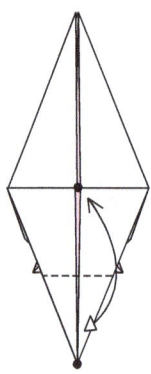

24. Precrease the bottom flap in half.

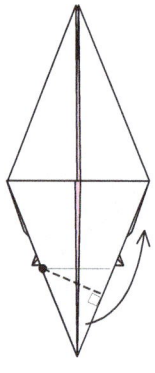

25. Valley fold up, keeping the side edges aligned.

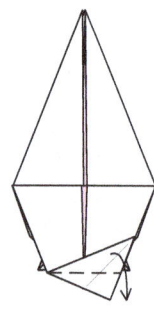

26. Valley fold down.

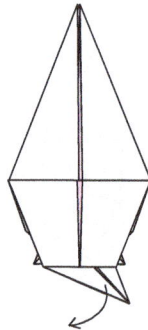

27. Unfold the pleat.

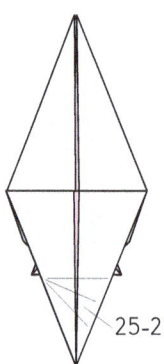

28. Repeat steps 25-27 in mirror image.

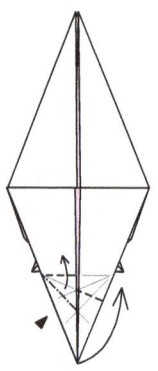

29. Squash the bottom flap.

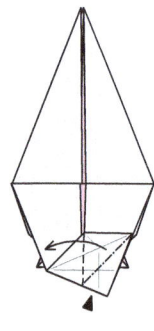

30. Squash fold.

cutie cat

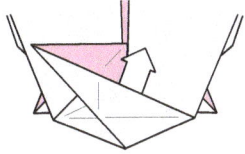
31. Pull out a single layer.

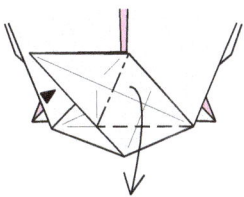
32. Squash fold.

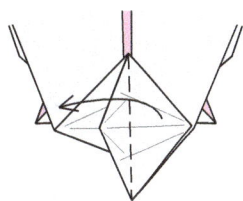
33. Valley fold.

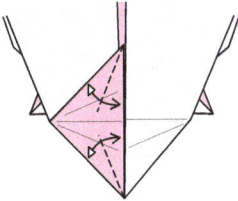
34. Precrease along the angle bisectors.

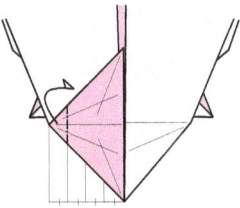
35. Mountain fold approximately 1/4 of the flap.

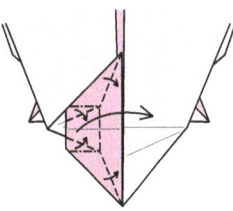
36. Valley fold over while swiveling in the sides.

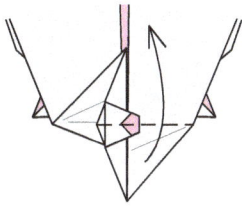
37. Lightly valley fold up.

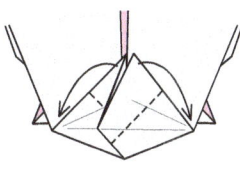
38. Valley fold the sides outwards.

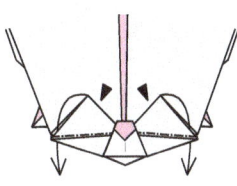
39. Reverse fold the corners down.

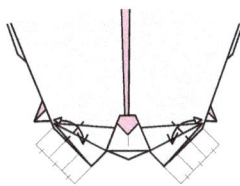
40. Precrease the side flaps at 1/3rd their width.

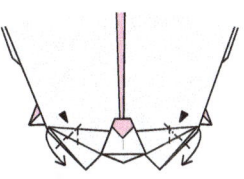
41. Squash the flaps down using the previously made creases.

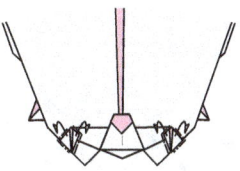
42. Wrap around all of the layers on each flap.

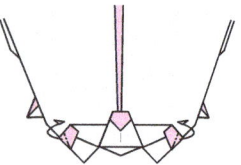 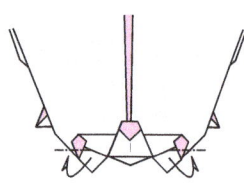 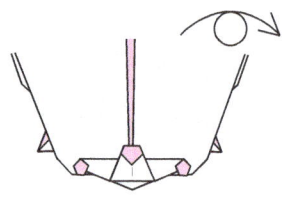

43. Mountain fold the corners behind.

44. Mountain fold the bottom corners behind.

45. Turn over.

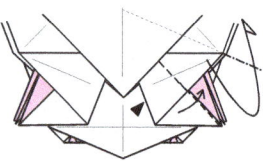 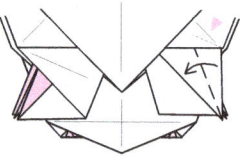 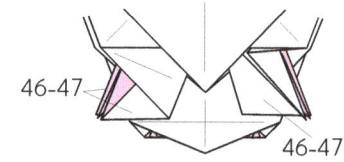

46. Reverse fold the flap up.

47. Reverse fold down.

48. Repeat steps 46-47 on the remaining three sections.

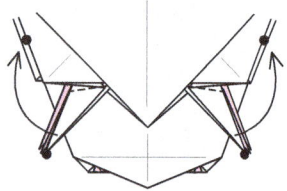 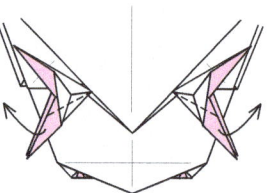 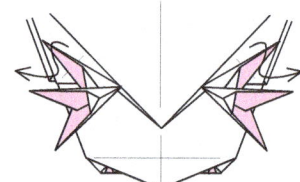

49. Valley fold the flaps up to meet the side edges, allowing a small squash to form.

50. Valley fold the next set of flaps up, allowing small squashes to form.

51. Pull the flaps around to the surface.

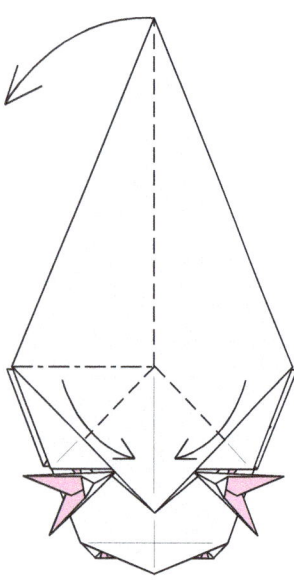 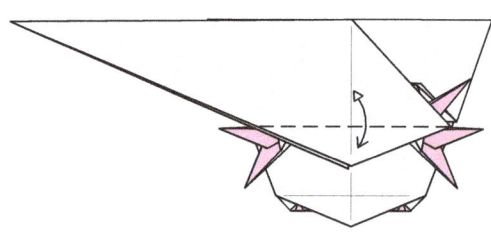

52. Rabbit ear.

53. Precrease the top flap.

22

cutie cat

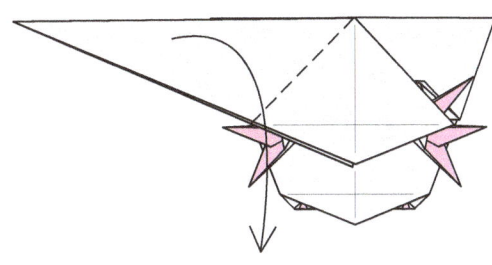

54. Valley fold down.

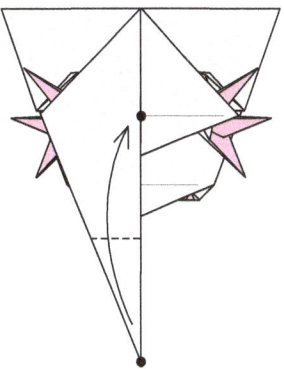

55. Valley fold to meet the crease.

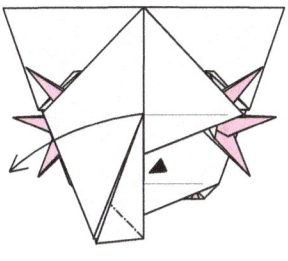

56. Squash fold.

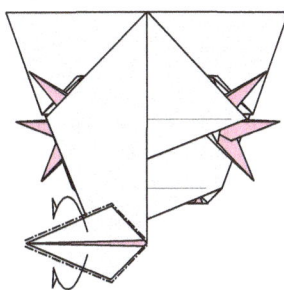

57. Wrap around a single layer at each side.

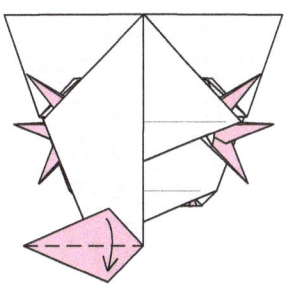

58. Valley fold down.

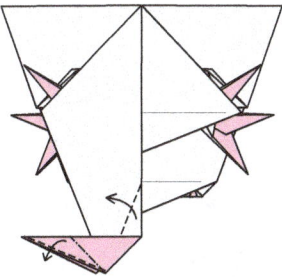

59. Swivel fold, such that the bottom edge becomes straight.

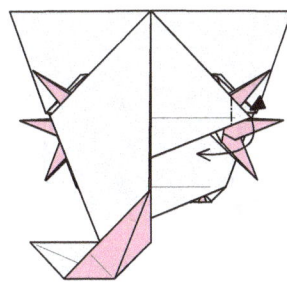

60. Open sink the corner.

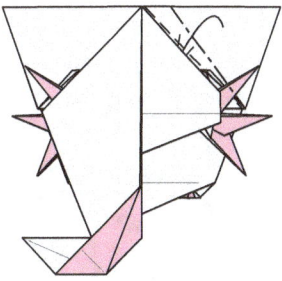

61. Pleat the flap up, tucking it into the pocket.

cutie cat

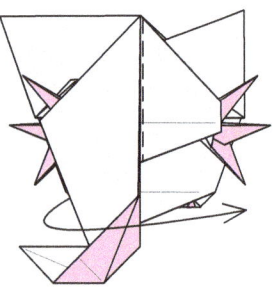

62. Swing the flap over.

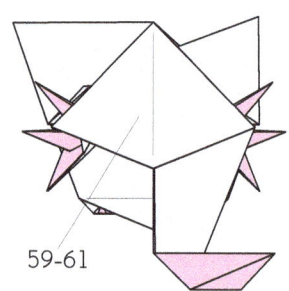

63. Repeat steps 59-61 in mirror image.

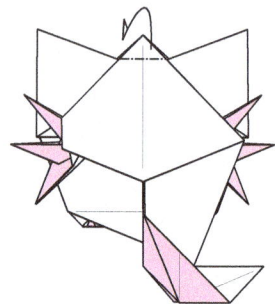

64. Mountain fold the flap behind (or sink if your paper can handle it).

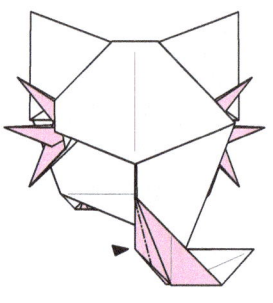

65. Sink along the angle bisector.

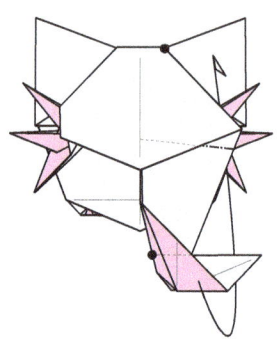

66. Mountain fold, allowing the indicated points to meet.

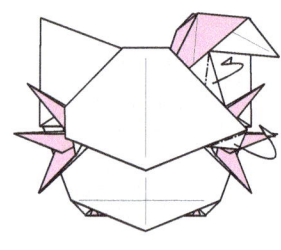

67. Swivel fold.

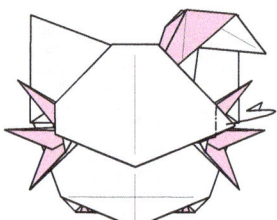

68. Mountain fold, tucking the corner into the pocket.

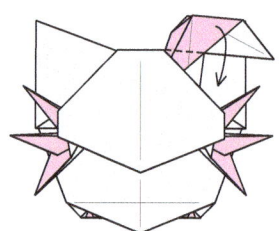

69. Open out the flap.

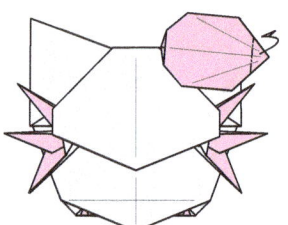

70. Mountain fold to match the opposite edge.

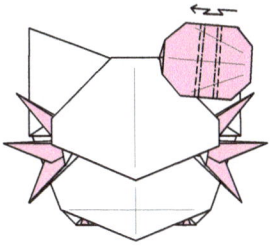

71. Pleat the flap.

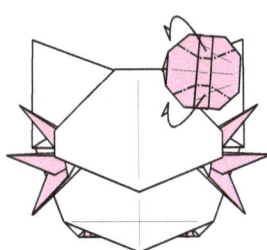

72. Mountain fold the sides, allowing the pleats to spread out behind.

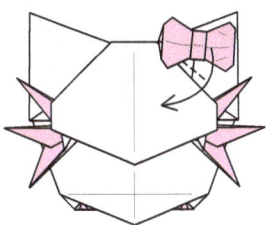

73. Rotate the flap using a pleat.

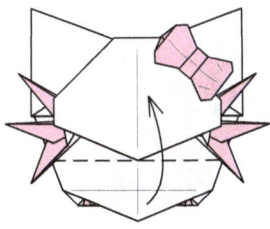

74. Valley fold the bottom section up.

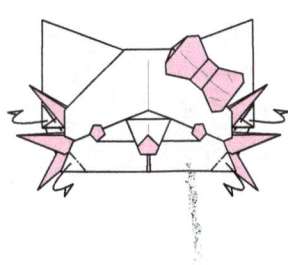

75. Mountain fold the sides.

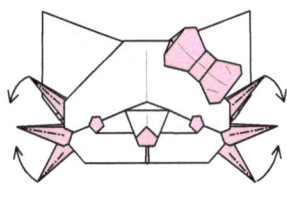

76. Pinch the side flaps and make them stick out straight.

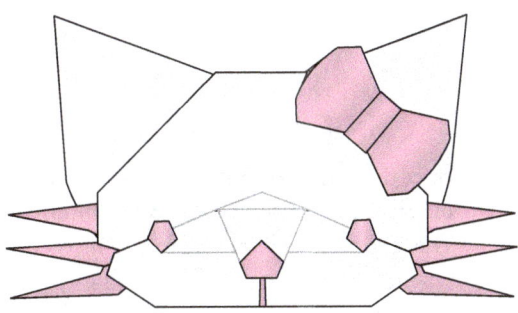

77. Completed *Cutie Cat*.

Elephant

Sporting an elongated trunk, large ears and a robust body, the elephant is one of the most distinctive looking animals in nature. This uniqueness has made the large grey animal a favorite subject with origami artists. The challenge is to infuse some unique element to separate your rendition from other interpretations of the subject. The defining feature with this *Elephant* is how it seems like the head section is separate from the body portion. This disconnection allows for additional expressiveness in the final shaping.

elephant

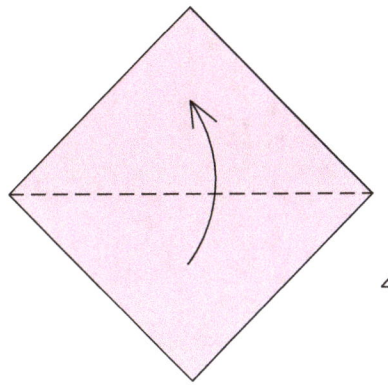

1. Valley fold in half.

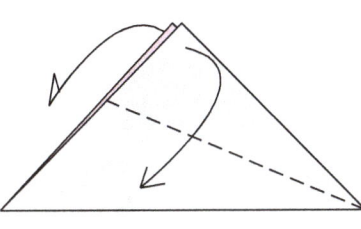

2. Valley fold the sides down along angle bisectors.

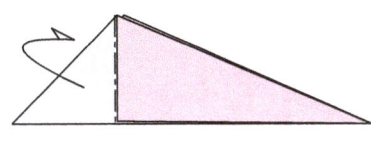

3. Mountain fold.

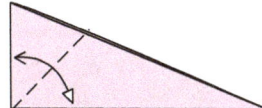

4. Precrease along the angle bisector.

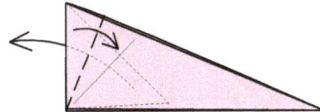

5. Valley fold the left edge towards the crease, allowing the back flap to flip out.

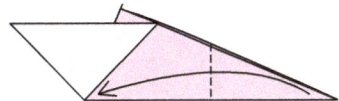

6. Valley fold.

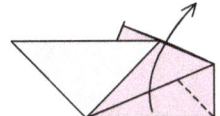

7. Valley fold the flap up.

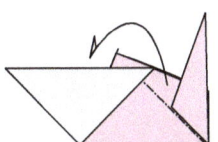

8. Mountain fold.

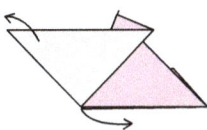

9. Unfold everything, opening up to the white side.

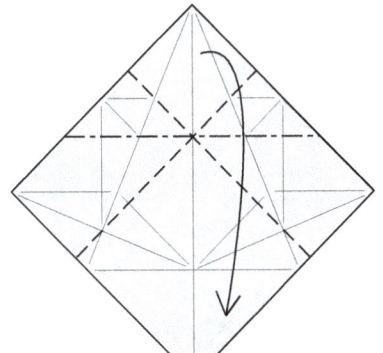

10. Extend some of the creases, and collapse down.

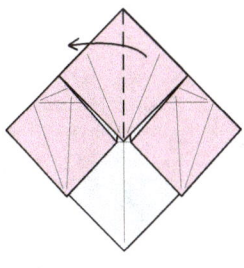

11. Swing over the top flap.

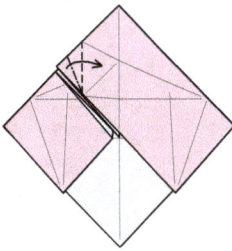

12. Pleat the corner, starting with the existing valley fold crease.

27

elephant

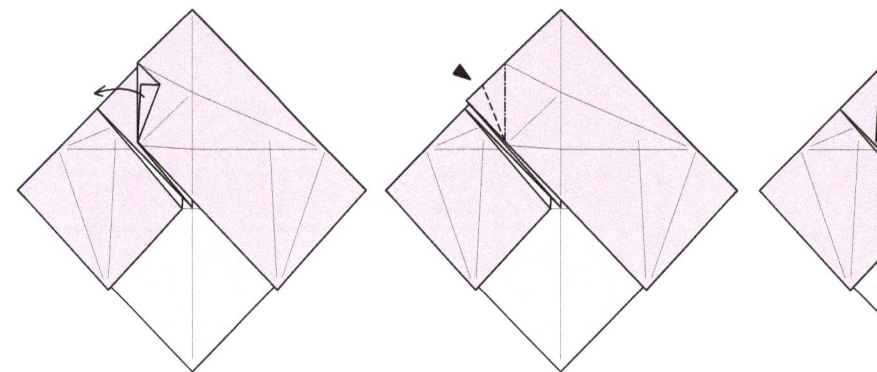
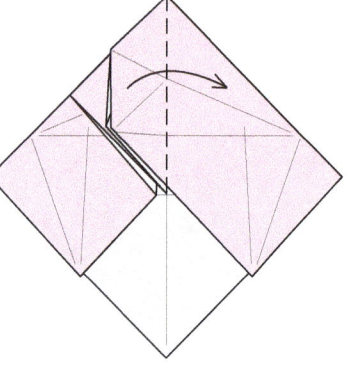

13. Unfold the pleat.

14. Reverse fold in and then out along the existing creases.

15. Swing the flap back over.

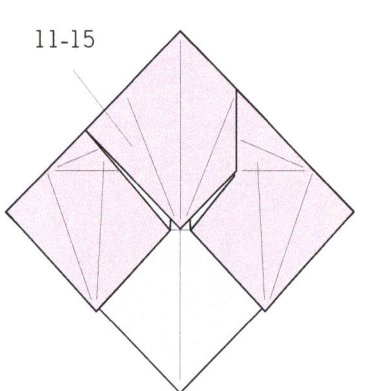
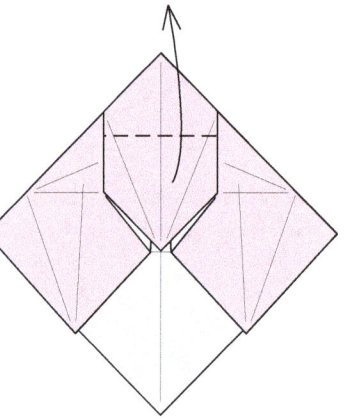
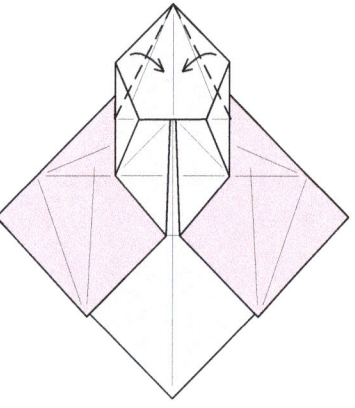

16. Repeat steps 11-15 in mirror image.

17. Lightly valley fold the flap up as far as possible.

18. Valley fold the sides inwards.

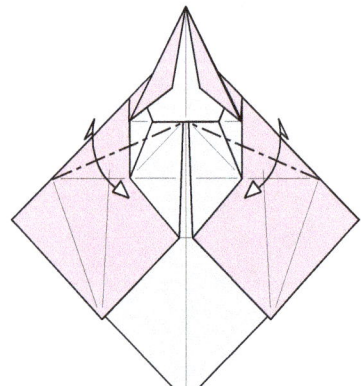
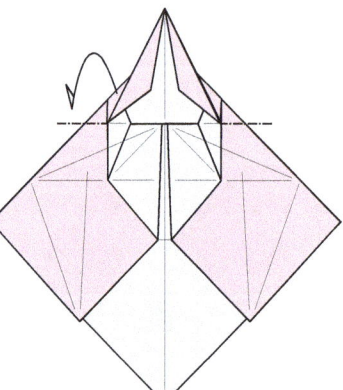
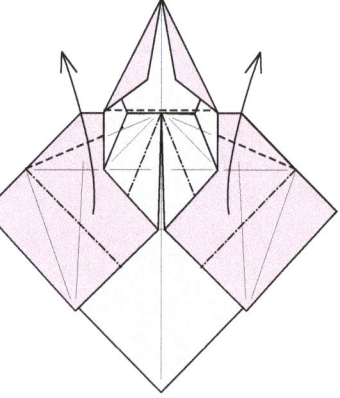

19. Precrease with mountain folds (extending the existing creases).

20. Flip the back flap down.

21. Squash fold the sides upwards.

elephant

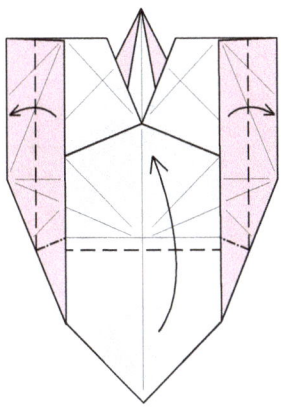

22. Swivel fold the sides outwards, allowing the bottom to fold up.

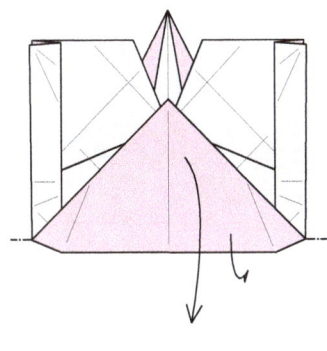

23. Flip the bottom flap.

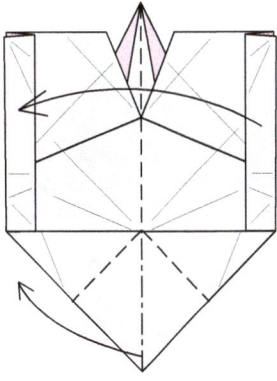

24. Valley fold in half while reverse folding at the bottom.

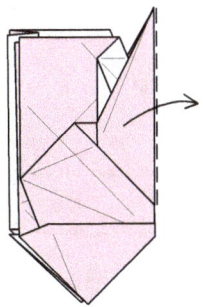

25. Raise the top layer. The model will not lie flat.

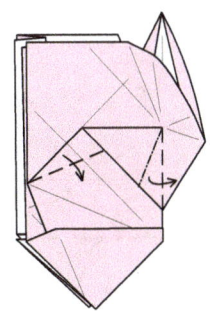

26. Swivel over.

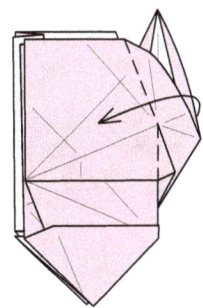

27. Bring the flap back down.

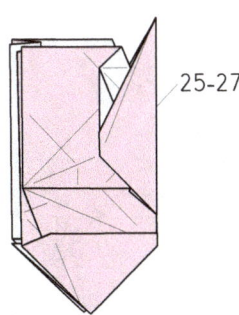

28. Repeat steps 25-27 behind.

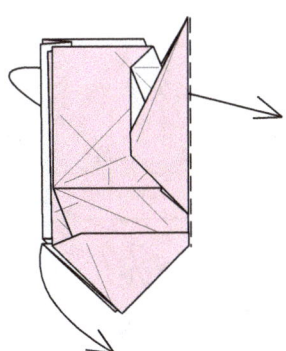

29. Open out the model, undoing the bottom reverse fold.

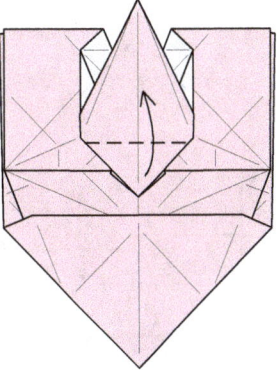

30. Lightly valley fold the flap up, allowing squashes to form beneath.

29

elephant

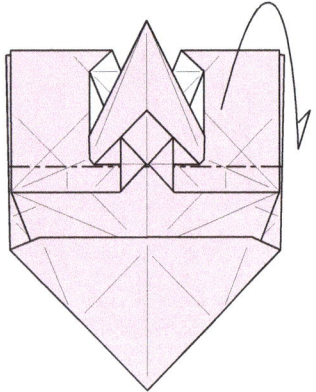

31. Mountain fold.

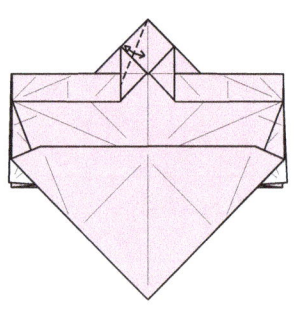

32. Precrease along the angle bisector.

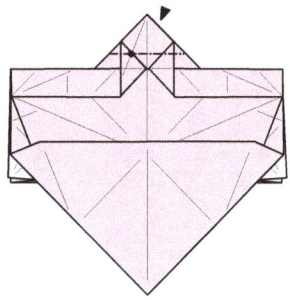

33. Closed sink, noting the dotted reference point.

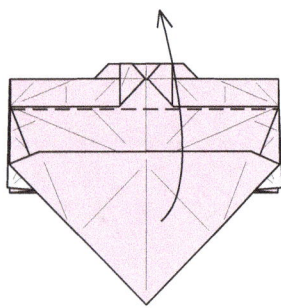

34. Valley fold the flap up.

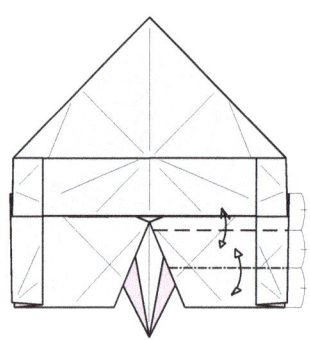

35. Precrease the indicated section into thirds.

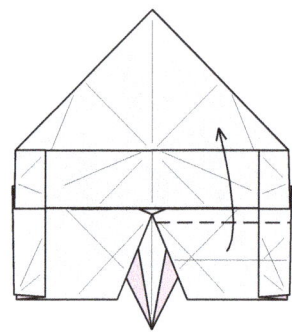

36. Valley fold up.

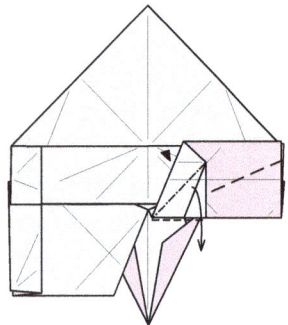

37. Squash fold.

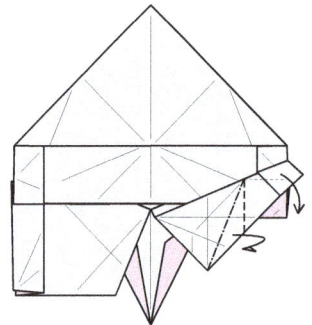

38. Swivel fold.

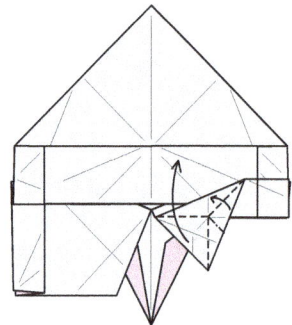

39. Valley fold up while swiveling in.

elephant

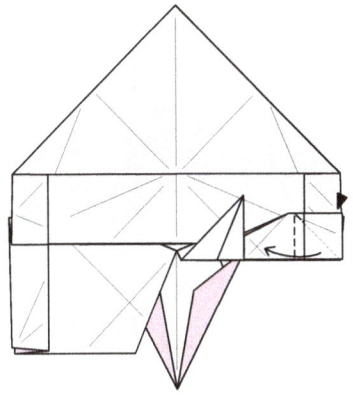

40. Squash the flap inwards.

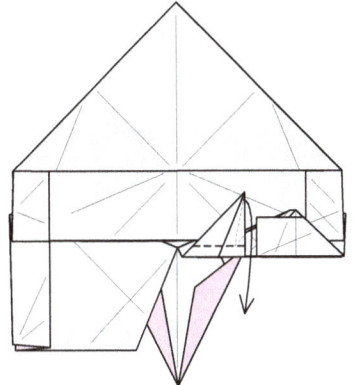

41. Valley fold, allowing a squash fold to form.

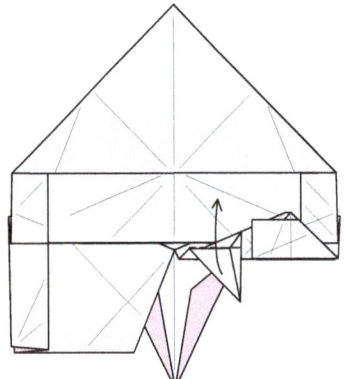

42. Swing back up.

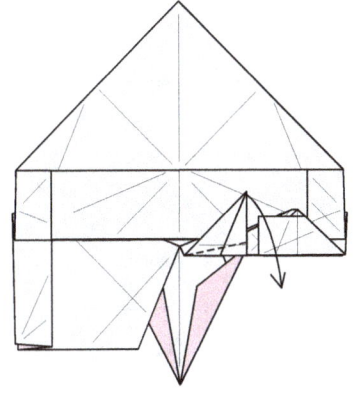

43. Valley fold outwards as far as possible.

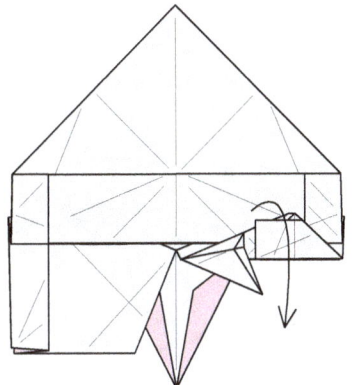

44. Bring the layer from behind to the surface.

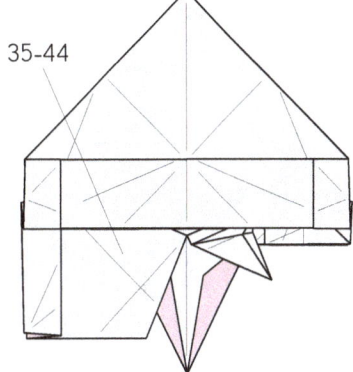

45. Repeat steps 35-44 in mirror image.

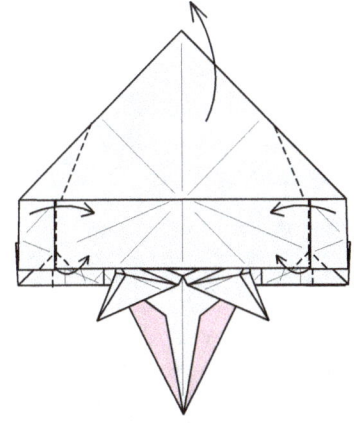

46. Valley fold the sides inwards (incorporating tiny reverse folds), while undoing the top pleat.

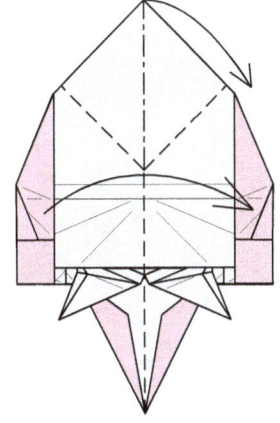

47. Valley fold in half while replacing the reverse fold.

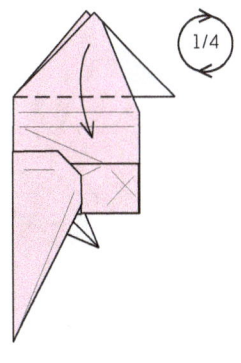

48. Valley fold over one flap. Rotate the model.

elephant

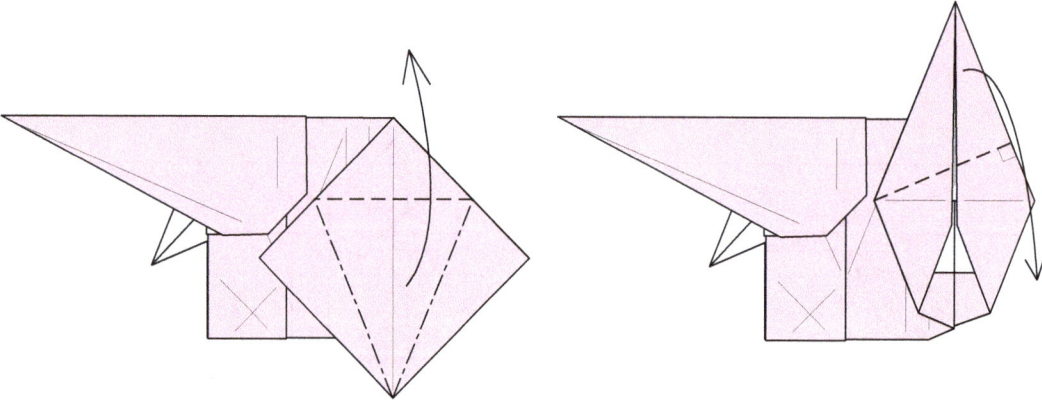

49. Petal fold the flap upwards.

50. Valley fold.

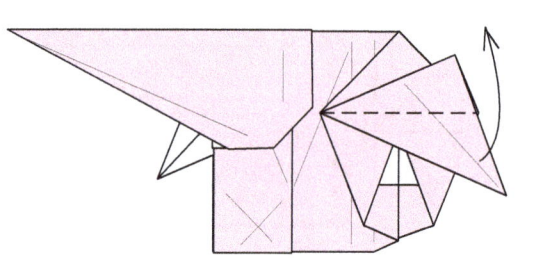

51. Valley fold up.

52. Unfold the pleat.

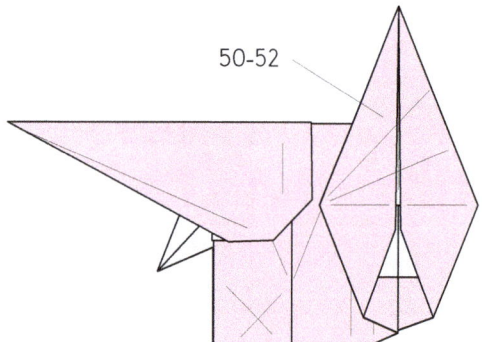

53. Repeat steps 50-52 in mirror image.

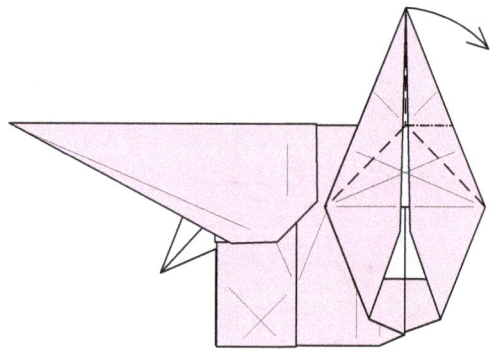

54. Rabbit ear the flap.

elephant

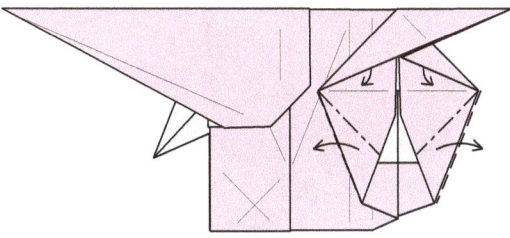

55. Slide out the single layers.

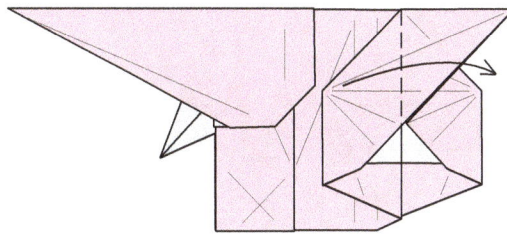

56. Valley fold the flap over.

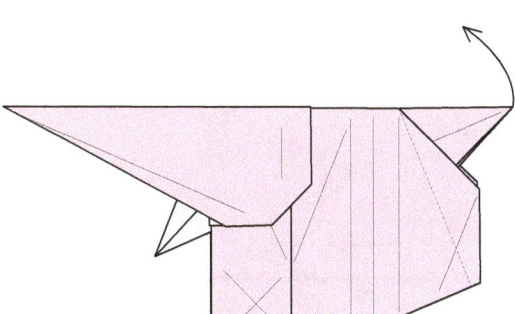

57. Pull the point straight up, allowing the inner layers to swivel.

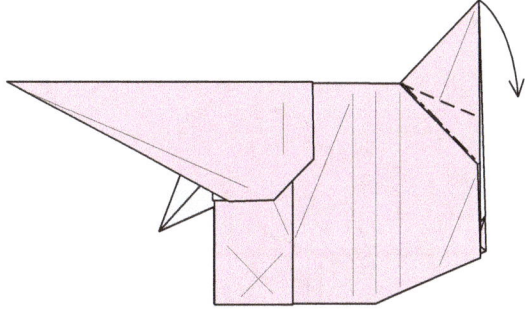

58. Crimp the flap down.

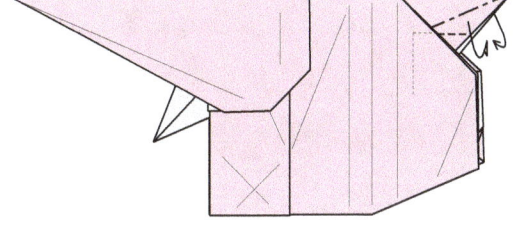

59. Swivel in the sides.

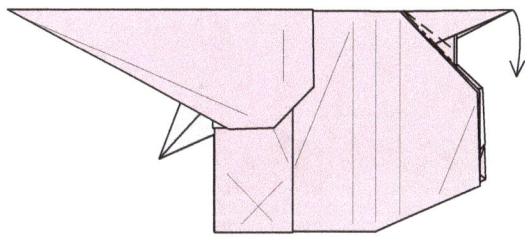

60. Crimp the flap down.

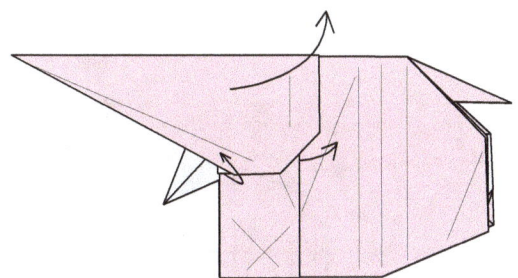

61. Pull the head upwards, releasing the trapped layers at the tusks, and sliding a layer from behind the legs.

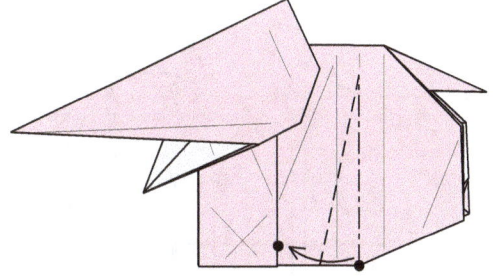

62. Crimp towards the front legs, allowing the model to become 3-D. The mountain fold lies along an existing crease.

elephant

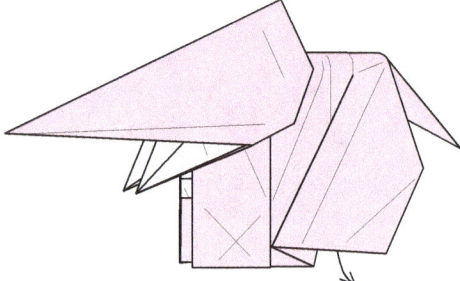

63. Slide out the trapped layer. You will have to undo the hidden pleat at the right edge to accomplish this.

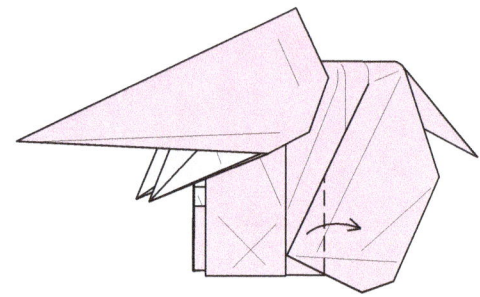

64. Valley fold over, keeping the resulting edge straight.

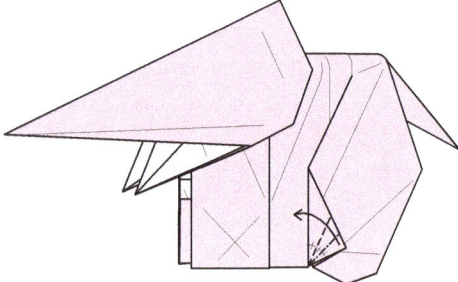

65. Pleat the flap into thirds.

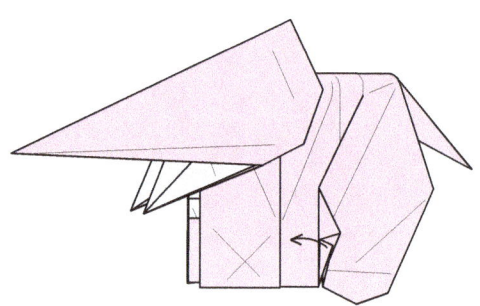

66. Unfold the pleat.

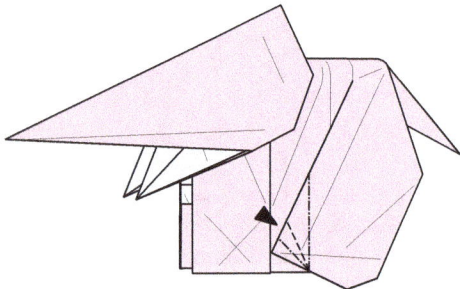

67. Closed reverse fold in and out along the existing creases.

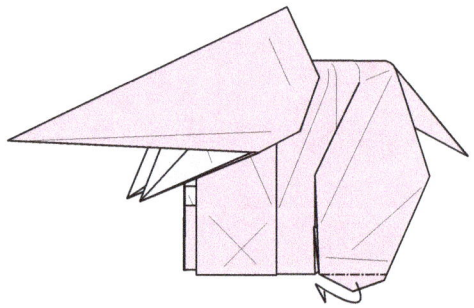

68. Mountain fold the edge to make it flush with the other leg.

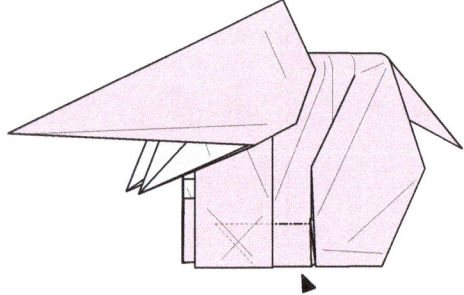

69. Closed sink as far as possible, adjusting the tiny reverse fold from step 46 if necessary.

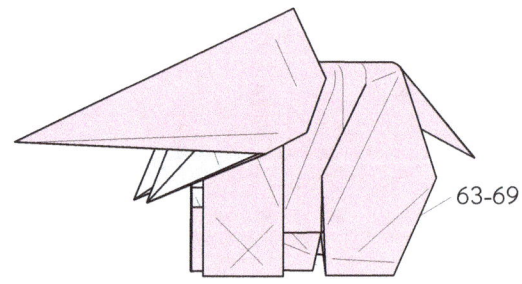

70. Repeat steps 63-69 behind.

elephant

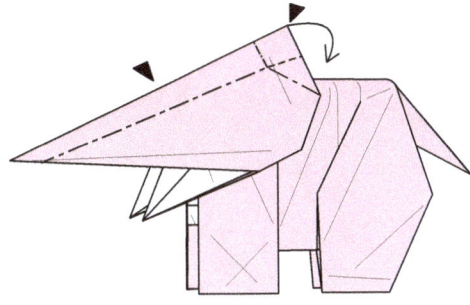

71. Reverse fold the top of the head into a 3-D shape. Do not crease the length of the trunk sharply.

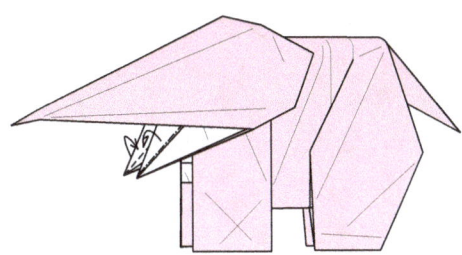

72. Reverse fold to thin the tusks. The tusks will be flat, but the inside of the model will not.

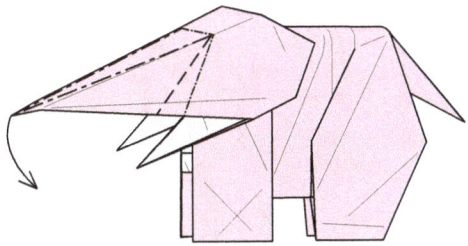

73. Crimp the trunk down. The long mountain folds that run the length of the trunk should be along angle trisectors.

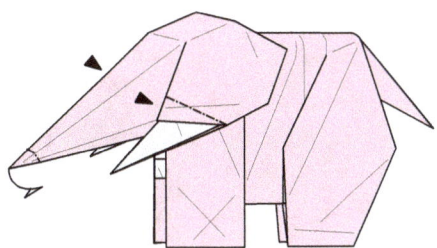

74. Add reverse folds where the ears meet the tusks. Blunt the tip of the trunk with a reverse fold.

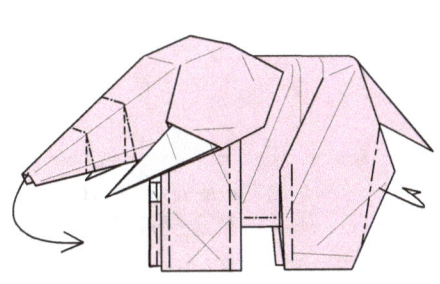

75. Add additional crimps to the trunk. Mountain fold the hind legs, and then shape your model to taste.

76. Completed *Elephant*.

En Route to the Observatory

Dorothy Engleman needed an origami piece to represent Hollywood for her short film *Folding California*, and this *En Route to the Observatory* was created to fit the bill. It is a depiction of everyone's favorite overgrown gorilla scaling the Empire State Building as it did in the climactic scene of the movie *King Kong*. Years later it was folded from a six-foot square sheet of paper to be large enough to permanently adorn the lobby of a prominent New York City luxury apartment building. Folding this from smaller paper is far easier.

en route to the observatory

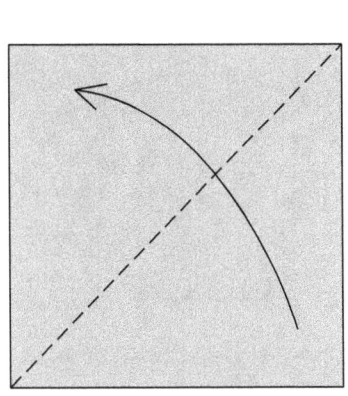

1. Valley fold in half.

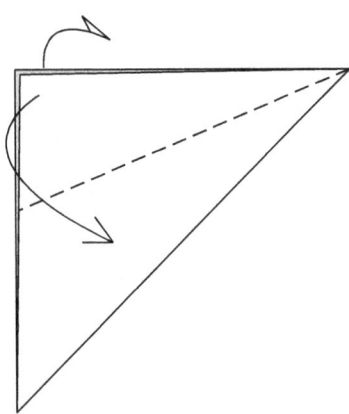

2. Valley fold both sides to the folded edge.

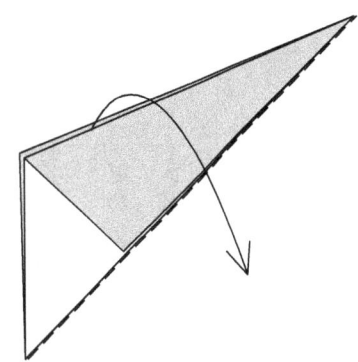

3. Swing down the top.

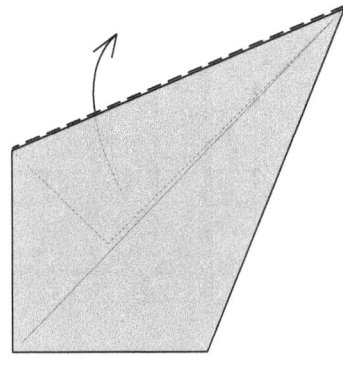

4. Unfold the flap from behind.

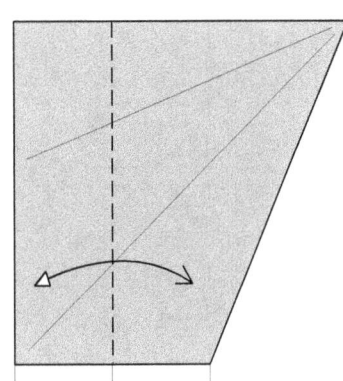

5. Precrease in half.

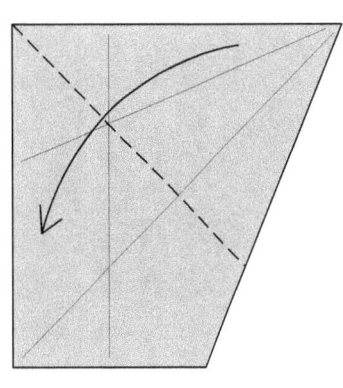

6. Valley fold.

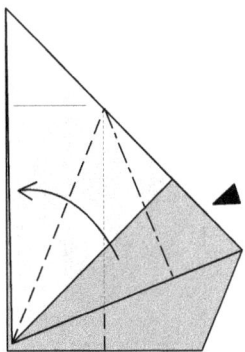

7. Form an asymmetrical squash, utilizing the existing creases.

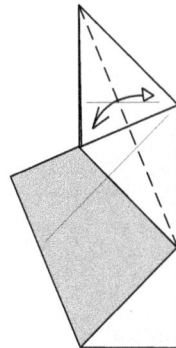

8. Precrease.

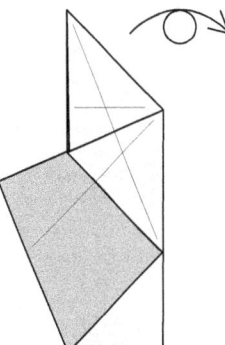

9. Turn over.

37

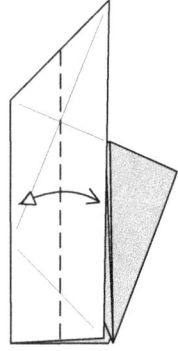

10. Precrease through all layers of the top flap.

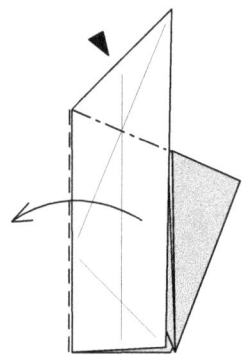

11. Squash fold.

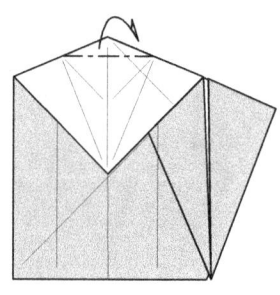

12. Mountain fold.

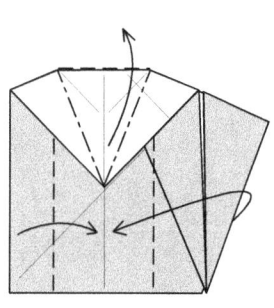

13. Petal fold, leaving the right side on the model's surface.

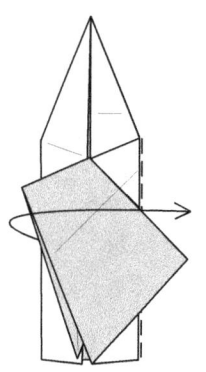

14. Swing the top flap over. The model will not lie flat.

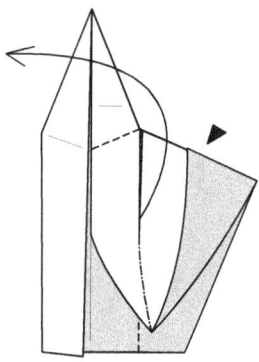

15. Invert the flap, and squash fold upwards.

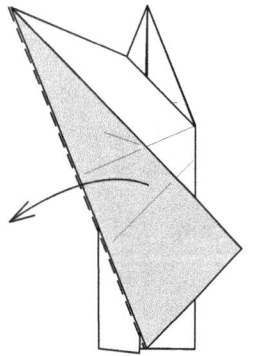

16. Swing down.

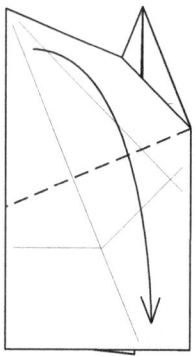

17. Valley fold the flap down.

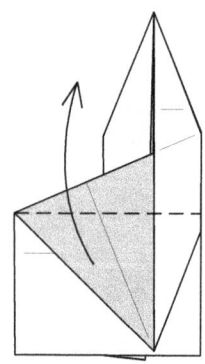

18. Valley fold up.

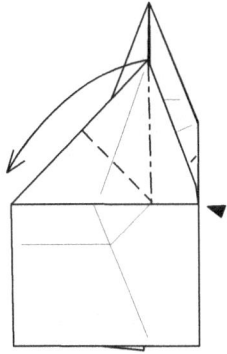 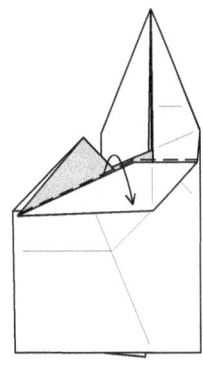 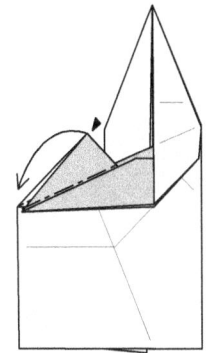

19. Squash fold.

20. Wrap a single layer around.

21. Reverse fold.

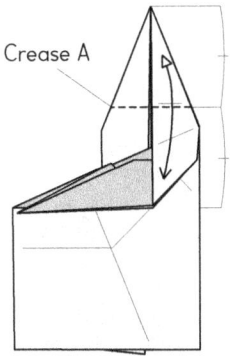 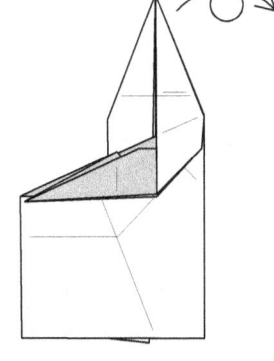

22. Precrease, to establish crease A.

23. Precrease, to establish crease B.

24. Turn over.

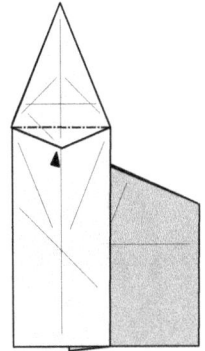 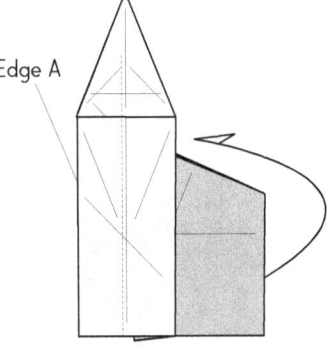 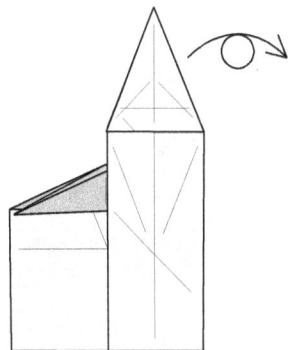

25. Closed sink the point upwards.

26. Fold the large flap to the left, such that crease B (step 23) hits edge A. The back will not lie flat.

27. Turn over.

en route to the observatory

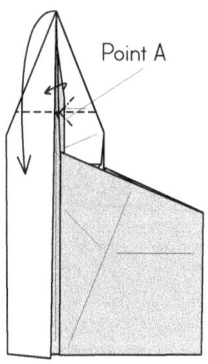

28. Valley fold down along crease A (step 22), allowing a swivel fold to form at point A.

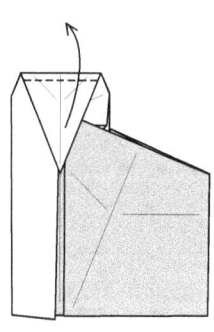

29. Valley fold up along an intersection of point A (step 28).

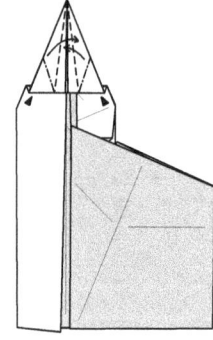

30. Squash fold over the sides of the flap into thirds, allowing them to overlap.

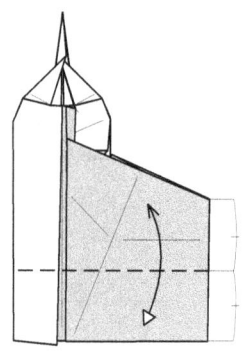

31. Lightly precrease.

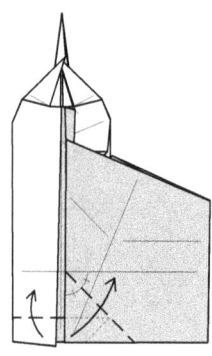

32. Swivel fold the corner up (the horizontal fold should be made lightly).

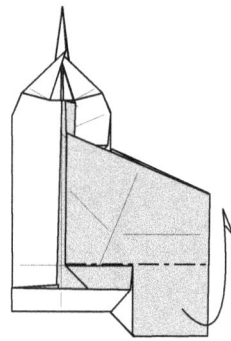

33. Mountain fold.

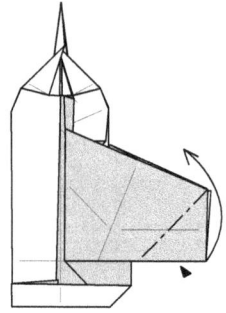

34. Reverse fold.

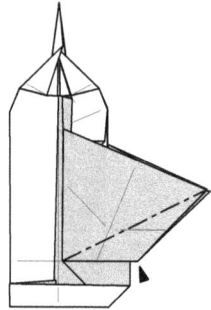

35. Open sink the corner. Note this is not along an angle bisector.

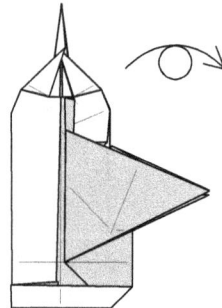

36. Turn over.

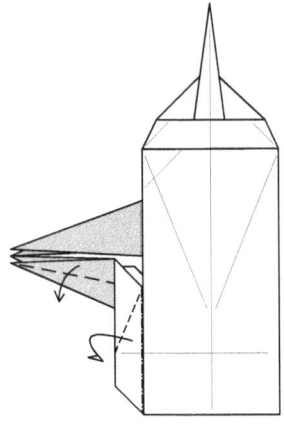
37. Swivel fold the single layer.

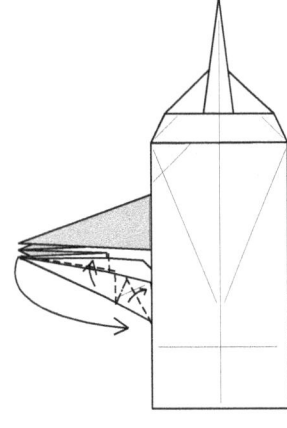
38. Swing over the flap as far as possible while reverse folding the single layer.

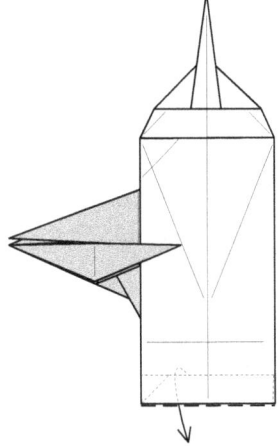
39. Pull out the single layer from behind.

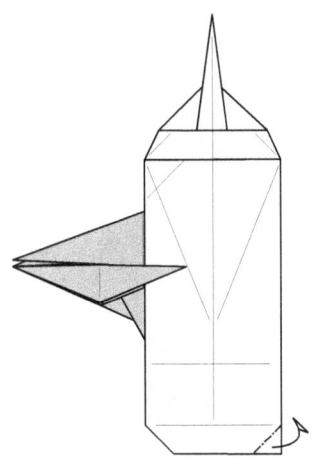
40. Mountain fold.

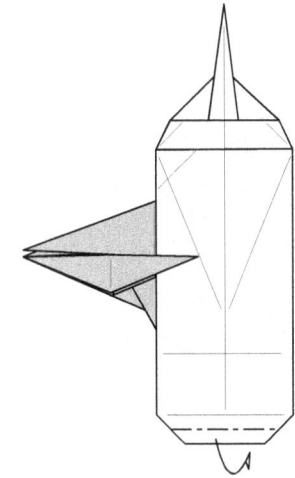
41. Mountain fold again.

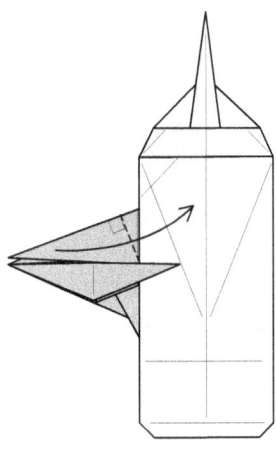
42. Valley fold the flap up.

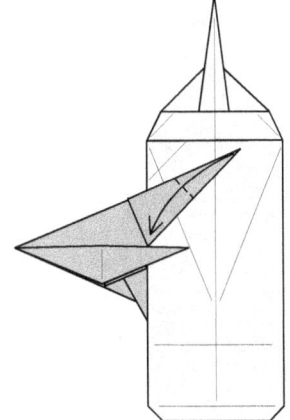
43. Valley fold in half.

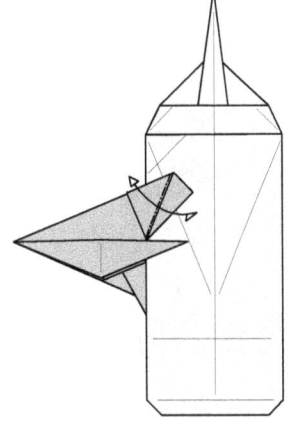
44. Precrease with a mountain fold.

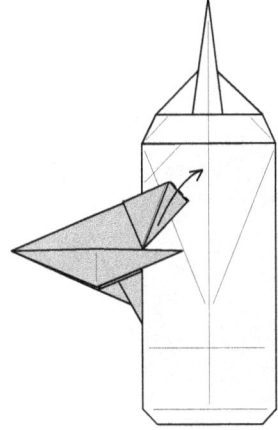
45. Unfold.

en route to the observatory

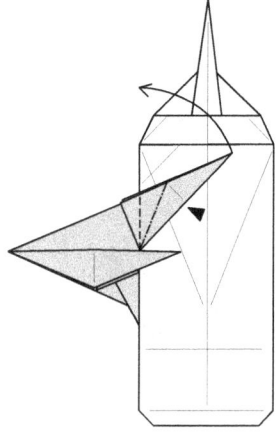

46. Squash fold.

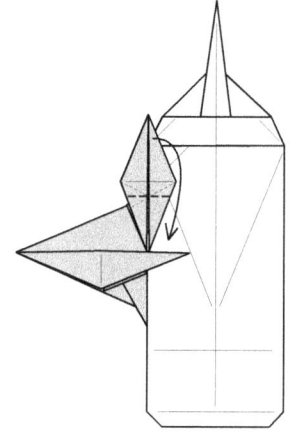

47. Valley fold down. Note the hidden intersections.

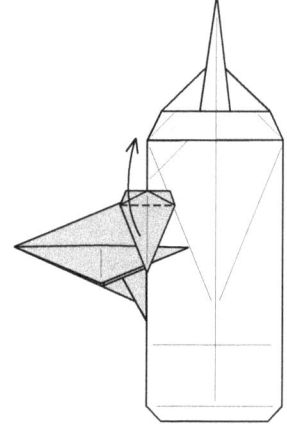

48. Valley fold up.

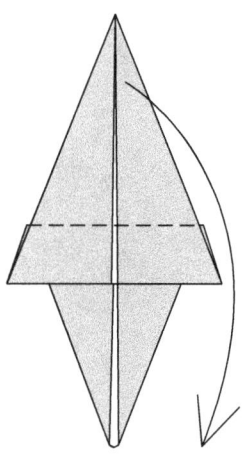

49. Detail of the head flap. Valley fold down.

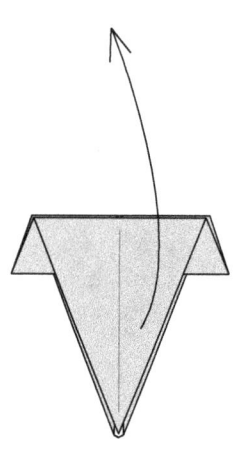

50. Unfold the pleats.

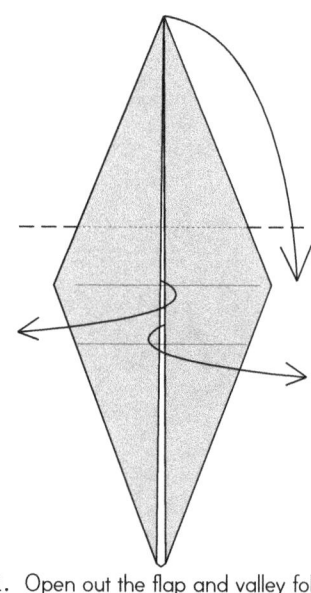

51. Open out the flap and valley fold along the existing crease. The model will not lie flat.

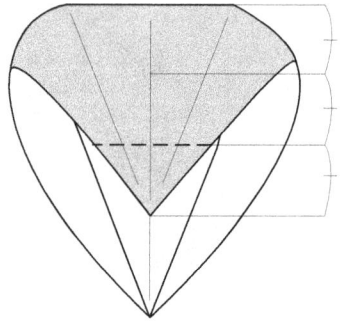

52. Valley fold up about 1/3rd of the flap.

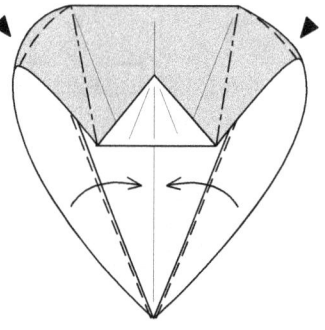

53. Reverse fold the sides inwards to flatten.

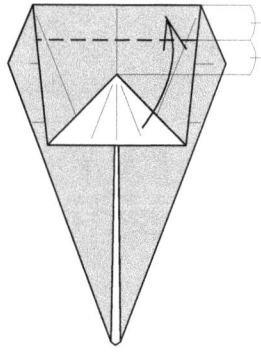

54. Valley fold up.

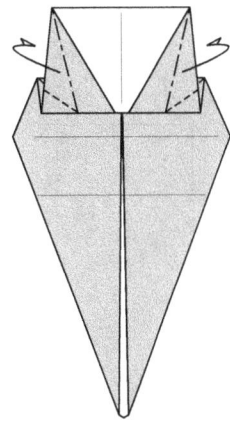

55. Swivel fold the sides behind. See step 60 for approximate positioning.

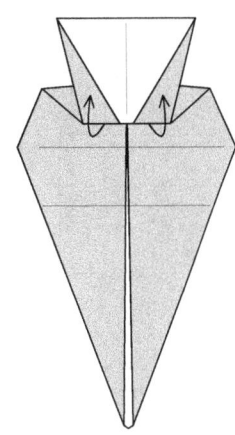

56. Pull a single layer at each side to the surface.

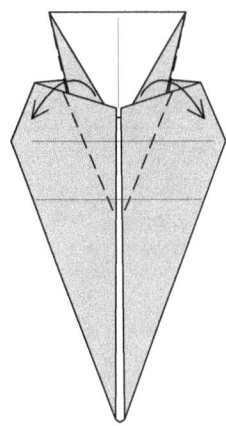

57. Open out the top layers, allowing them to stretch flat.

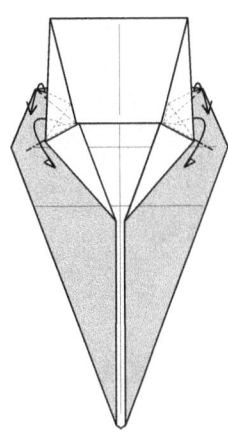

58. Swivel the top ridges down, allowing the hidden ridges to swivel as well.

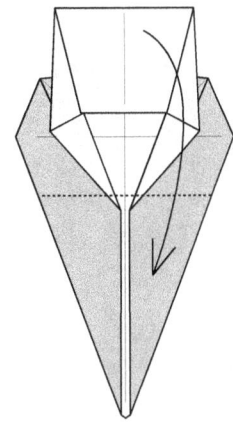

59. Valley fold along the existing crease.

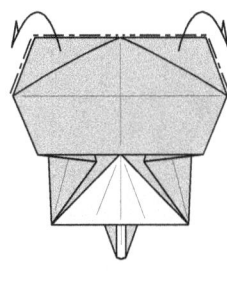

60. Wrap a layer around at each side.

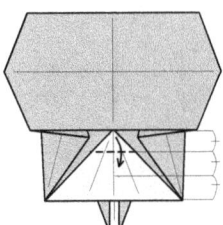

61. Valley fold down about 1/3rd of the flap.

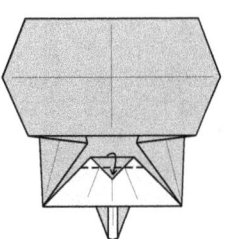

62. Valley fold towards the tip of the triangle.

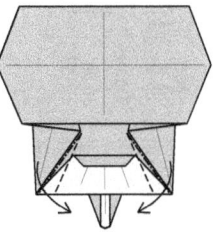

63. Pleat the sides inwards. This will cause the bottom to be curved.

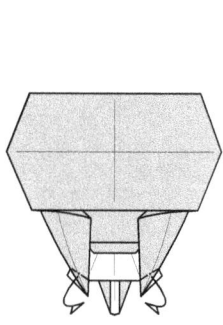 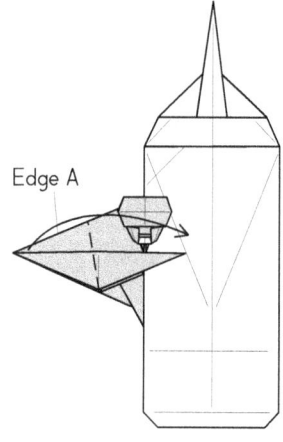 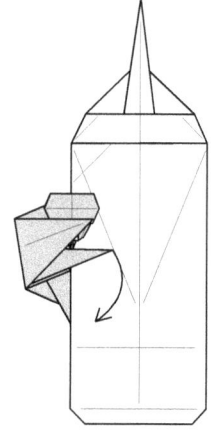

64. Lock the corners with mountain folds.

65. Valley fold over, such that edge A lies straight.

66. Slide the flap down.

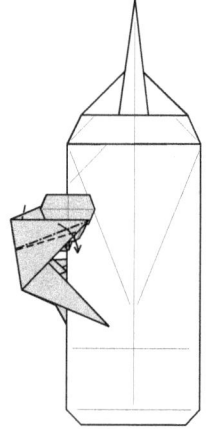 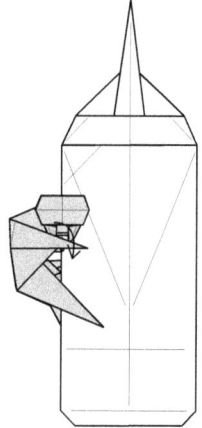 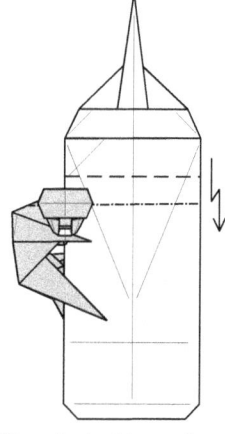

67. Swivel fold the arm down slightly.

68. Bring the head section to the surface.

69. Pleat the building, allowing squashes to form at the back of the head. The valley fold is to taste.

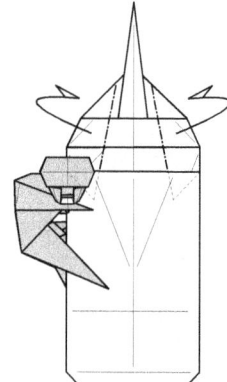 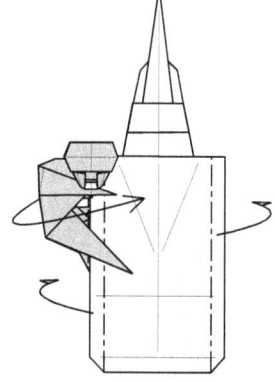 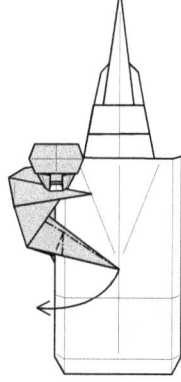

70. Swivel fold the sides behind.

71. Mountain fold the side edges at a slight angle, while pulling the body inward.

72. Crimp the leg, allowing a hem to curl around at the resulting joint.

en route to the observatory

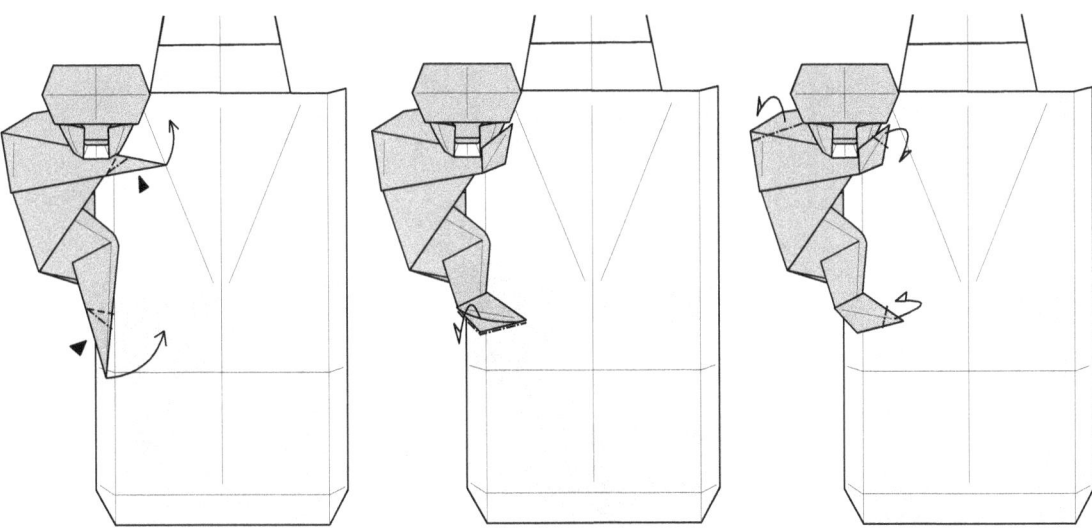

73. Form two squash folds.

74. Wrap a layer around.

75. Mountain fold the indicated areas to shape.

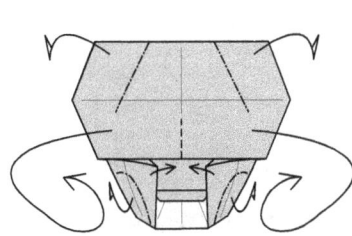

76. Detail of the head. Curl the sides to form eye sockets. Shape the rest of the model to taste.

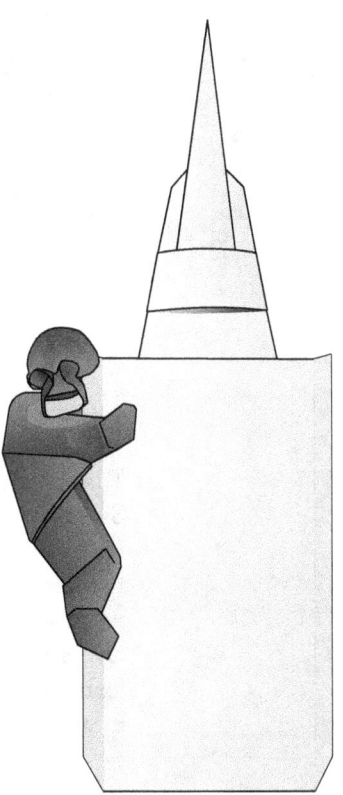

77. Completed *En Route to the Observatory*.

45

Giant Panda

The giant panda's patches of color are integral to its unique look. Simply recreating this pattern of colors is most of the design effort when creating an origami rendering. For this *Giant Panda*, the spots on the face are essentially separate appendages that are inverted, while the legs have colored layers that are brought to the surface. The ears go through an unusual sequence to get formed with some tricky squash folds and a single layer of paper that must be carefully wrapped around. These unorthodox folding sequences make this one of the more difficult pieces in this collection.

giant panda

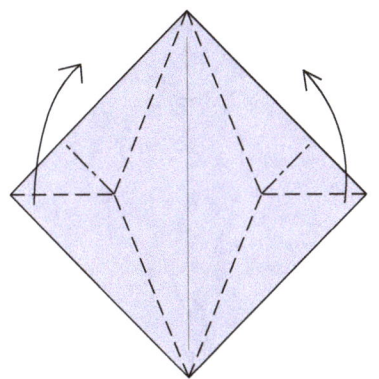

1. With the darker side up, form rabbit ears on both sides.

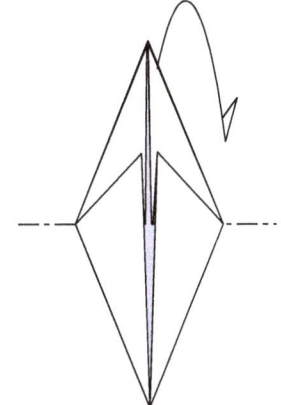

2. Swing back.

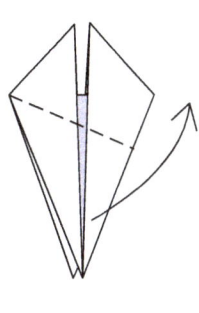

3. Valley fold the flap up.

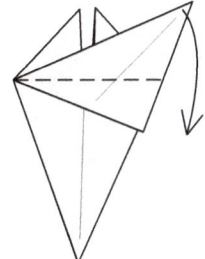

4. Valley fold down.

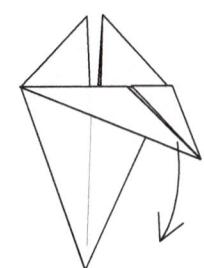

5. Unfold.

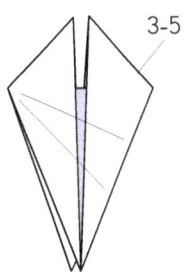

3-5

6. Repeat steps 3-5 in mirror image.

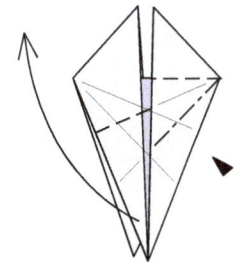

7. Form an asymmetrical squash fold.

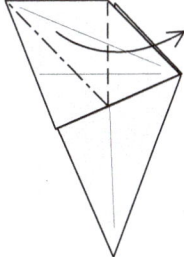

8. Squash fold over.

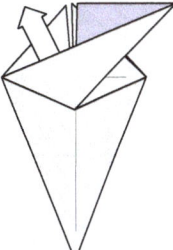

9. Pull out a single layer to match the other side.

47

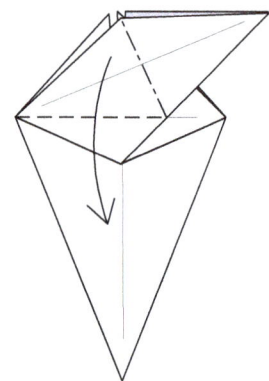
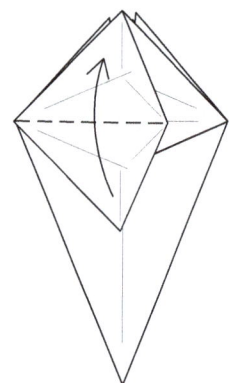
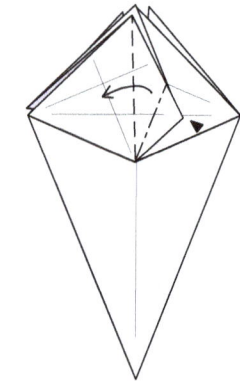

10. Squash fold.

11. Valley fold up.

12. Squash fold the center flap.

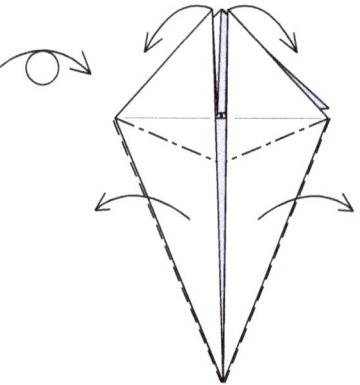
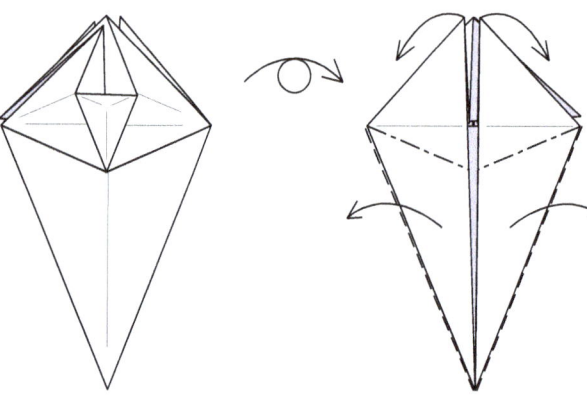
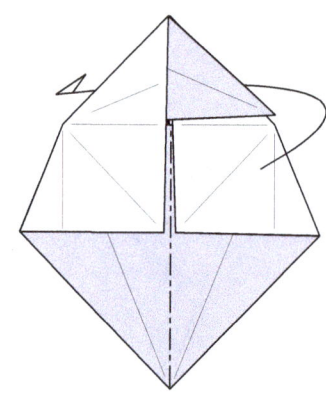

13. Turn over.

14. Spread out the top layer.

15. Mountain fold in half.

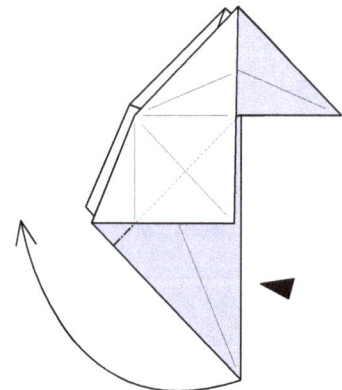
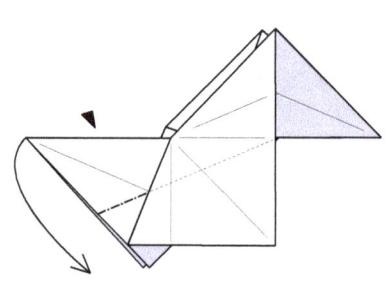
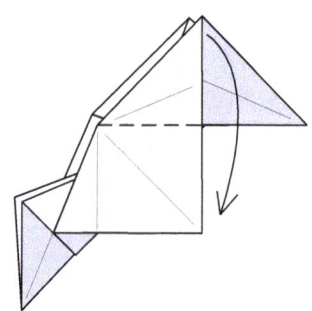

16. Reverse fold through all layers.

17. Reverse fold again through all layers.

18. Swing down, allowing the center to stretch flat.

giant panda

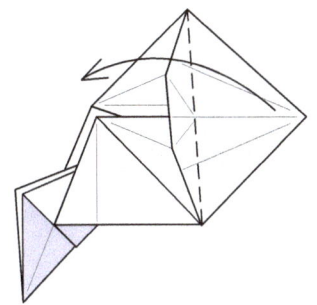
19. Valley fold over.

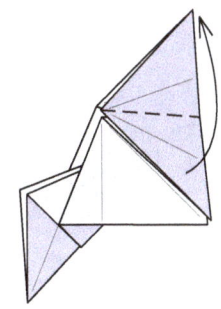
20. Valley fold up.

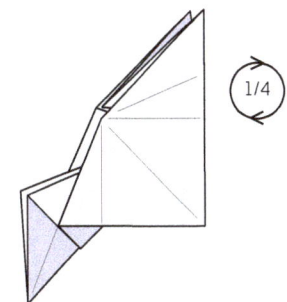
21. Rotate 1/4 turn.

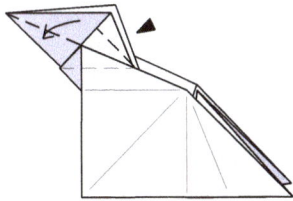
22. Reverse fold.

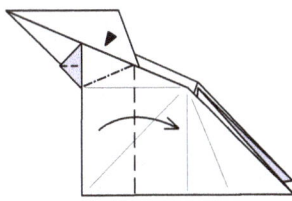
23. Squash fold.

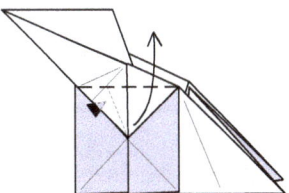
24. Valley fold up, allowing a squash fold to form.

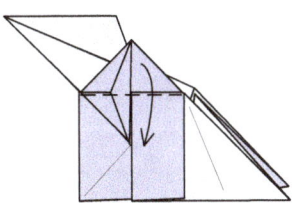
25. Swing the flap down.

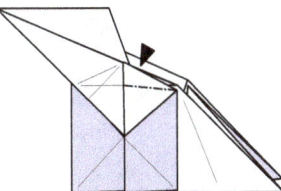
26. Open sink the trapped corner.

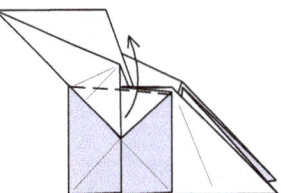
27. Swing up again.

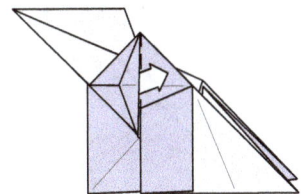
28. Unsink.

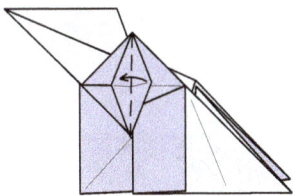
29. Valley fold over.

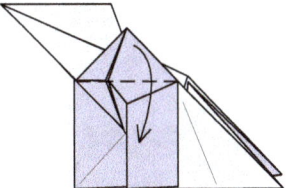
30. Valley fold back down.

giant panda

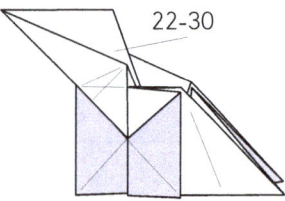

31. Repeat steps 22–30 behind.

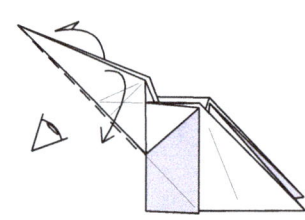

32. Spread apart the front flap. The remainder of the model will not lie flat.

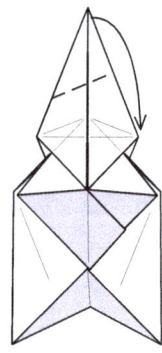

33. Valley fold the tip to the corner.

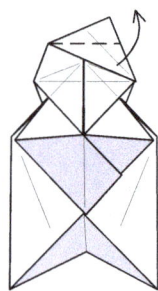

34. Valley fold up.

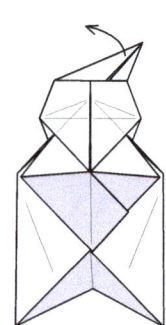

35. Unfold the pleat.

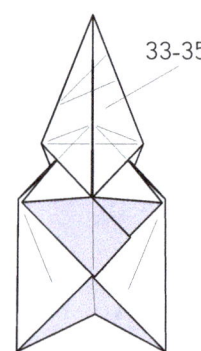

36. Repeat steps 33–35 in mirror image.

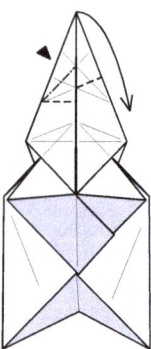

37. Squash fold.

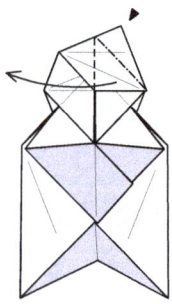

38. Squash fold again.

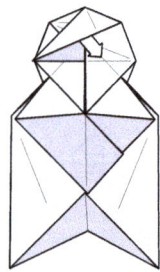

39. Pull out a single layer.

giant panda

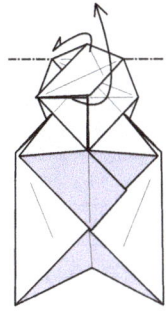

40. Flip the top section.

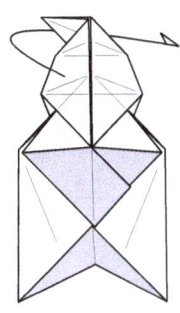

41. Close the model back up.

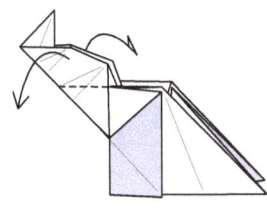

42. Outside reverse fold the front section.

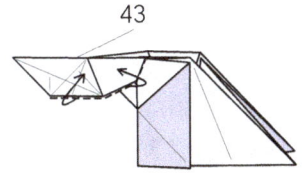

43. Wrap around a single layer to the surface. You will have to invert a corner to accomplish this. Repeat behind.

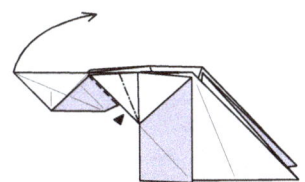

44. Crimp the flap upwards.

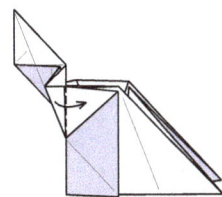

45. Swing over one flap.

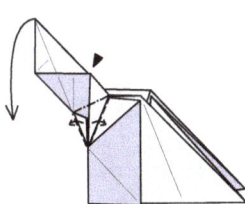

46. Squash fold the top section down.

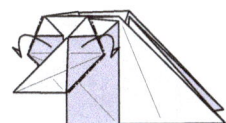

47. Wrap around a single layer at each side.

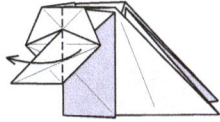

48. Swing over one flap.

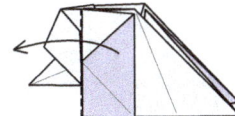

49. Swing over a flap.

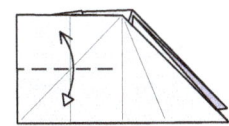

50. Lightly precrease the single layer in half.

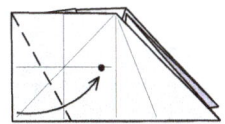

51. Valley fold the corner over to meet the crease.

51

giant panda

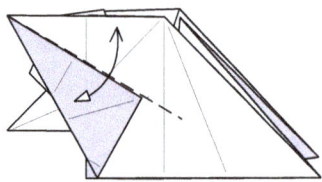

52. Precrease along the angle bisector.

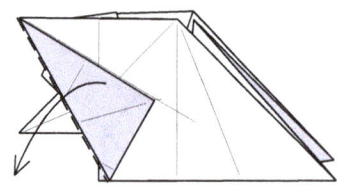

53. Unfold.

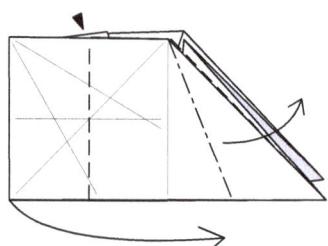

54. Stretch the single layer back while folding the left side in half.

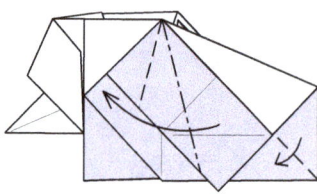

55. Pleat the top layer over along the existing creases, The right side will not lie flat.

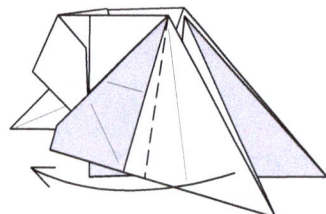

56. Valley fold over to meet the other edges to flatten.

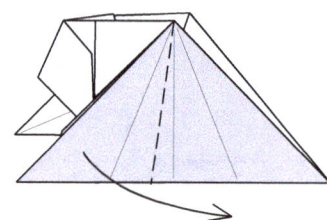

57. Valley fold the flap back as far as possible.

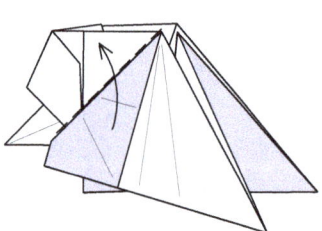

58. Lift up a single layer (it will not lie flat).

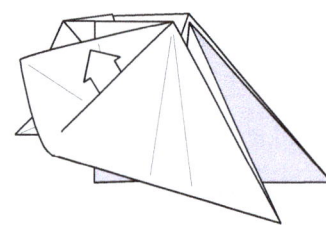

59. Unsink.

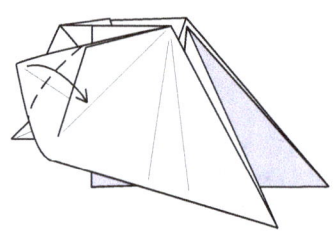

60. Valley fold the corner to the crease.

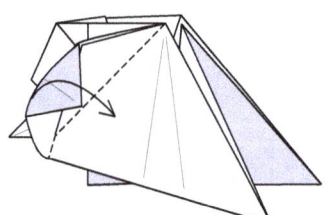

61. Close the flap back up.

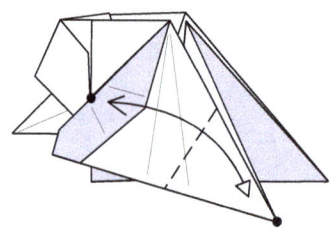

62. Precrease by bringing the flap to the dotted point and unfolding.

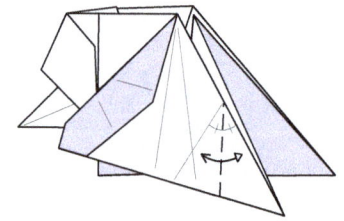

63. Precrease along the angle bisector.

giant panda

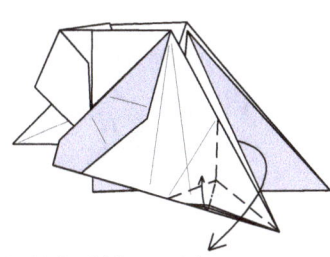

64. Valley fold over while incorporating a rabbit ear on the top two layers.

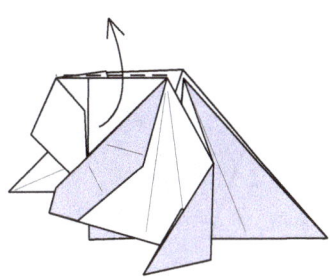

65. Lift up the trapped flap.

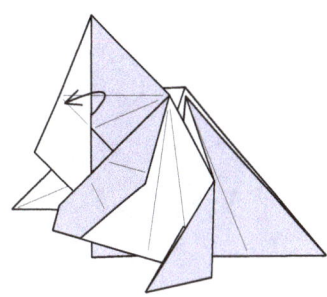

66. Bring two colored flaps to the surface.

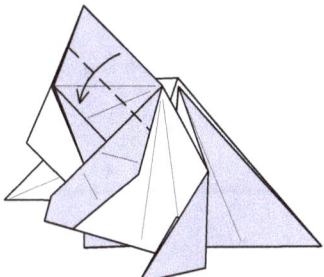

67. Valley fold the flap in half.

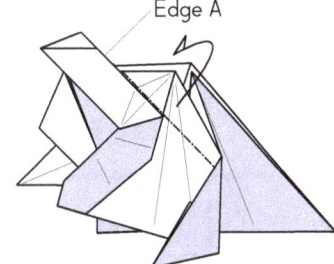

68. Mountain fold, so as to align with edge A.

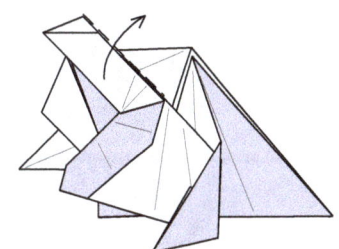

69. Unfold the flap.

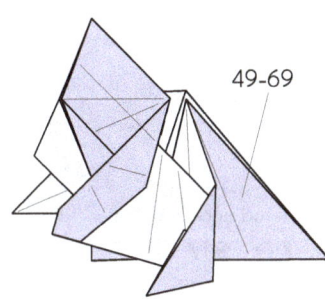

70. Repeat steps 49-69 behind.

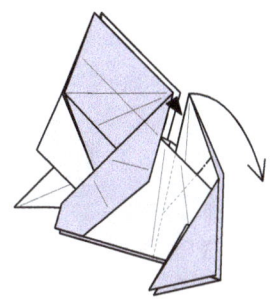

71. Reverse fold, allowing the tiny pleat in the flap's center to come undone.

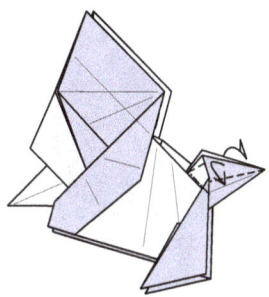

72. Swivel fold the side of the flap in along the angle bisector.

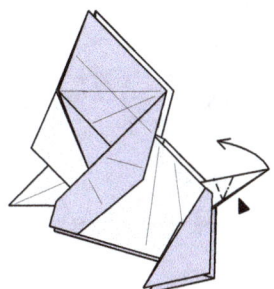

73. Squash fold the flap flat.

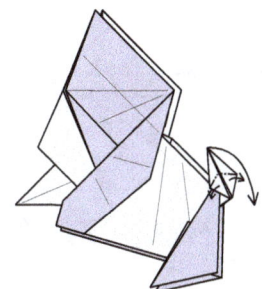

74. Pull out the side layers while swinging down.

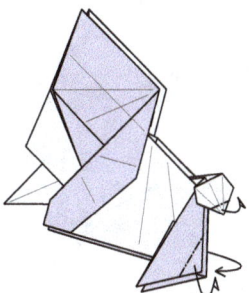

75. Mountain fold the indicated corners.

53

giant panda

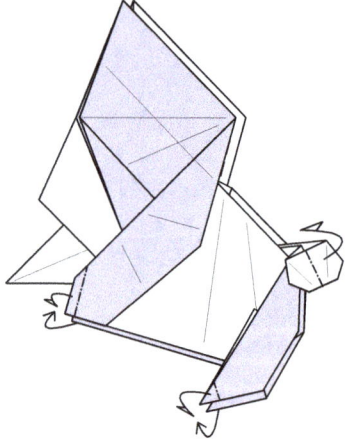

76. Mountain fold the tail in half, and mountain fold the feet as indicated.

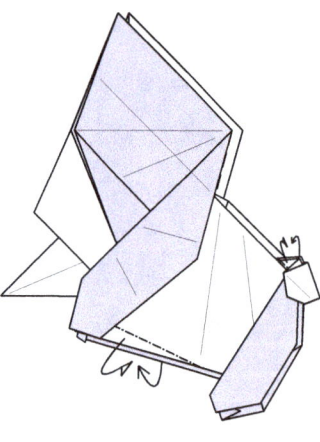

77. Tuck in the flaps at the tail, and swivel in the bottom of the body.

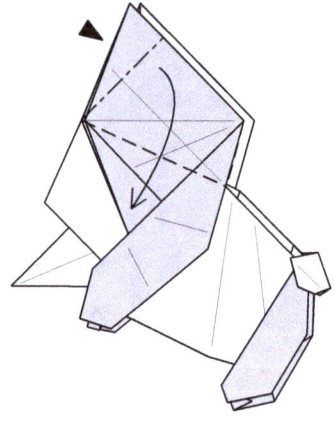

78. Squash fold the top flap.

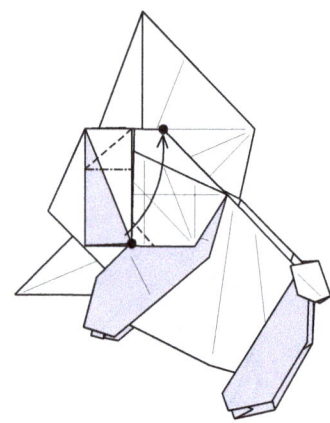

79. Form a squash fold, such that the dotted points meet.

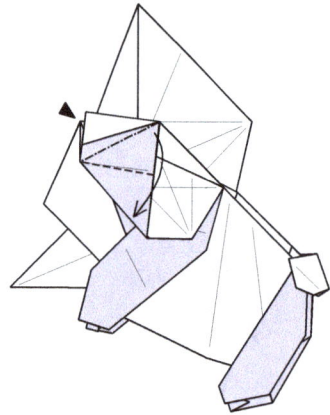

80. Squash fold the corner down as far as possible.

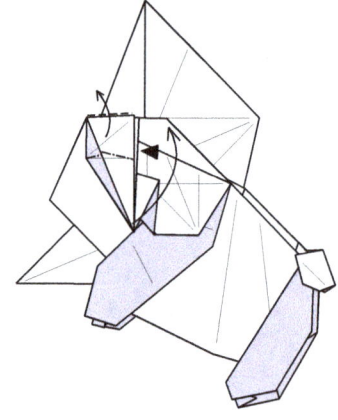

81. Spread apart the center ridge, squashing the flap upwards.

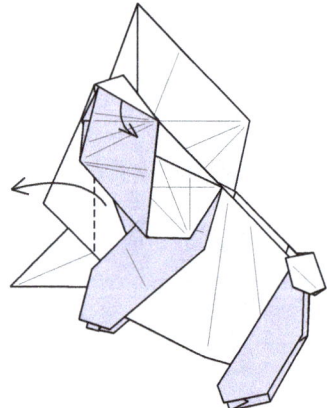

82. Pull out the trapped paper while valley folding the flap at the left (the bottom will not lie flat).

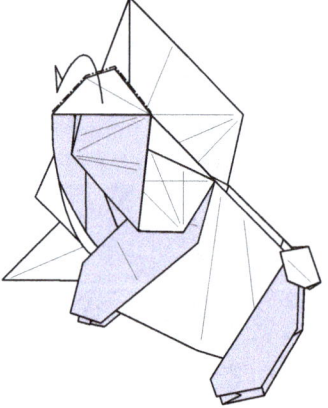

83. Wrap around a single layer.

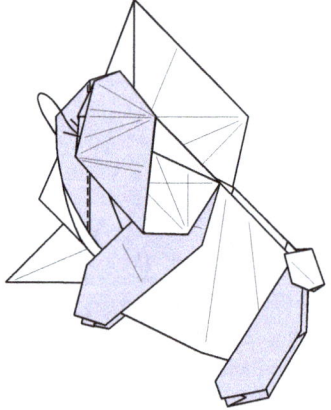

84. Flatten, by tucking the flap beneath all of the layers.

giant panda

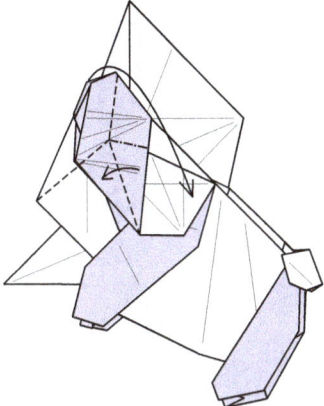
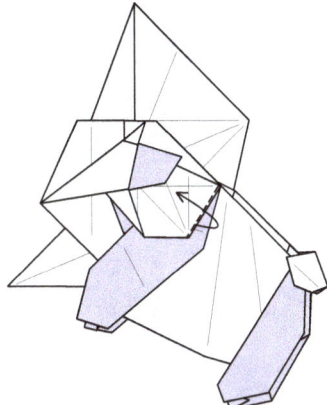
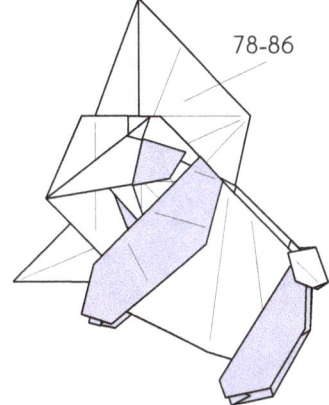

85. Valley fold down while incorporating a reverse fold.

86. Wrap the colored portion around to the surface.

87. Repeat steps 78-86 behind.

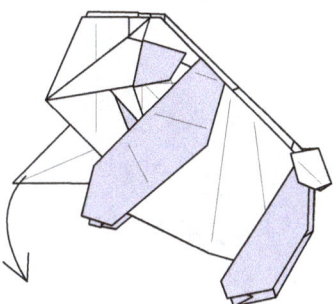
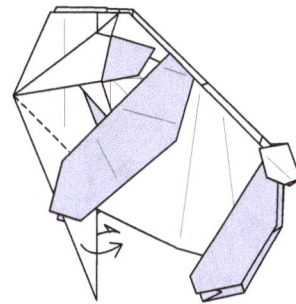
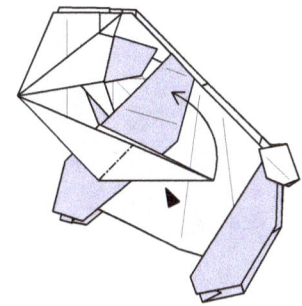

88. Stretch the point downwards.

89. Outside reverse fold, allowing the flap to lie on the surface.

90. Reverse fold upwards.

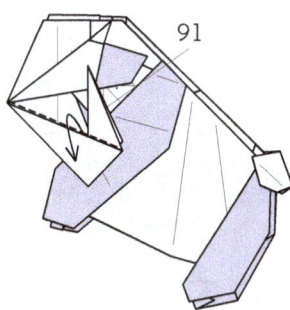
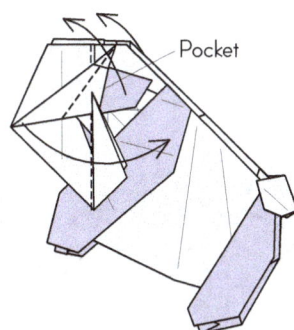
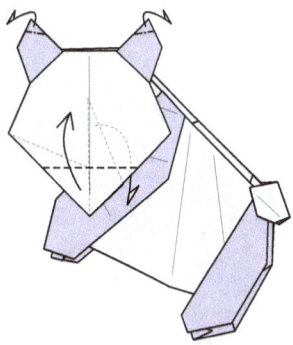

91. Wrap a single layer around. Repeat on the other side of the flap.

92. Open out the face, while pulling the ears up. Tuck the corners of the head into the indicated pockets.

93. Flip the hidden flap as indicated. Mountain fold the corners of the ears.

55

giant panda

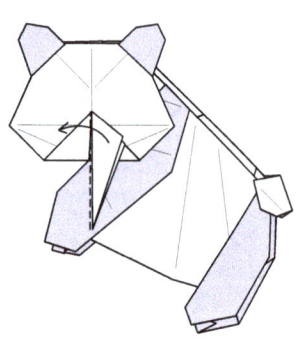

94. Swing over one layer.

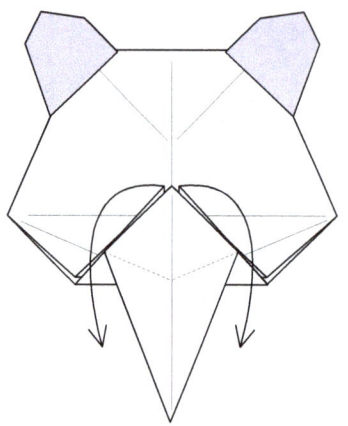

95. Reverse fold the points straight down.

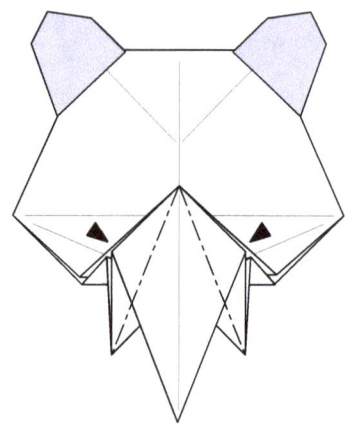

96. Open sink along the angle bisectors.

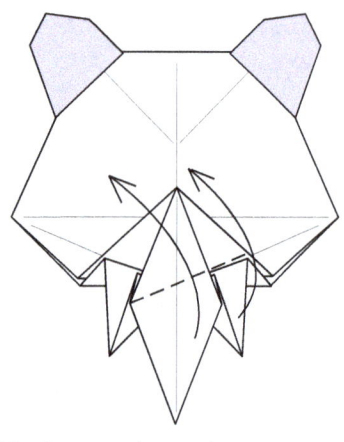

97. Swing up the two flaps.

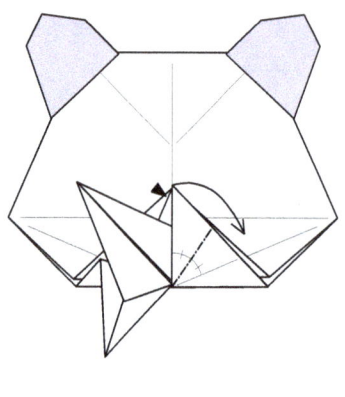

98. Reverse fold along the angle bisector.

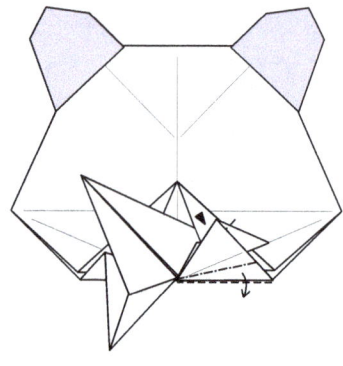

99. Slide some paper down.

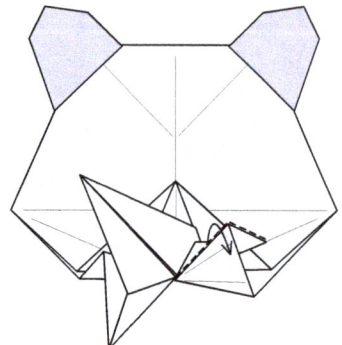

100. Wrap around a single layer.

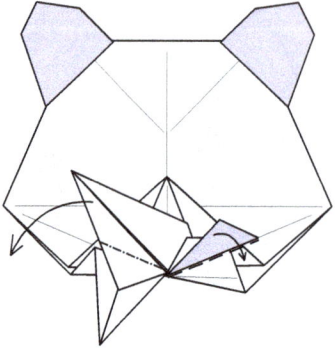

101. Valley fold the colored section down. Pull the point to the side, releasing a pleat.

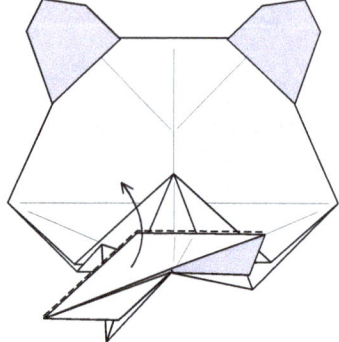

102. Lift up the top layer to reveal the colored portion.

giant panda

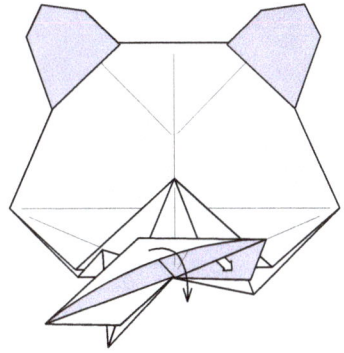

103. Unsink, and then close the top flap.

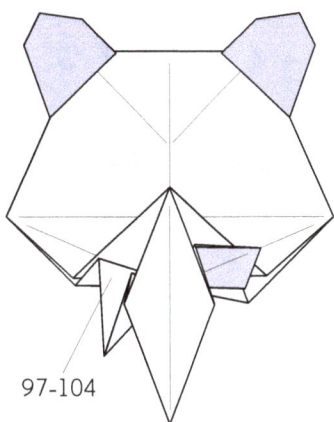

104. Valley fold the colored flap, and swing the center flap back down.

105. Repeat steps 97–104 in mirror image.

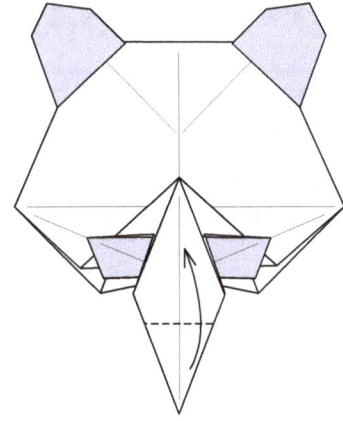

106. Valley fold up.

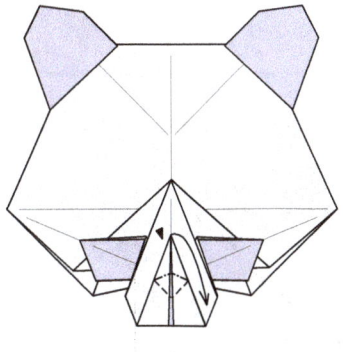

107. Squash fold.

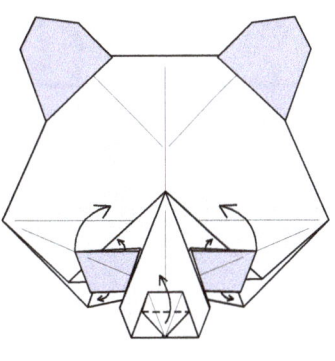

108. Valley fold the nose, and pull up the eyes, spreading apart the layers.

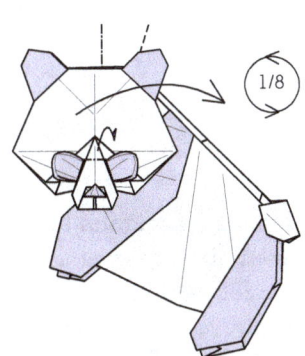

109. Mountain fold between the eyes. Pleat the head into position, and shape to taste. Rotate 1/8 of a turn.

110. Completed *Giant Panda*.

Giraffe

The giraffe is one of the biggest challenges an origami artist might tackle. On the outset, it might seem like the goal is to simply create a form with long and slender features. Taking this approach would leave you with a stick figure, rather than a graceful animal with intricate nuances of form. This Giraffe sets to embrace these subtleties by having a body that is three-dimensional and can be shaped. The neck even has extra layers that overlap to create a closed front.

giraffe

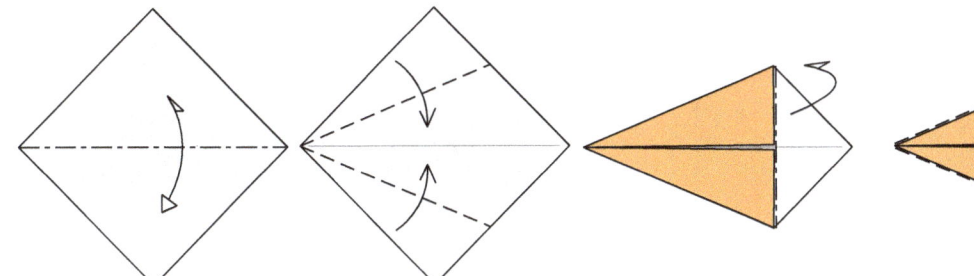

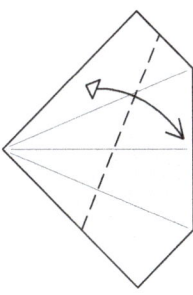

1. Precrease with a mountain fold.

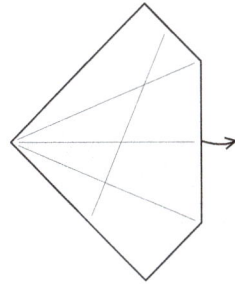

2. Valley fold to the center.

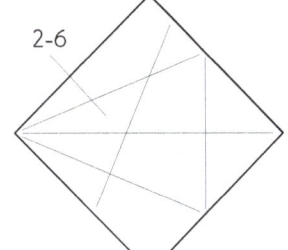

3. Mountain fold the corner.

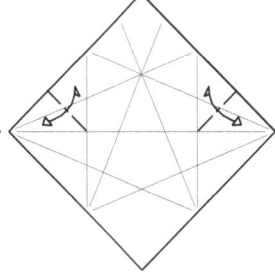

4. Open out the flaps.

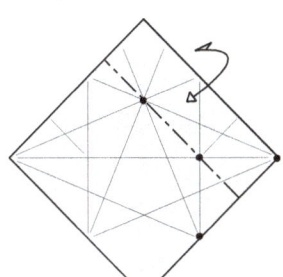

5. Precrease by bringing the top edge to the folded edge.

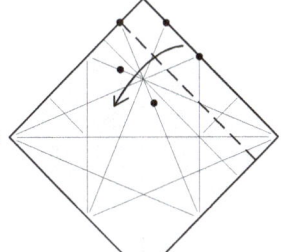

6. Unfold the original corner.

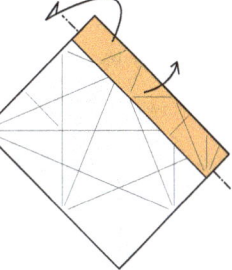

7. Repeat steps 2-6 in mirror image.

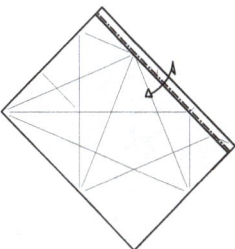

8. Precrease with mountain folds.

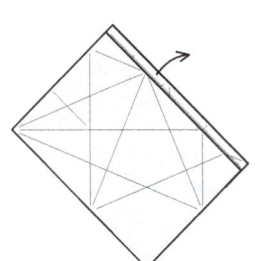

9. Precrease through the intersection of creases with a mountain fold.

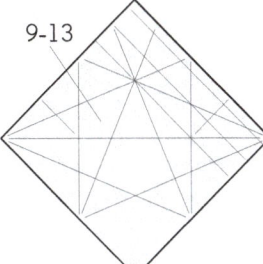

10. Valley fold, noting the indicated intersections.

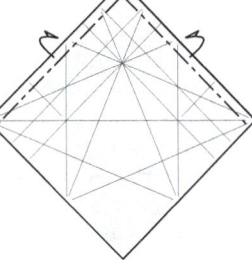

11. Mountain fold along the existing crease, allowing the flap to flip.

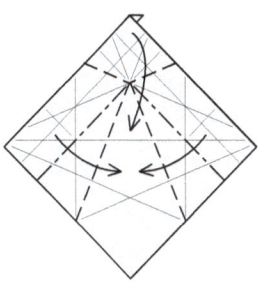

12. Precrease with a mountain fold.

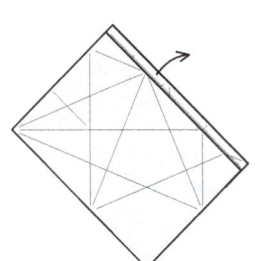

13. Unfold the pleat.

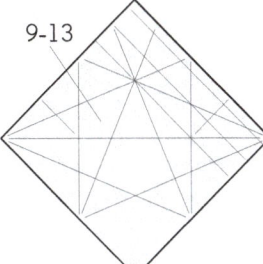

14. Repeat steps 9-13 in mirror image.

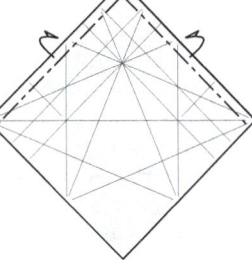

15. Form a rabbit ear at the top.

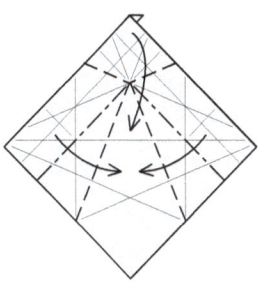

16. Collapse along the existing creases.

giraffe

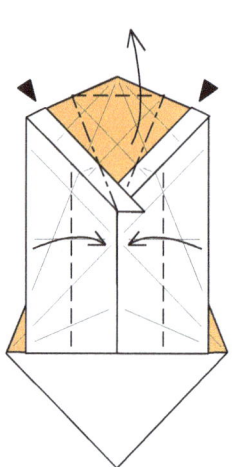

17. Petal fold.

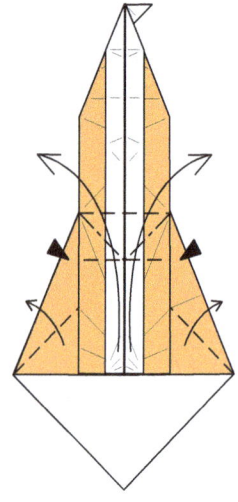

18. Collapse the sides upwards.

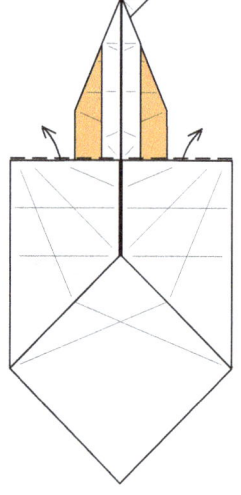

19. Pull out a single layer from each side.

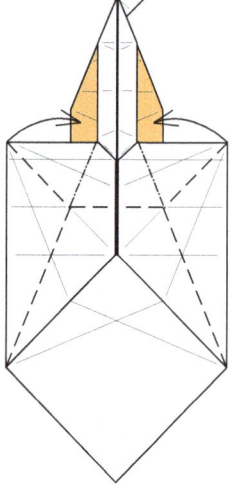

20. Rabbit ear the sides. The flaps will overlap.

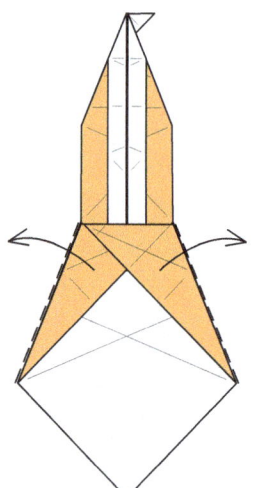

21. Unfold the two flaps.

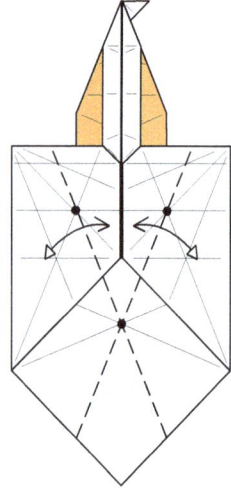

22. Precrease by bringing a bottom edge towards the opposite side edge. Note the indicated intersections.

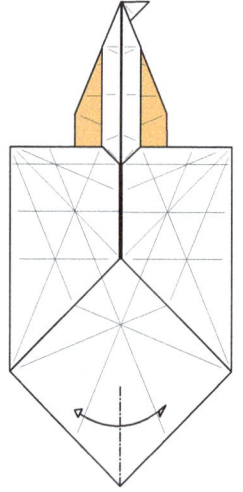

23. Precrease the bottom corner with a mountain fold.

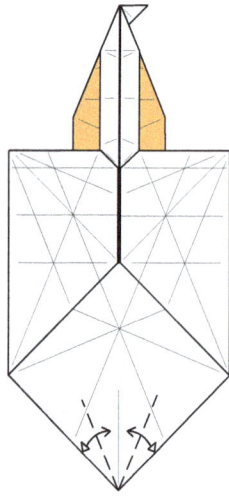

24. Precrease along the angle bisectors.

giraffe

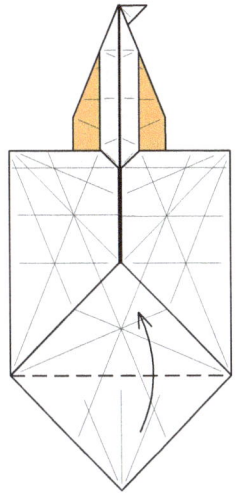 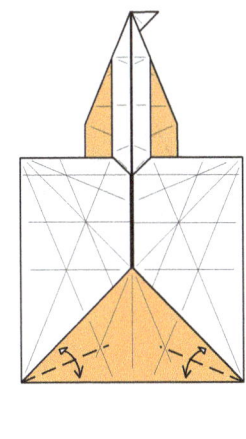 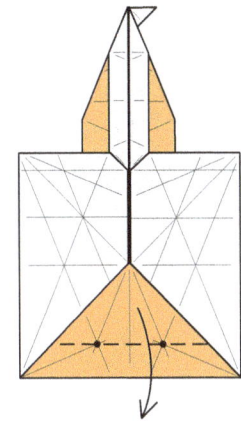 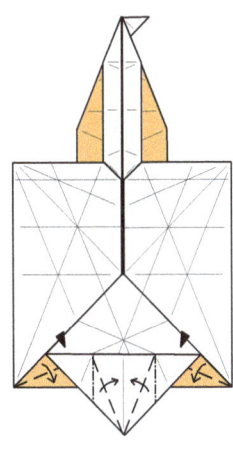

25. Valley fold the corner up.
26. Valley fold along the angle bisectors.
27. Valley fold through the indicated intersections.
28. Swivel fold along the existing creases.

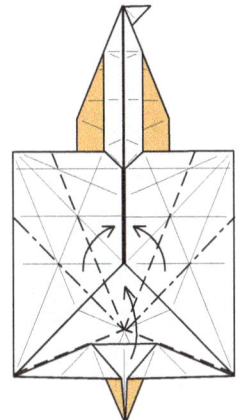 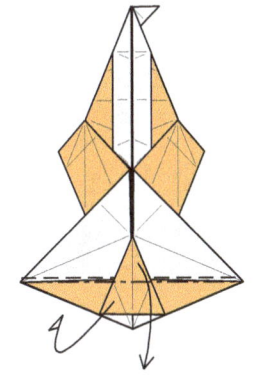 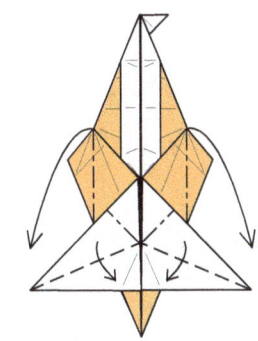 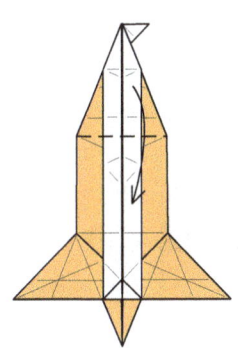

29. Collapse along the existing creases.
30. Flip the flap.
31. Bring the original corners towards the bottom flaps, collapsing along existing creases.
32. Swing the top flap down.

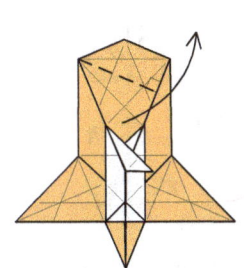 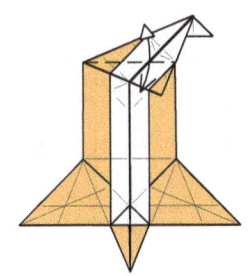 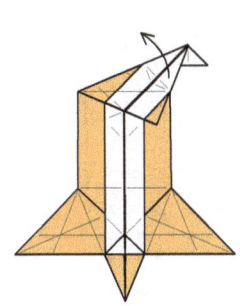 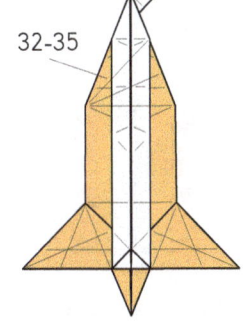

33. Valley fold up.
34. Precrease.
35. Unfold the pleat.
36. Repeat steps 32-35 in mirror image.

61

giraffe

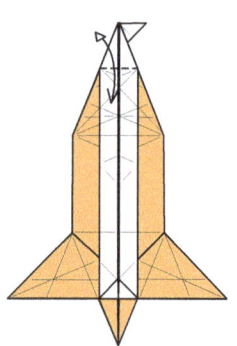 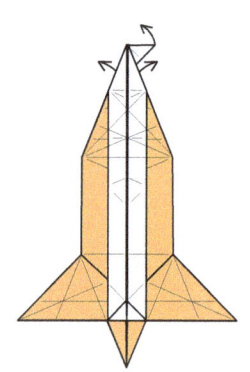 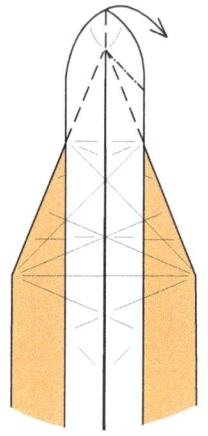 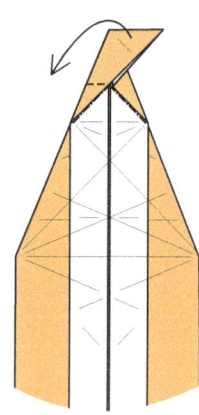

37. Precrease.

38. Pull the side edges out from behind. The tip will not lie flat.

39. Rabbit ear the tip to flatten.

40. Rabbit ear the flap behind.

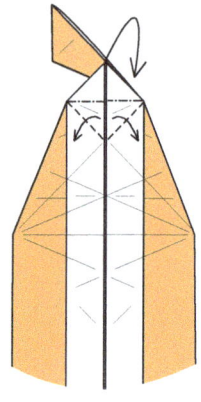 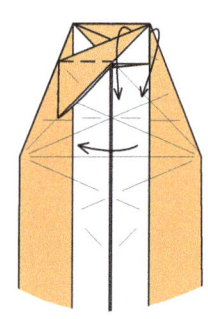 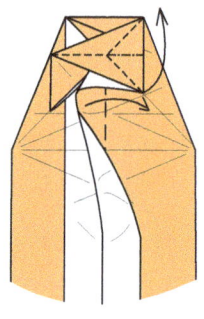 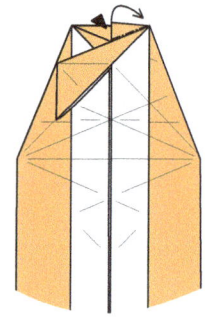

41. Valley fold down while pulling out the inner edges.

42. Unwrap the outer layer. The center hem should be brought to the other side partially.

43. Valley fold up while incorporating a reverse fold.

44. Reverse fold.

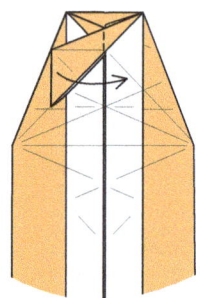 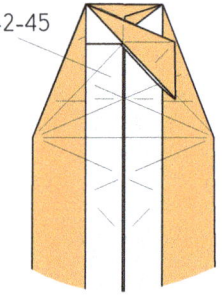 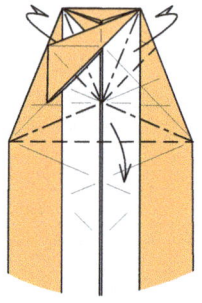 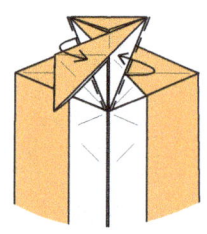

45. Swing over the center flap.

46. Repeat steps 42-45 in mirror image.

47. Pleat the sides behind, bringing the top section down.

48. Wrap around a single layer at each side.

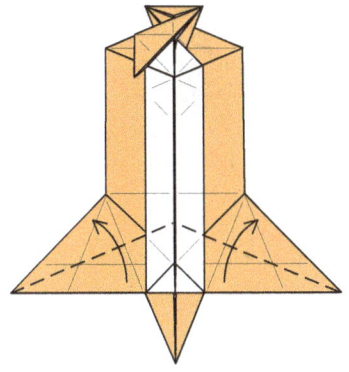

49. Valley fold the top layers up.

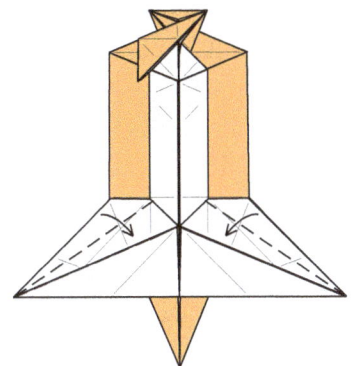

50. Valley fold the layers down.

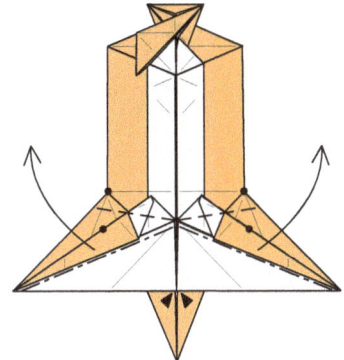

51. Squash fold the flaps up, such that the dotted areas meet.

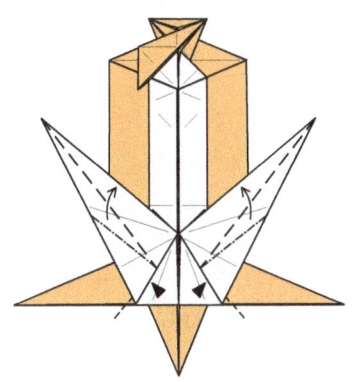

52. Swivel in the top layers.

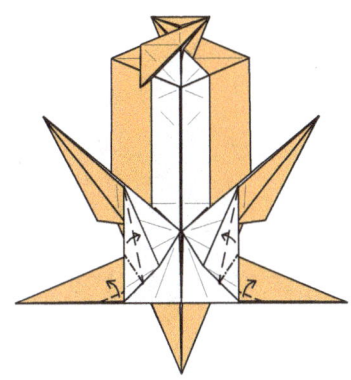

53. Swivel in again. The exact angles are not critical.

54. Turn over.

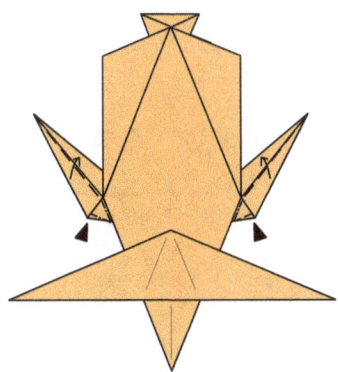

55. Reverse fold the edges in.

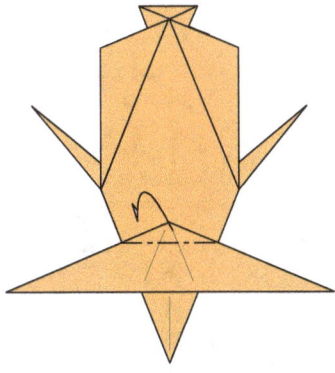

56. Mountain fold the edge to align with the sides.

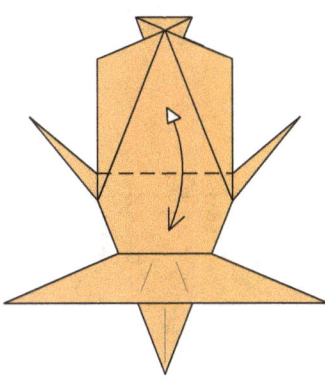

57. Precrease.

giraffe

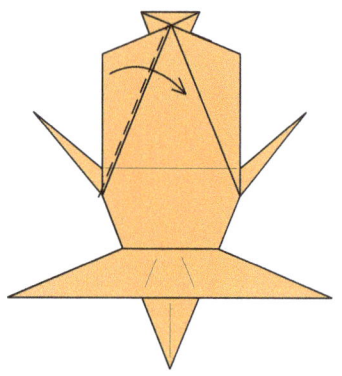

58. Valley fold the flap over.

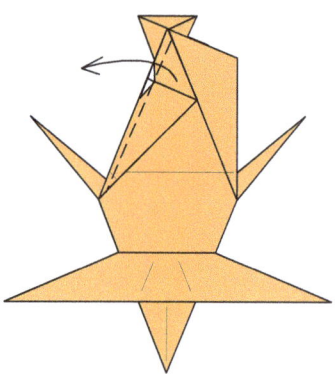

59. Valley fold, noting that the edge will meet the leg flap.

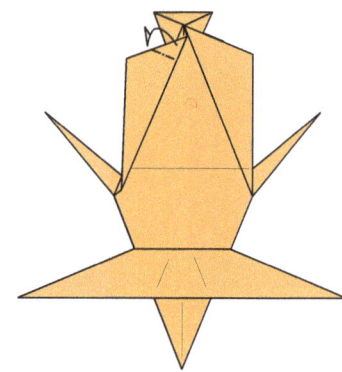

60. Swivel behind.

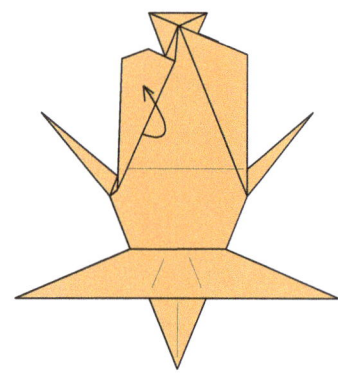

61. Tuck the pleat under the top layer.

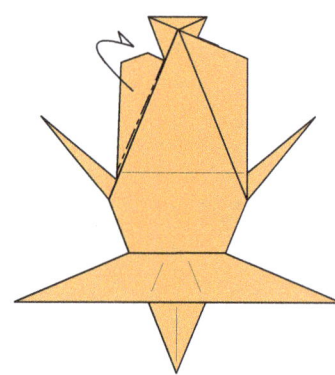

62. Mountain fold.

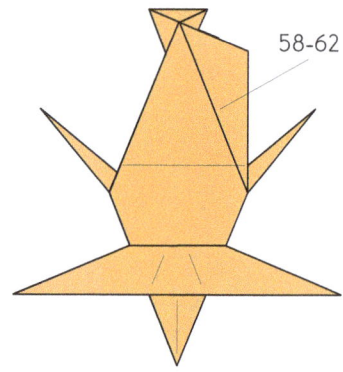

63. Repeat steps 58-62 in mirror image.

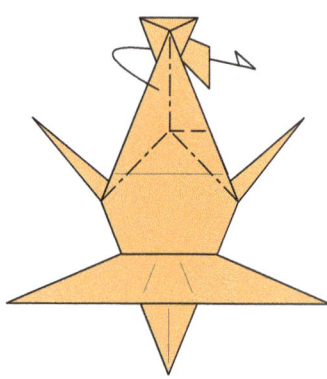

64. Rabbit ear, creasing softly along the center.

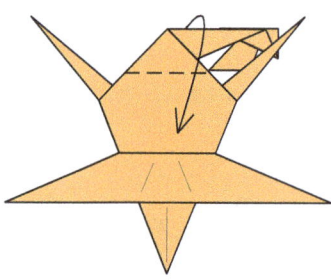

65. Valley fold along the existing crease.

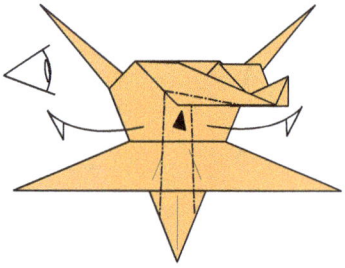

66. Softly mountain fold the sides down while softly flattening the center of the neck.

giraffe

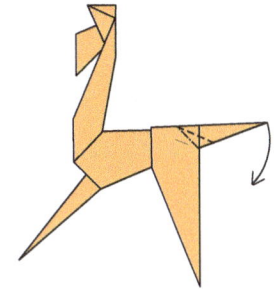

67. Crimp the tail down.

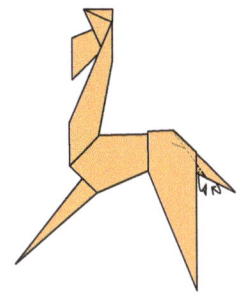

68. Mountain fold the hidden edges.

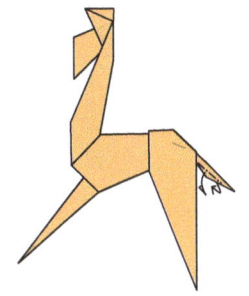

69. Mountain fold the sides of the tail.

70. Rabbit ear the legs back.

71. Mountain fold the legs.

72. Crimp down.

73. Crimp again.

74. Pull the legs down.

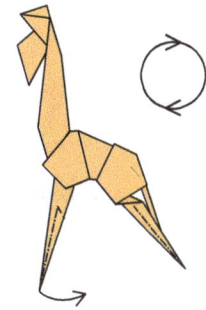

75. Shape the legs. Rotate the model slightly.

76. Outside reverse fold the top section.

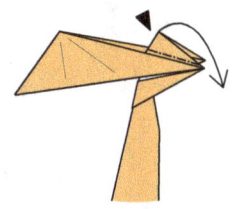

77. Reverse fold.

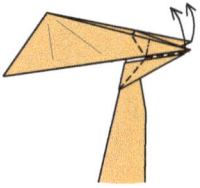

78. Rabbit ear the outer flaps up.

giraffe

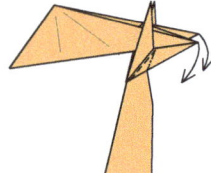

79. Pleat the lower edges, allowing the ears to curl outwards.

80. Pull up the top edges.

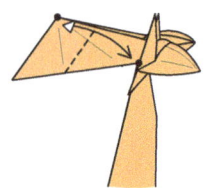

81. Precrease.

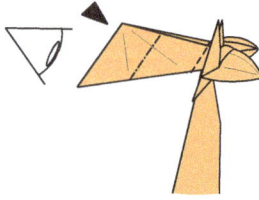

82. Spread squash.

83. View from previous step. Mountain fold the bottom.

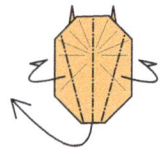

84. Round the sides of the head and lift slightly.

85. Pull out the hidden edges.

86. Tuck the flap into the opposite side.

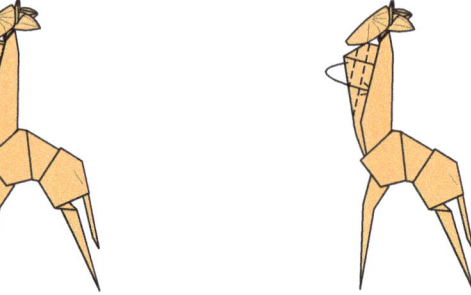

87. Tuck the remaining flap into the pocket.

88. Completed *Giraffe*.

Koala

Australia is the home to many unusual creatures, and the koala is no exception. Its spoon-shaped nose is certainly unique, but this creature most certainly gets noticed for how adorable it is. These marsupials sport a cute set of features, but its laid-back disposition kicks its charm into high gear. This origami *Koala* captures its exemplary teddy bear pose. The folds are engineered for the legs to splay out slightly, giving a look of not wanting to leave a comfortable seated position.

koala

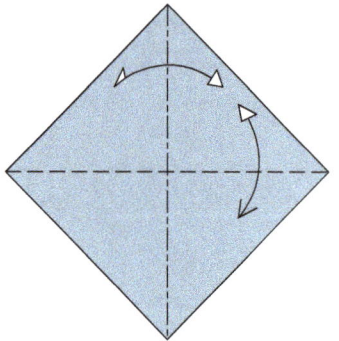

1. Precrease the diagonals with a valley fold and a mountain fold.

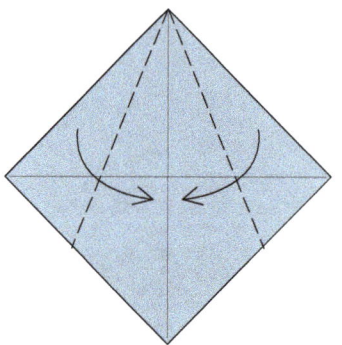

2. Valley fold the sides to the center.

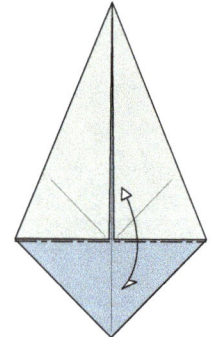

3. Precrease with a mountain fold.

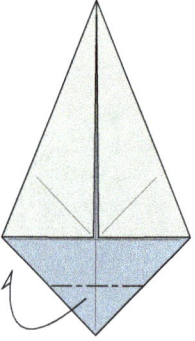

4. Mountain fold the corner to the last crease.

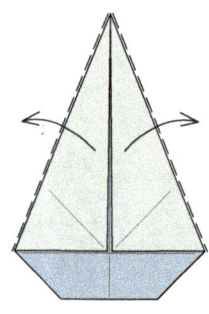

5. Open out the sides.

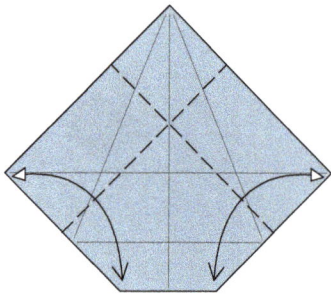

6. Precrease the side edges in half.

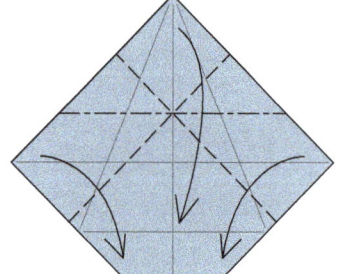

7. Collapse downwards.

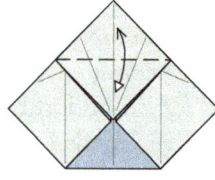

8. Lightly precrease the top layer.

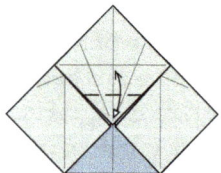

9. Precrease the bottom section in half.

koala

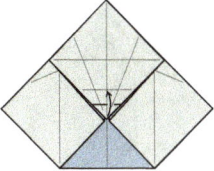

10. Valley fold up to the last crease.

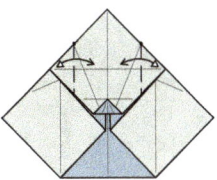

11. Precrease starting from the dotted intersections.

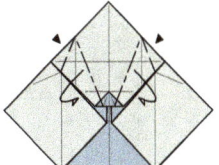

12. Reverse fold the sides.

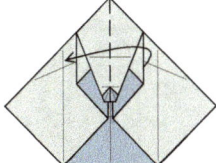

13. Swing over one flap.

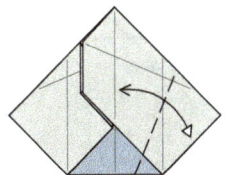

14. Precrease by bringing the side edge to the center and unfolding.

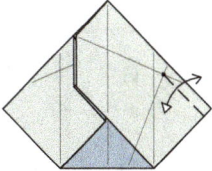

15. Precrease the top layer starting from the dotted intersection.

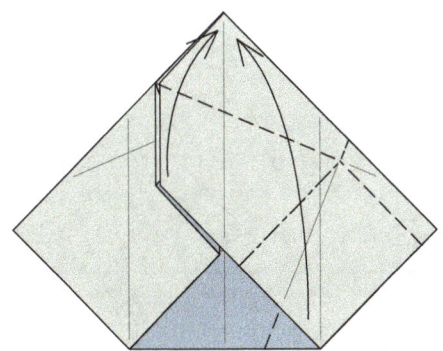

16. Bring the indicated corners to the top, collapsing along mostly existing creases.

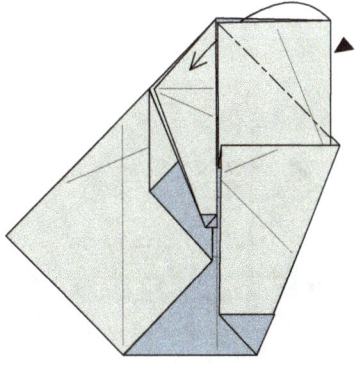

17. Reverse fold the corner.

69

koala

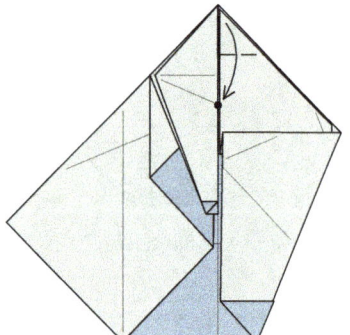

18. Valley fold to the dotted intersection.

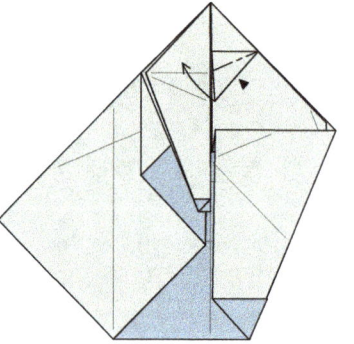

19. Squash fold the flap.

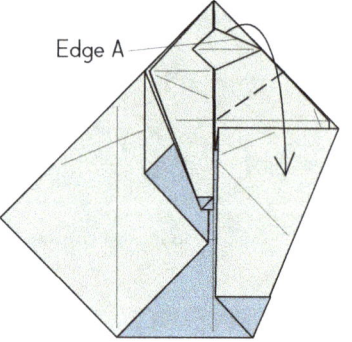

20. Valley fold such that edge A lies straight.

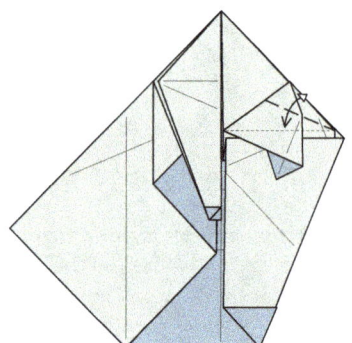

21. Precrease along the angle bisector.

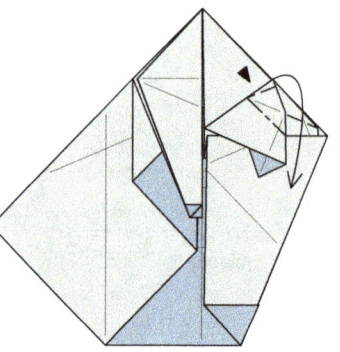

22. Reverse fold the flap.

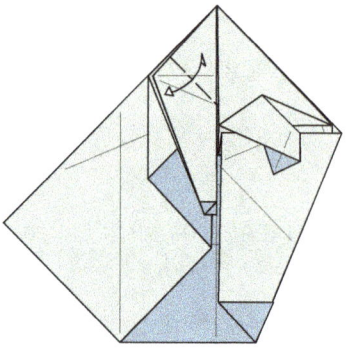

23. Precrease with a mountain fold.

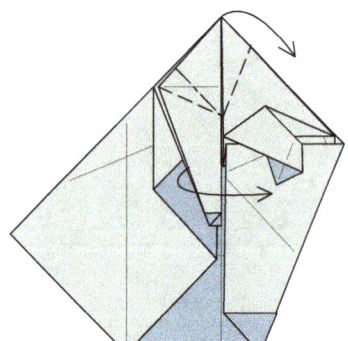

24. Swing the flap over while crimping the top corner down.

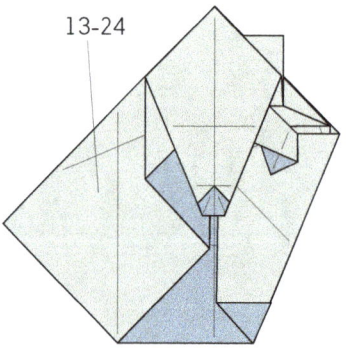

25. Repeat steps 13-24 in mirror image.

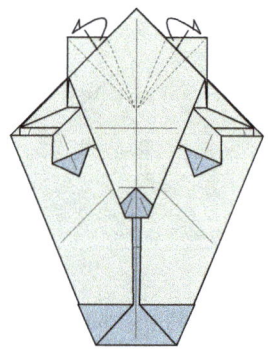

26. Mountain fold the edges along the indicated angle bisectors.

koala

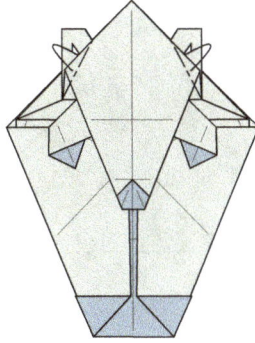

27. Mountain fold the corners inside.

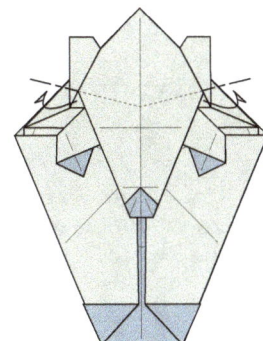

28. Mountain fold the lower edges as far as possible.

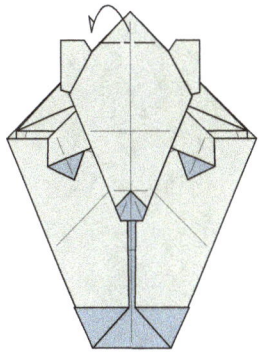

29. Mountain fold the top corner.

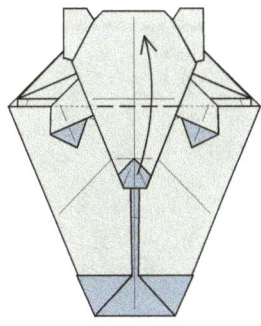

30. Valley fold up, aligning with the indicated hidden edge.

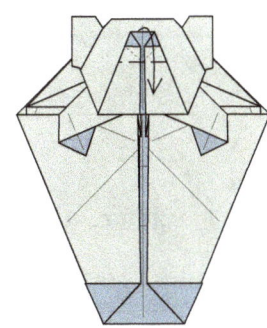

31. Valley fold down, aligning with the corner behind.

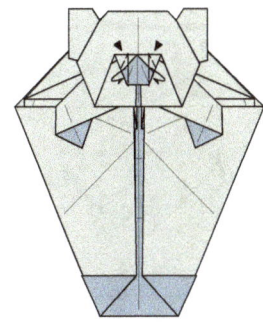

32. Swivel the sides in, allowing the flap to be slightly curled.

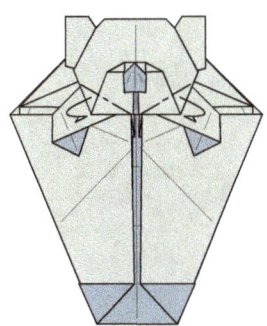

33. Mountain fold the lower corners inside.

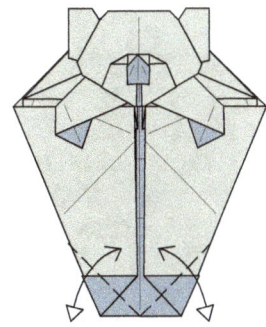

34. Precrease by folding the bottom edges to the center and unfolding.

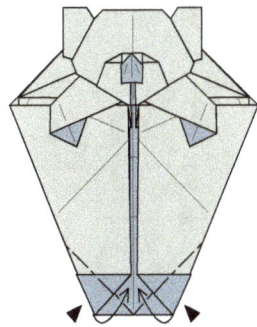

35. Reverse fold the bottom corners.

koala

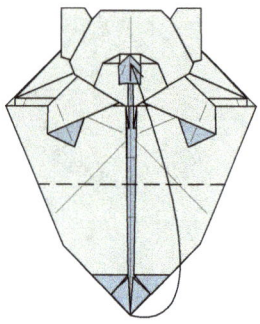

36. Valley fold to the top of the colored flap.

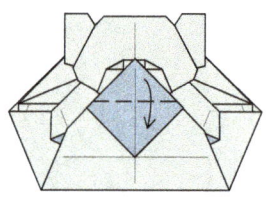

37. Valley fold the flap down as far as possible.

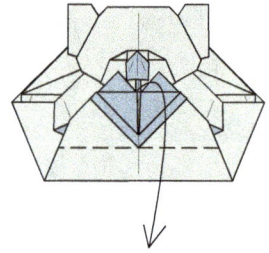

38. Valley fold down along the existing crease.

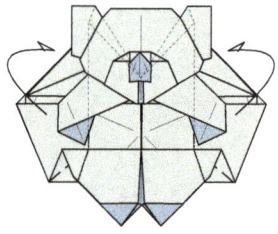

39. Mountain fold the sides behind allowing swivels to form at the legs. The flaps will overlap slightly.

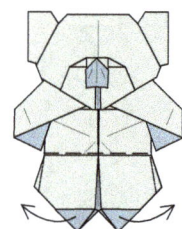

40. Raise the legs out straight, and adjust so the model will stand.

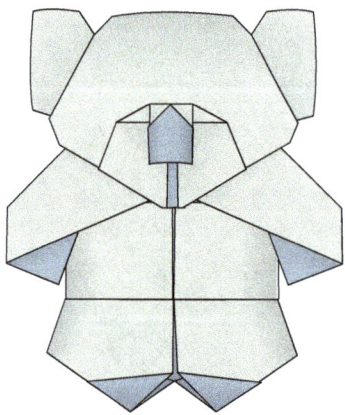

41. Completed *Koala*.

Peacock

Peacocks are renowned for their lavish array of tail feathers, so it makes sense to design a model that showcases this plumage in an open position. This *Peacock* also sports a tail section that adds some realism and more importantly allows the model to stand on its own. There is also a sequence of steps to form the distinctive head feathers that fortuitously puts the head in a proud position. The final lock that joins the sides of the body serendipitously adds just the right amount of volume to the body.

peacock

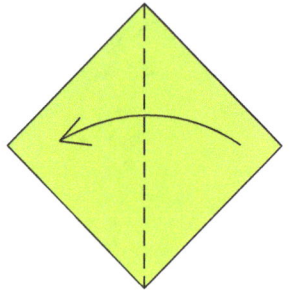
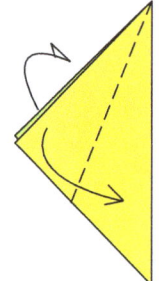
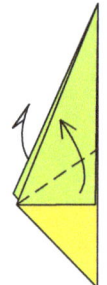

1. Begin with the body color side up. Valley fold in half.
2. Valley fold at each side.
3. Valley fold up at each side.
4. Valley fold to meet the folded edge.

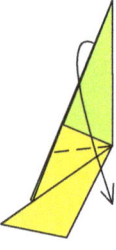
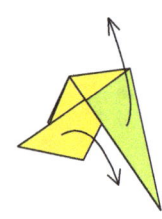
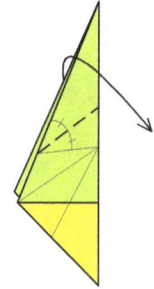
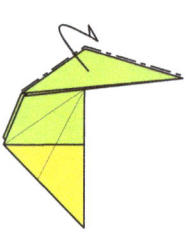

5. Valley fold along the angle bisector.
6. Unfold to step 3.
7. Valley fold along the angle bisector.
8. Wrap around a single layer.

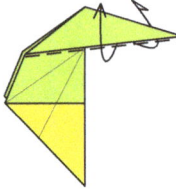
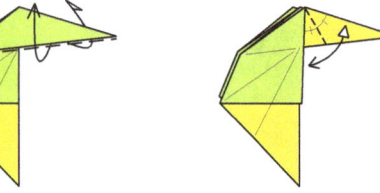
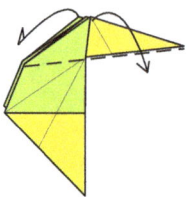
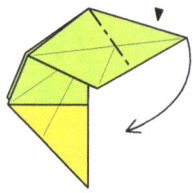

9. Wrap around a single layer at each side,
10. Precrease along the angle bisector.
11. Swing down a flap at each side.
12. Reverse fold.

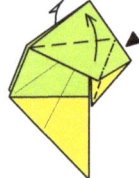
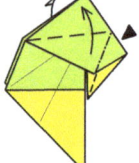
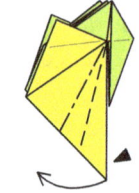

13. Petal fold the sides up.
14. Valley fold along the existing creases.
15. Crimp the flap.
16. Crimp again.

peacock

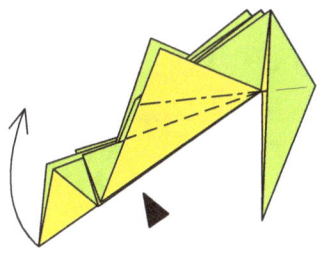
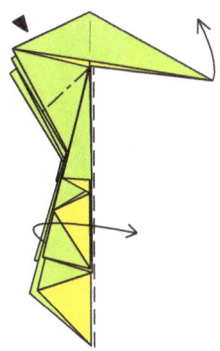

Edge A

17. Crimp again, this time through a double layer.

18. Valley fold the outer flaps. Rotate the model such that Edge A is straight.

19. Spread apart the bottom layers evenly, squash folding at the top.

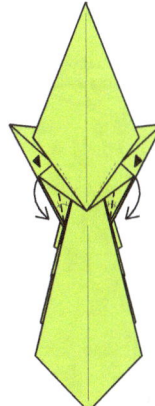
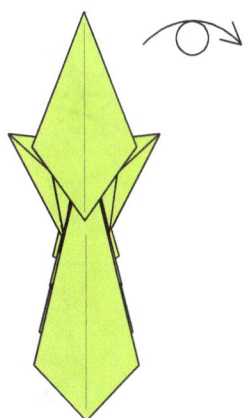

20. Open out the top while reverse folding the side flaps up.

21. Reverse fold the side flaps along the angle bisectors. Part of the fold is hidden.

22. Turn over.

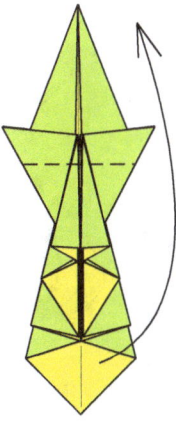
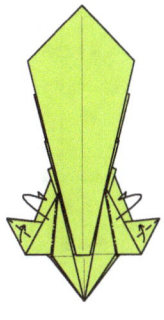
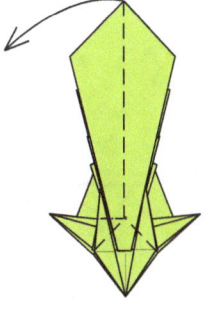

23. Valley fold up as far as possible.

24. Swivel the sides inwards.

25. Rabbit ear the top section.

peacock

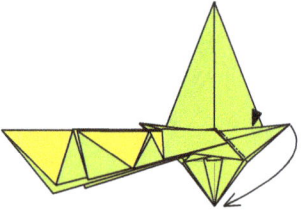

26. Reverse fold.

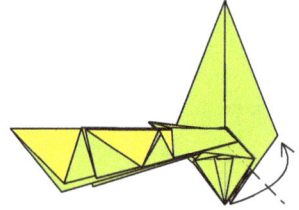

27. Reverse fold back out to meet the corner.

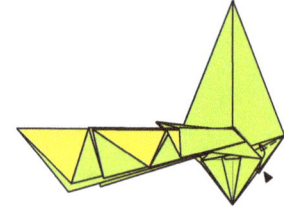

28. Reverse fold along the angle bisector.

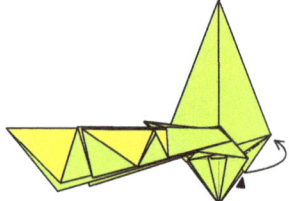

29. Reverse fold the other side.

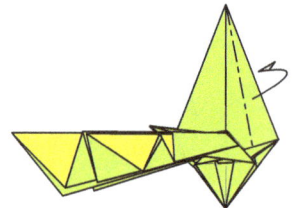

30. Mountain fold along the angle bisector.

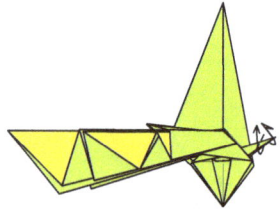

31. Outside reverse fold.

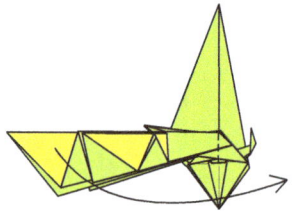

32. Swing the flap over.

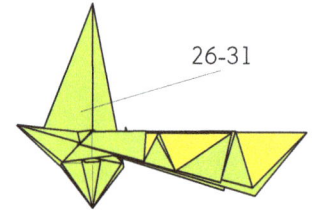

33. Repeat steps 26-31 in mirror image.

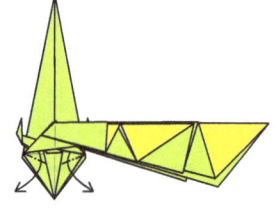

34. Slide out the top layers.

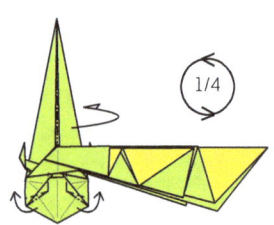

35. Crimp the lower section down and mountain fold the top flap in half, Avoid folding the thick section in half. Rotate the model.

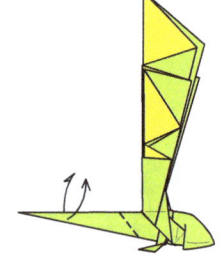

36. Outside reverse fold.

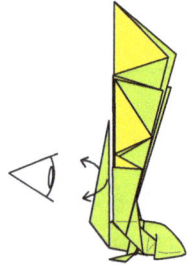

37. Spread apart the sides of the flap.

peacock

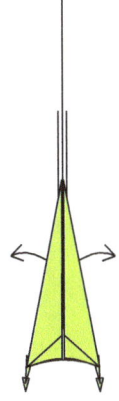

38. View from previous step. Slide out a single layer at each side.

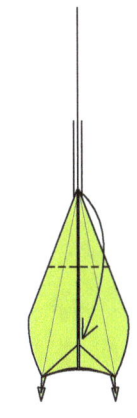

39. Valley fold to the corner.

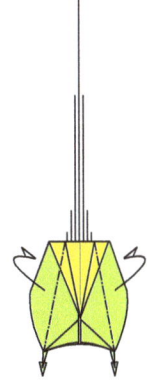

40. Mountain fold the sides back in.

41. Rabbit ear.

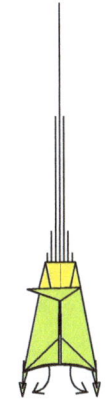

42. Pull out the bottom edges.

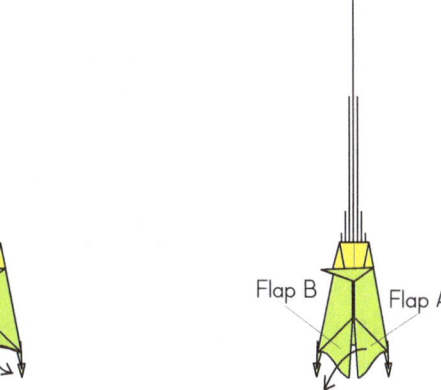

43. Place Flap A on top of Flap B.

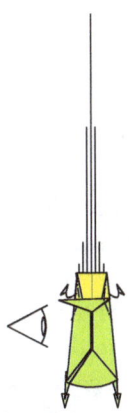

44. Shape the top flap with mountain folds and mountain fold it in half.

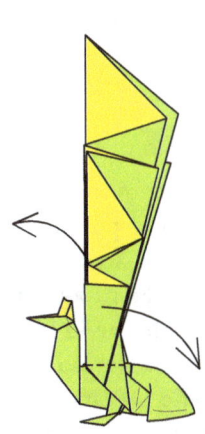

45. View from previous step. Spread apart the pleats of the top flap.

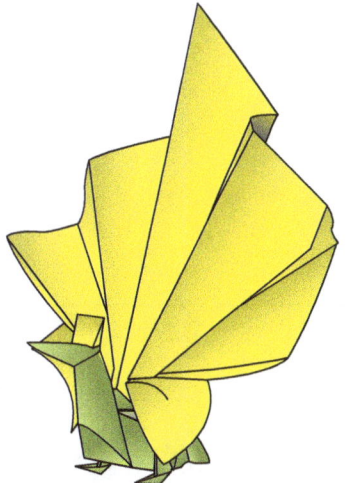

46. Completed *Peacock*.

Penguin

The profile of the classic origami Fish Base lends itself well to designing penguins, and most folded efforts use some variation on this starting point. Par for the course, these models sport an open backside. To create a piece that can be viewed from both sides required a novel approach. This *Penguin* solves this problem by forming the head from the middle portion of the paper, allowing the outer edges to be free to create the distinctive patterns and stature. This also generated extra complexity to form this bird's distinctive dome. Many unique folds are to be found here.

penguin

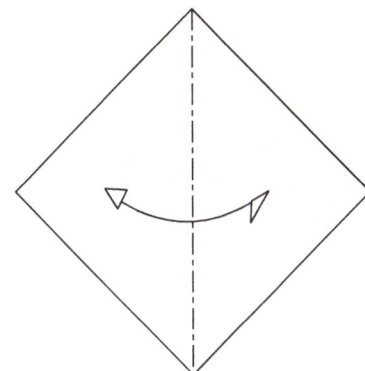 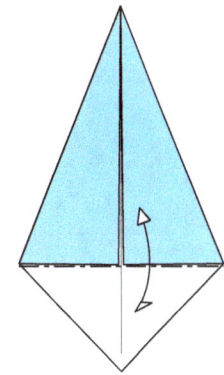

1. Precrease in half with a mountain fold.

2. Valley fold the sides to the center.

3. Precrease the bottom with a mountain fold.

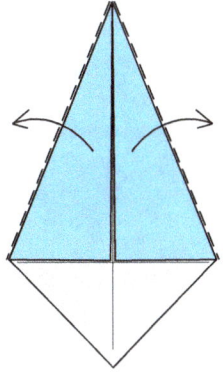 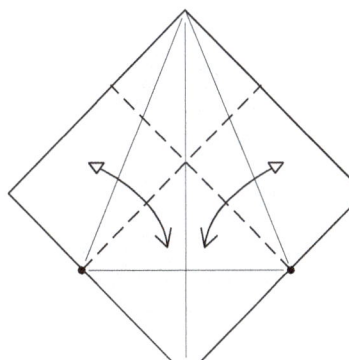 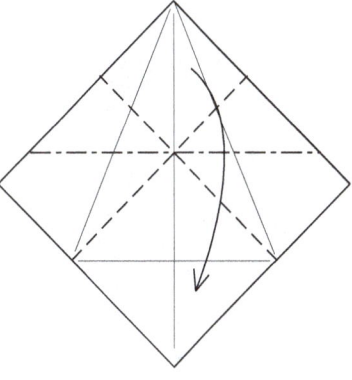

4. Open out the sides.

5. Precrease.

6. Collapse down.

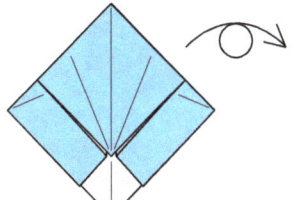 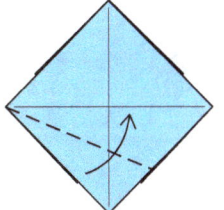 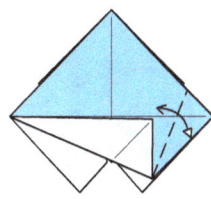

7. Turn over.

8. Valley fold up.

9. Precrease along the angle bisector.

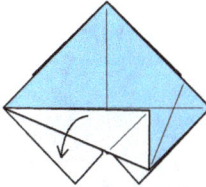 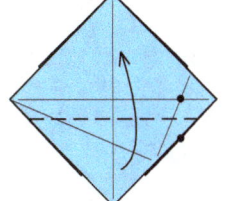 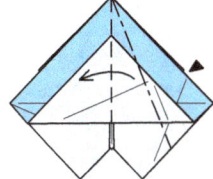

10. Fold the flap back down.

11. Valley fold up, such that the edge hits the indicated intersection.

12. Squash fold.

79

penguin

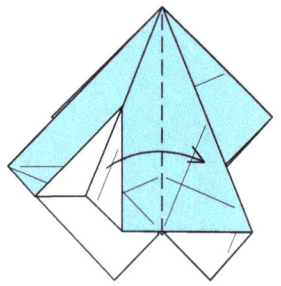

13. Swing the flap over.

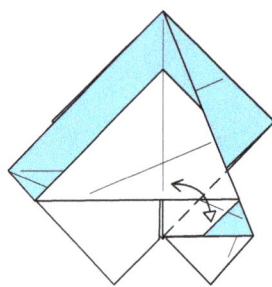

14. Precrease the top flap.

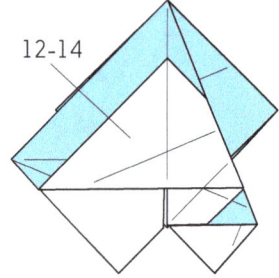

15. Repeat steps 12-14 in mirror image.

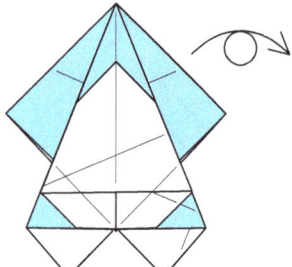

16. Turn over.

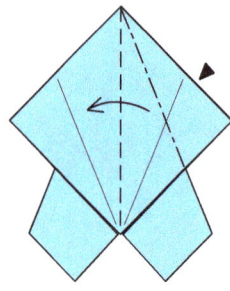

17. Squash fold.

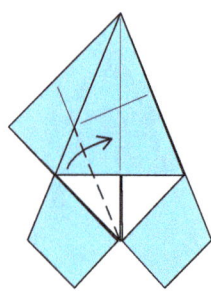

18. Valley fold.

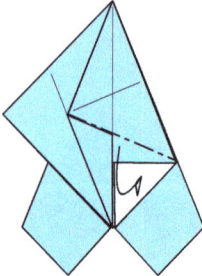

19. Mountain fold.

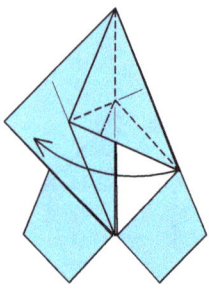

20. Valley fold the flap over, while collapsing the triangular section.

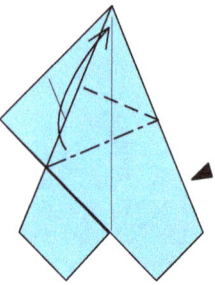

21. Fold the corner to the top, allowing a squash to form.

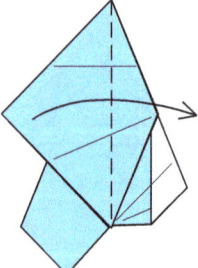

22. Valley fold.

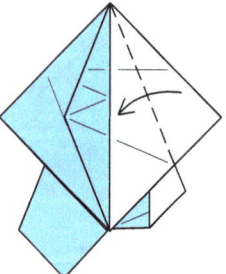

23. Valley fold.

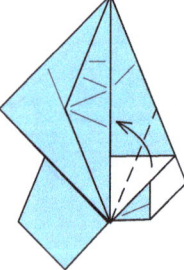

24. Valley fold.

penguin

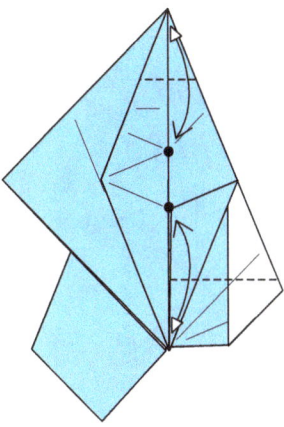

25. Precrease, noting the indicated intersections.

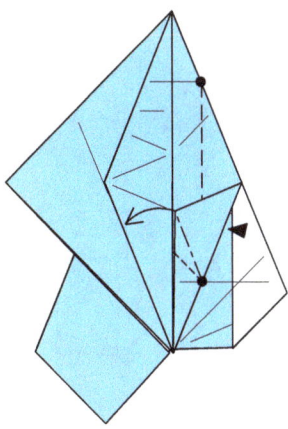

26. Swivel fold over.

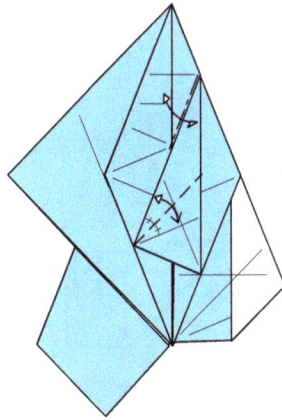

27. Precrease with mountain and valley folds as indicated.

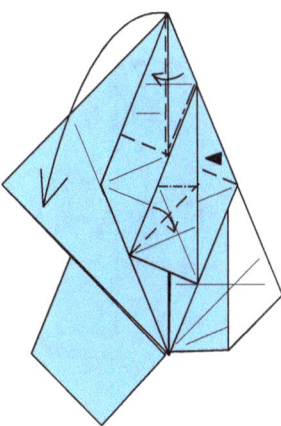

28. Swing the flap down while performing a double swivel fold.

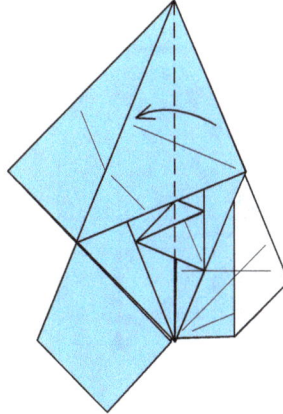

29. Lightly valley fold the flap over.

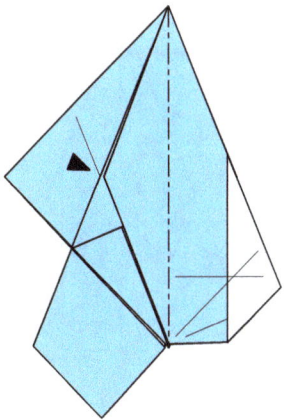

30. Closed sink.

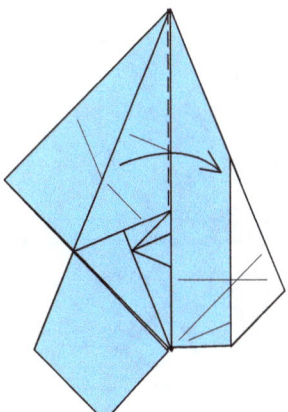

31. Valley fold over, allowing the flap to spread open.

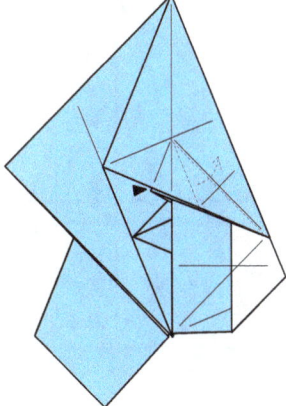

32. Squash fold the hidden layer.

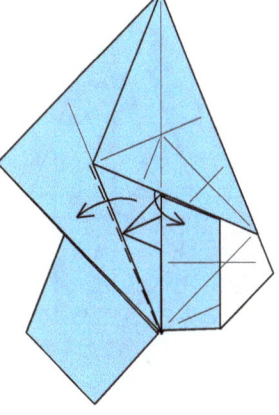

33. Pull out a single layer.

penguin

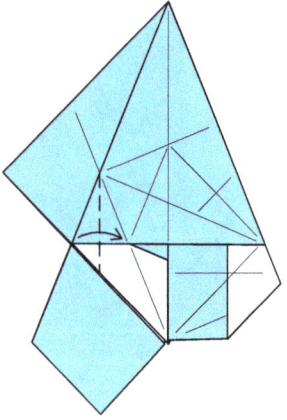

34. Valley fold the corner.

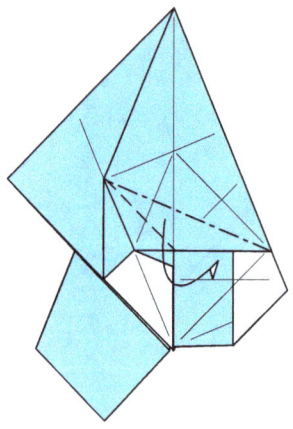

35. Swivel fold under.

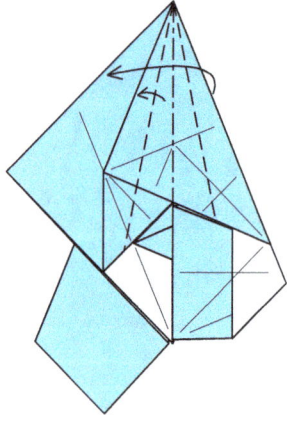

36. Swing the flap over, while inserting a pleat on the top layer.

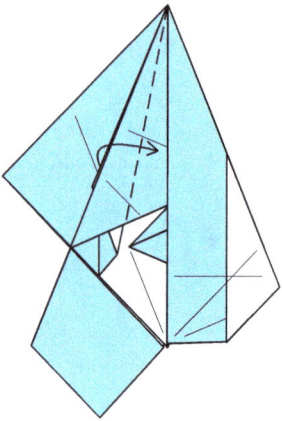

37. Valley fold over two flaps.

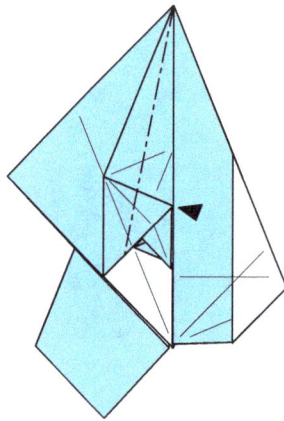

38. Reverse fold the flap through.

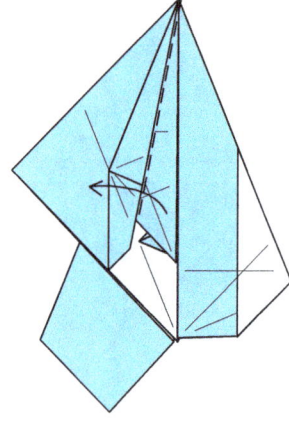

39. Swing over the flap.

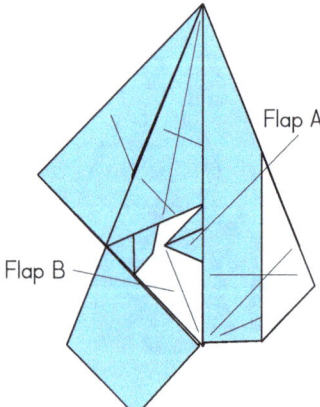

40. Tuck flap A under flap B.

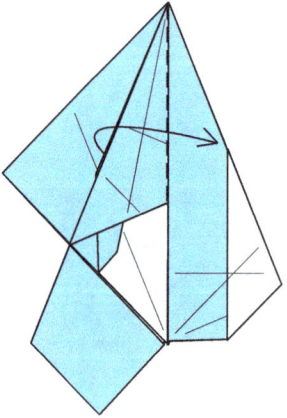

41. Swing over.

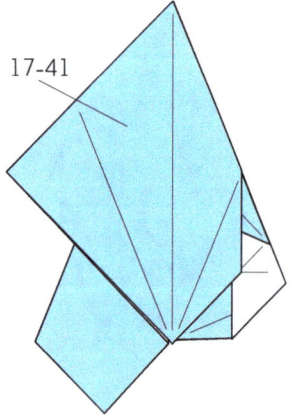

42. Repeat steps 17-41 in mirror image.

penguin

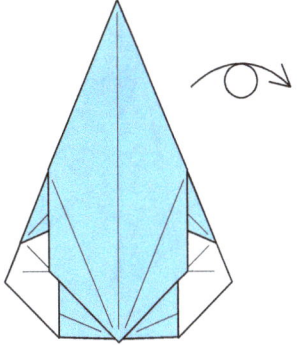

43. Turn over.

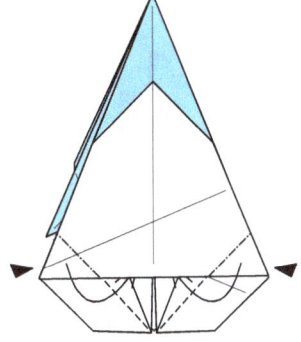

44. Reverse fold along the existing creases.

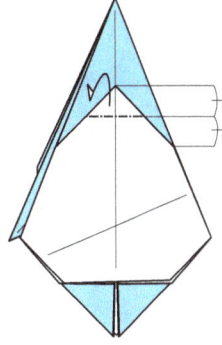

45. Mountain fold the corner approximately halfway.

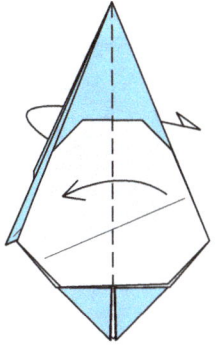

46. Swing over a flap in front and behind.

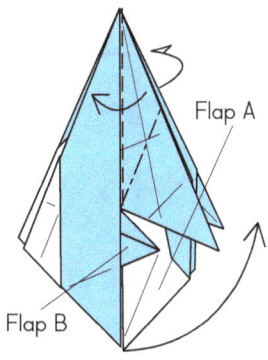

47. Crimp upwards, such that flap A is parallel with flap B.

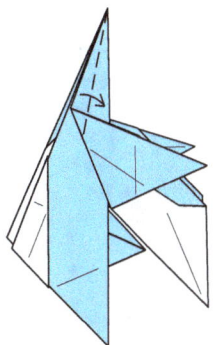

48. Valley fold along the angle bisector.

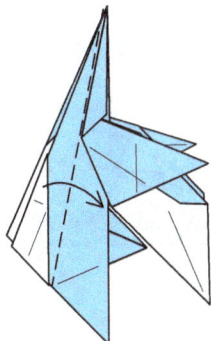

49. Valley fold along the angle bisector.

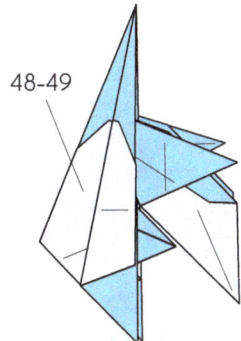

50. Repeat steps 48-49 behind.

51. Reverse fold. Because of the thickness, do not attempt to flatten completely.

penguin

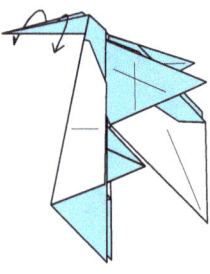

52. Wrap around all three layers at each side.

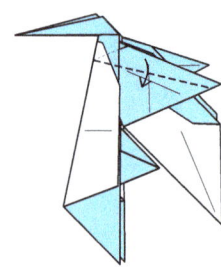

53. Lightly fold down the flap, allowing a swivel to form.

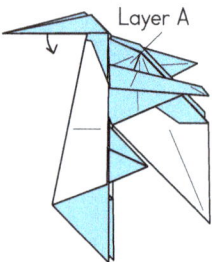

54. Unravel a single layer (which is a continuation of layer A) from the head and then flatten.

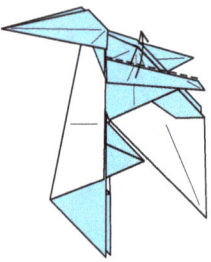

55. Swing the flap back up, reversing through.

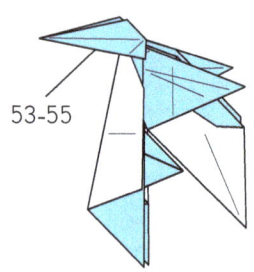

56. Repeat steps 53-55 behind.

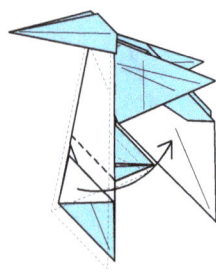

57. This is a cutaway view of the back layers. Valley fold the bottom flap outwards as far as possible.

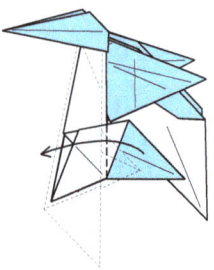

58. Valley fold the flap over. It will extend beyond the edge of the body, so you will have to open out the layers a bit to accommodate this for now.

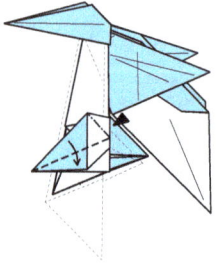

59. Valley fold along the angle bisector, allowing a squash to form.

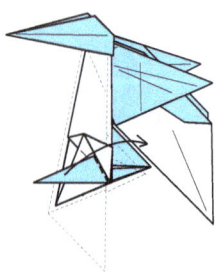

60. Valley fold the flap outwards. The model can now be flattened again.

penguin

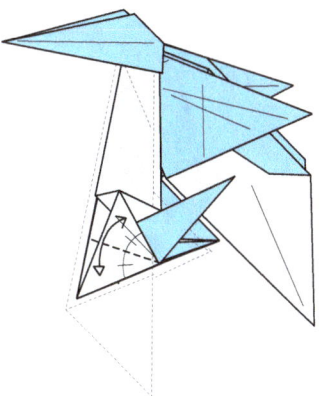
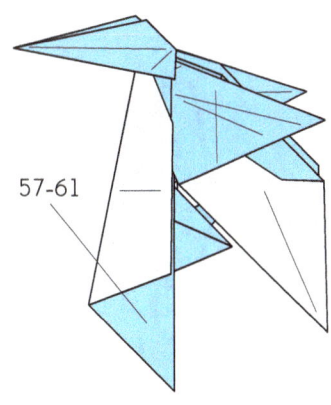
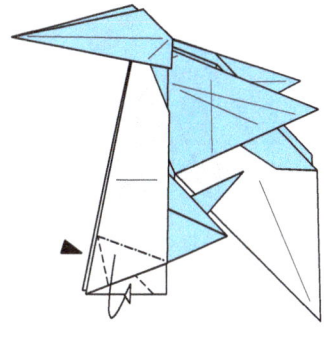

61. Precrease along the indicated angle bisector.

62. Repeat steps 57-61 on the front.

63. Swivel fold under. The bottom edge should end up being parallel to the right edge.

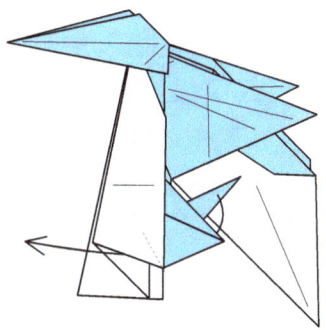
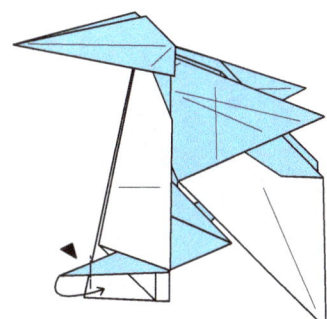
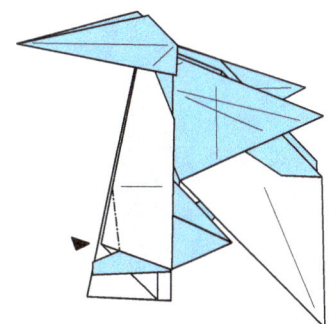

64. Pull the flap through.

65. Reverse fold the tip.

66. Closed sink the corner.

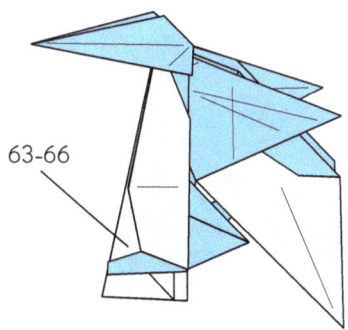
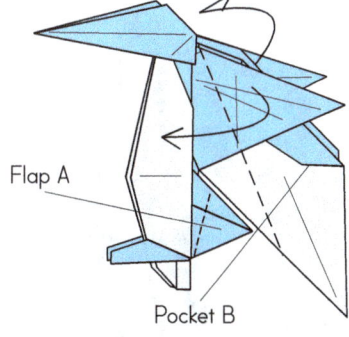
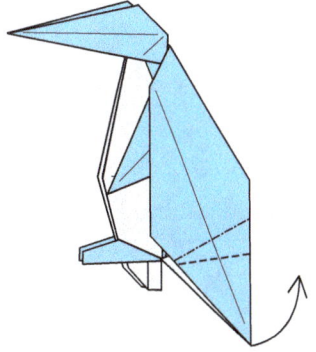

67. Repeat steps 63-66 behind.

68. Outside reverse fold the back section, tucking flap A into pocket B (at the front and the back).

69. Crimp the flap up.

85

penguin

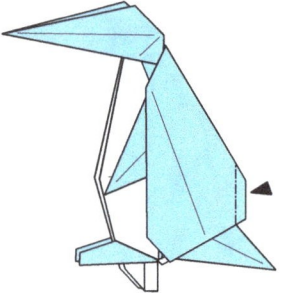

70. Closed sink the edge.

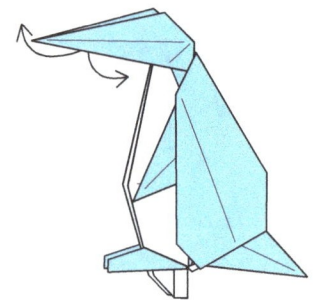

71. Open out the flap for the head, making it 3-D.

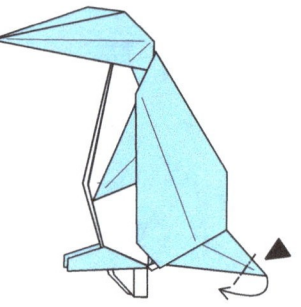

72. Reverse fold the tip.

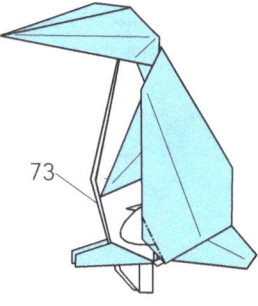

73. Mountain fold the edge behind to lock. Repeat behind.

74. Crimp the head down. Open out the body, feet and tail, and shape to taste.

75. Completed *Penguin*.

Raccoon

This *Raccoon* began as an origami study in creating stripes. Forming a pleat on a flap provides just enough slack to swivel the inner edges outwards to reveal the underlying color. Establishing a second pleat allows the edges to fold back to the center, covering the patch of color below. Devising a staggered array of pleats facilitates the formation of stripes. The model is formed from the classic Bird Base, using one flap for the tail and the rest for the body. It is finished with mostly simpler folds to give a streamlined look.

raccoon

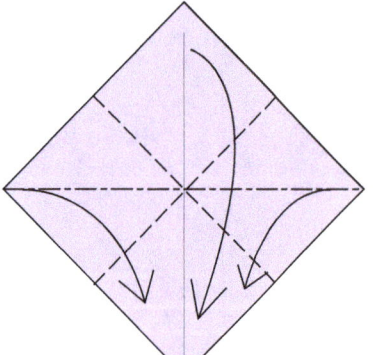

1. Collapse downwards.

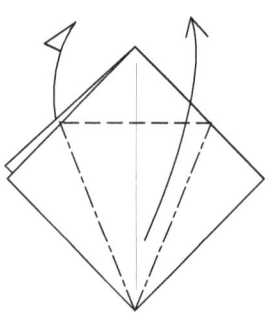

2. Petal fold front and back.

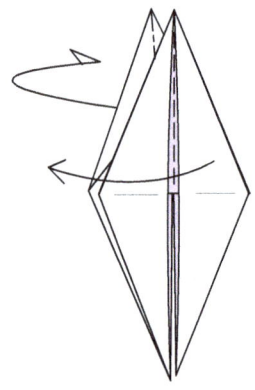

3. Swing a layer over, front and back.

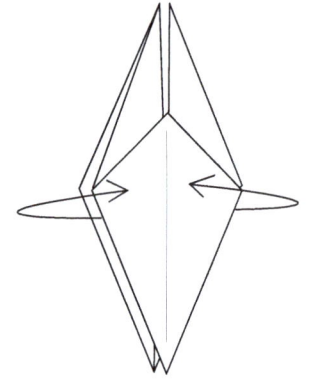

4. Wrap around a single layer to the front on each side.

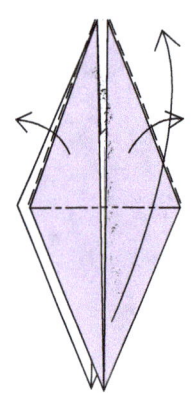

5. Squash fold the top flap.

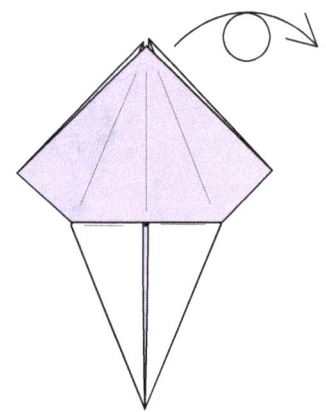

6. Turn over.

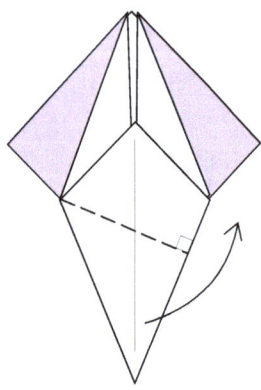

7. Valley fold up.

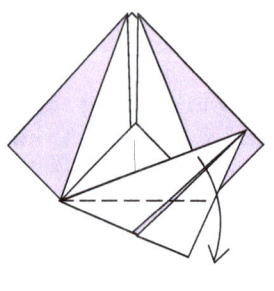

8. Valley fold down.

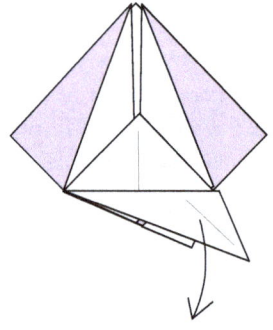

9. Unfold the pleat.

raccoon

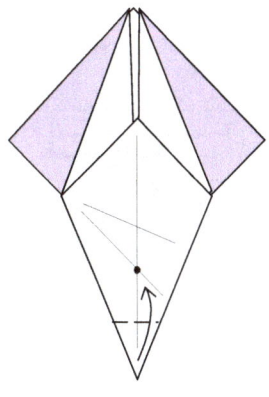 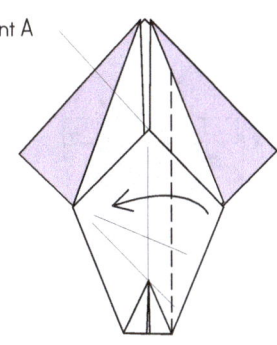 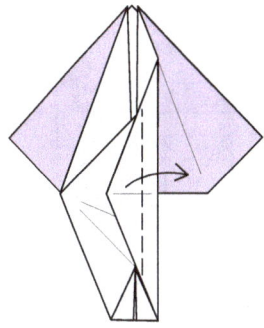

10. Valley fold to the dotted intersection of creases.

11. Valley fold over. The edge should intersect with point A.

12. Valley fold over, leaving a small gap at the center of the model.

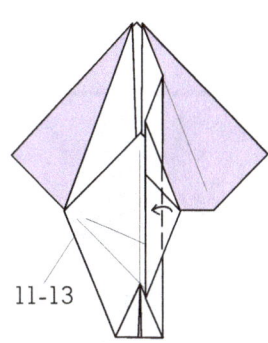 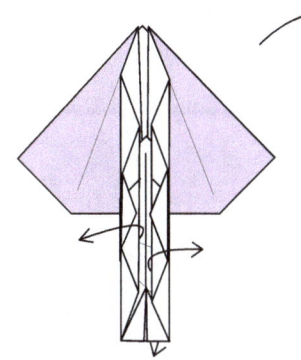 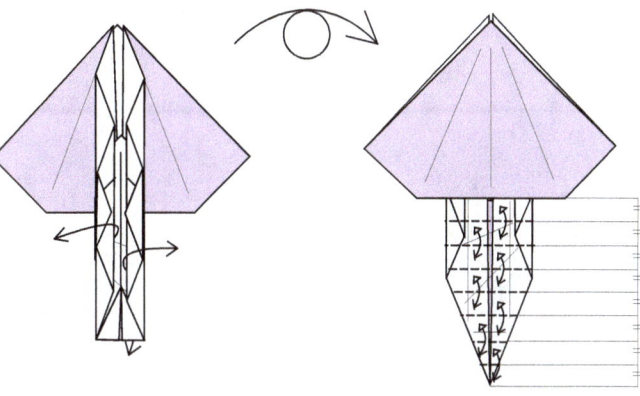

13. Valley fold in partway. Repeat steps 11-13 on other side.

14. Open out the side pleats. Turn over.

15. Divide the length of the flap into 1/8ths with valley folds.

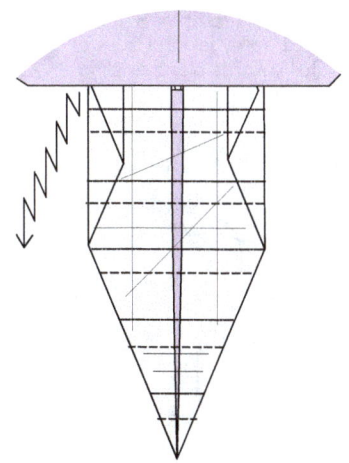 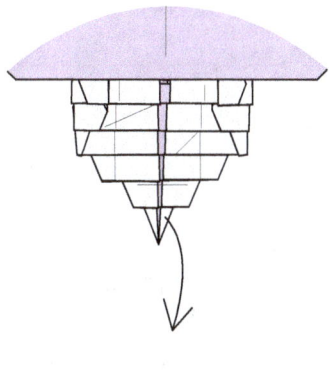 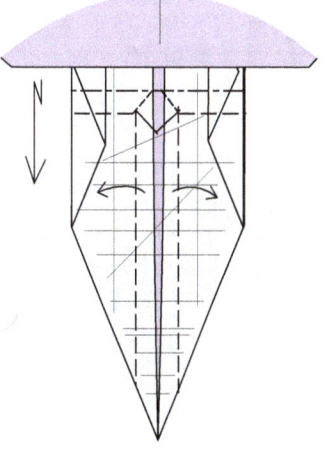

16. Form a staggered pleat, adding additional folds where indicated.

17. Unfold the pleat.

18. Replace the top pleat, while folding the top single layers outwards. The bottom of model will not lie flat.

89

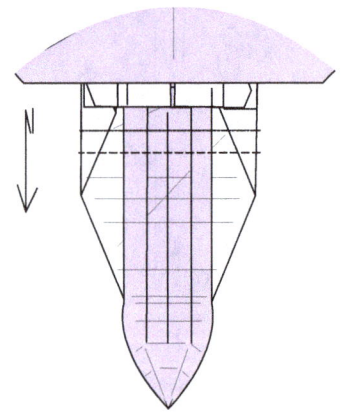
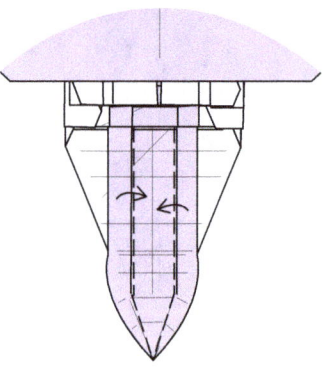
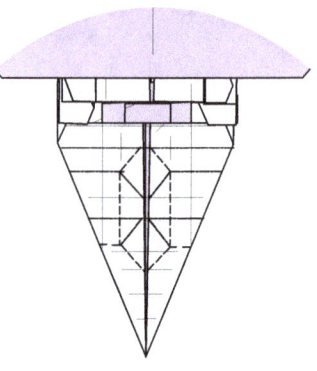

19. Replace another pleat.

20. Fold the sides back to the center. A swivel fold will form underneath the pleat.

21. Repeat steps 18-20 with the next set of pleats.

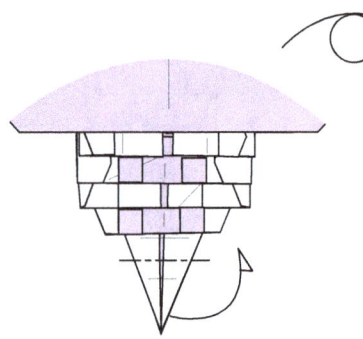
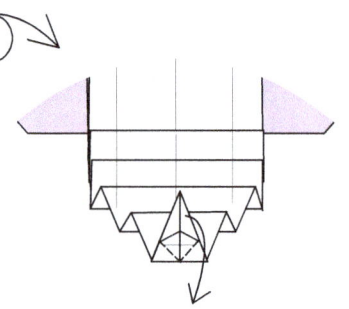
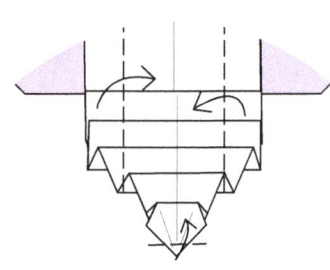

22. Mountain fold. Turn over.

23. Squash fold the tip.

24. Blunt the tip of tail with a valley fold. Valley fold the sides of the tail inwards along existing creases.

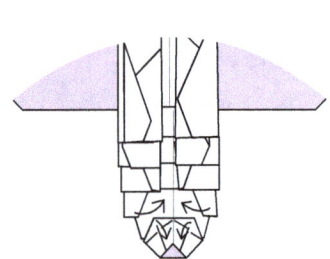
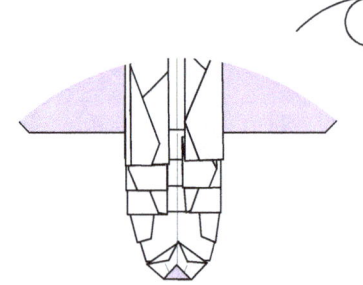
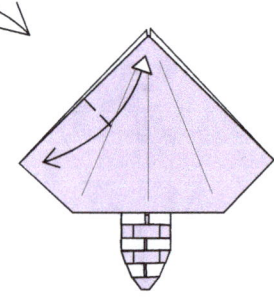

25. Lock the tip of the tail with valley folds. Swivel fold in the sides of the tail.

26. Completed tail. Turn over.

27. Pinch the top layer in half.

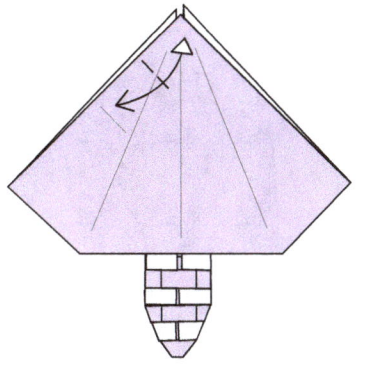

28. Pinch again.

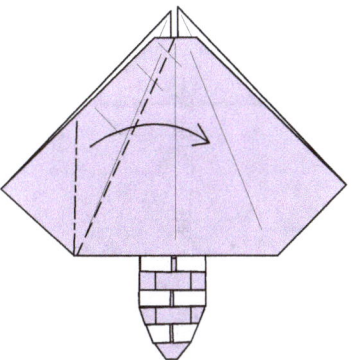

29. Lightly valley fold the top corner to the last crease.

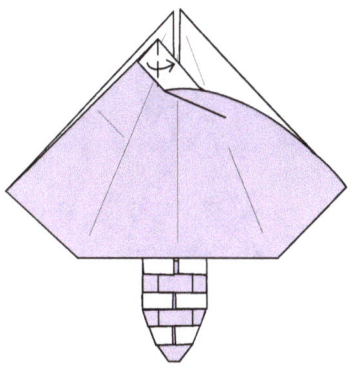

30. Valley fold the corner over to the folded edge.

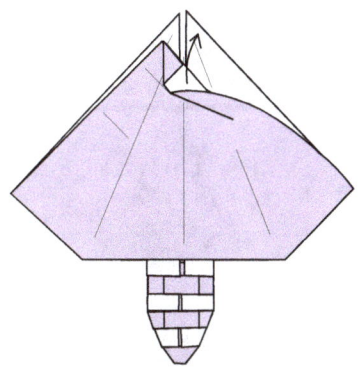

31. Flatten the top layer.

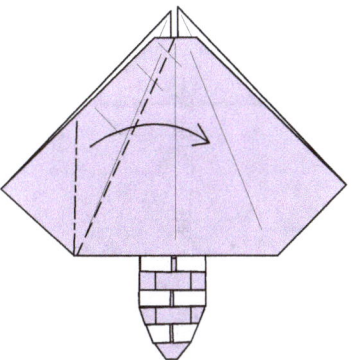

32. Squash fold. See the next diagram for positioning. The valley fold extends from the lower corner, to the intersection of the center and top edge.

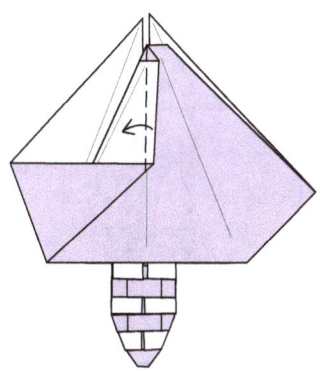

33. Valley fold over to align with the center.

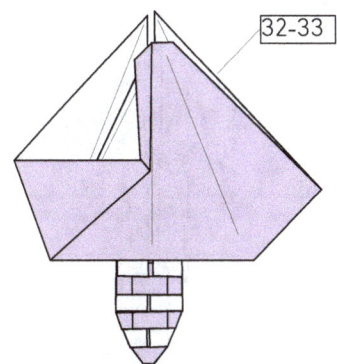

34. Repeat steps 32-33 in mirror image.

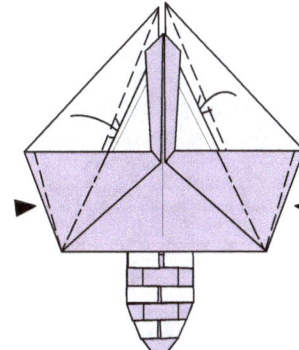

35. Reverse fold the sides.

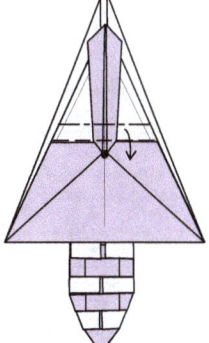

36. Pleat the flap, so that the mountain-fold lies on the dotted intersection.

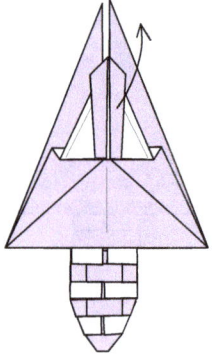

37. Undo the pleat.

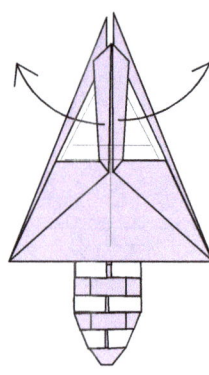

38. Unfold the top flap.

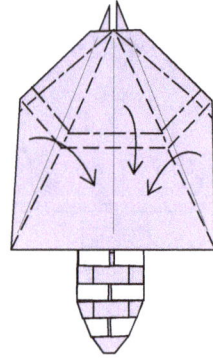

39. Fold the sides back in while incorporating a pleat.

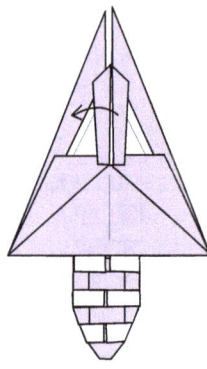

40. Swing over the top layer.

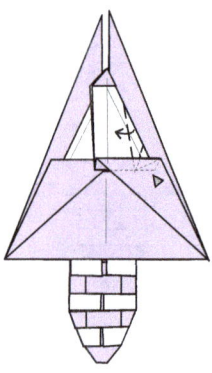

41. Swivel fold over as much of the white area as possible.

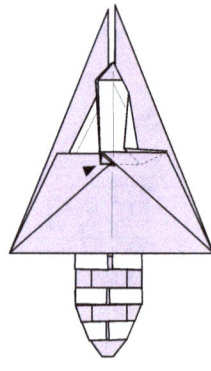

42. Reverse fold the corner.

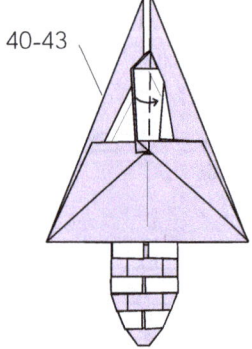

43. Swing the edge back. Repeat steps 40-43 in mirror image.

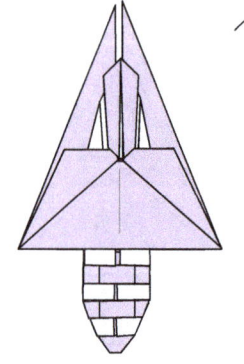

44. Turn over.

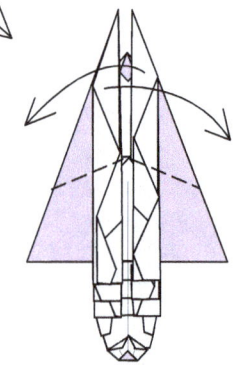

45. Valley fold the front flaps over each other.

raccoon

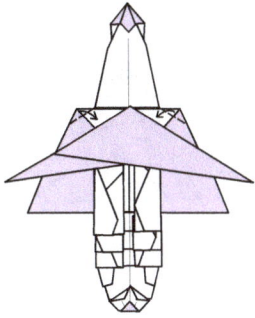
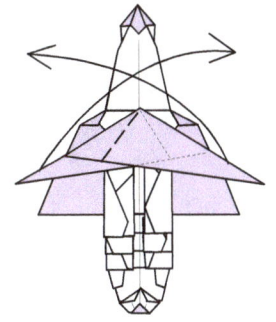
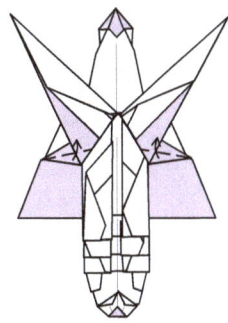

46. Valley fold the corners in.

47. Valley fold the the flaps outwards. Note that the folds intersect the white center portion.

48. Valley fold to lock.

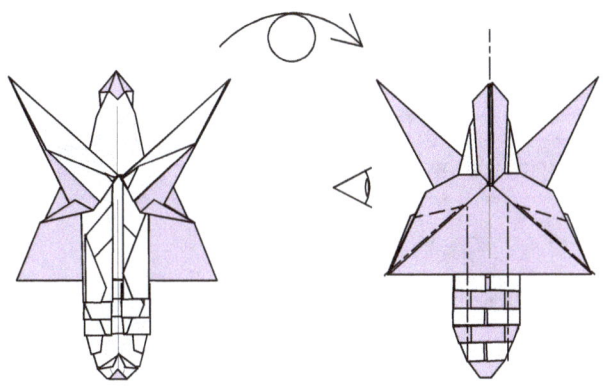

49. Turn over.

50. Make the model 3-D by crimping the hind legs and rounding the body and tail.

51. View from the previous step. Pull out the ears. Pull out the original corner from head. Rotate the model 1/4 turn.

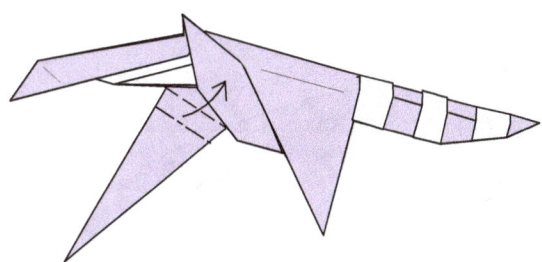
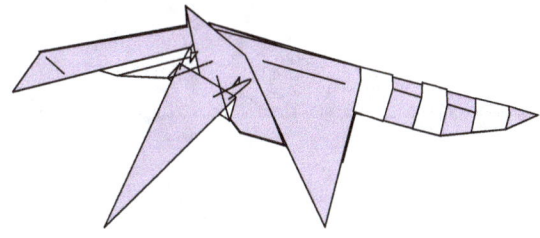

52. Pleat the front legs, leaving them slightly longer than the hind legs.

53. Lock the legs with mountain folds.

raccoon

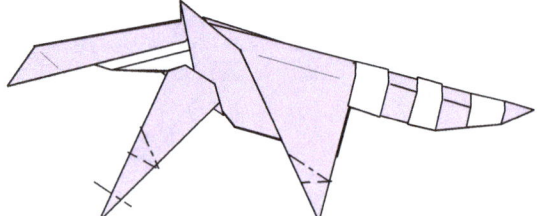
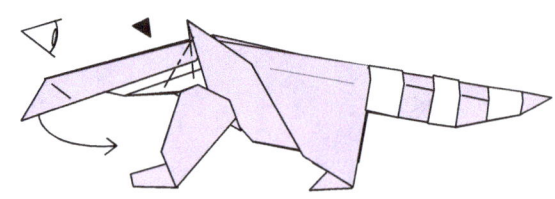

54. Pleat the legs with simple valley and mountain folds.

55. Squash fold the head. It will not spread out flat at the bottom.

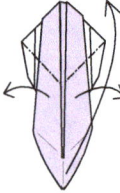
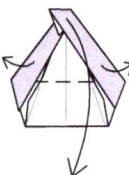
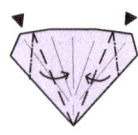

56. View from the previous step. Squash fold the flap.

57. Squash fold again, allowing the pleats at the corners of the head to come undone.

58. Squash fold, again allowing the top corners to spread out.

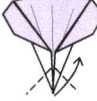
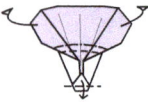

59. Squash fold the nose.

60. Valley fold the nose. Crimp the head. Wrap the sides of the head around the body.

61. Completed *Raccoon*.

Reindeer

This origami *Reindeer* utilizes the box-pleating style of origami master Neal Elias to form the antlers. The paper is pleated into a fan formation, and appendages are extruded as these pleats get stretched. The body is stylized to take on a boxy shape, although the folds utilized to achieve that employ a variety of different angles. Paper is stretched beyond the cluster of flaps that form the antlers to give the framework an airier feel. Reducing the thickness in the neck makes this model easier to pose.

reindeer

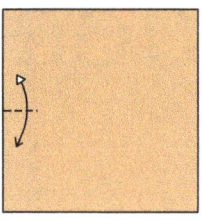

1. Precrease with a pinch mark.

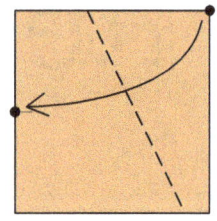

2. Valley fold the corner to the pinch mark.

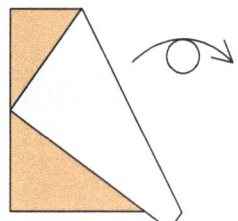

3. Turn over.

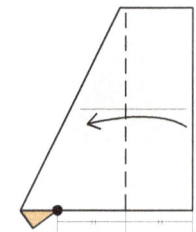

4. Valley fold to the dotted intersection of edges.

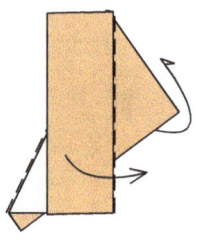

5. Open out.

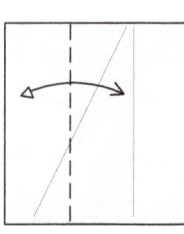

6. Precrease.

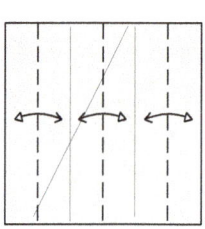

7. Precrease each section in half.

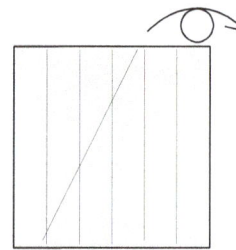

8. Turn over.

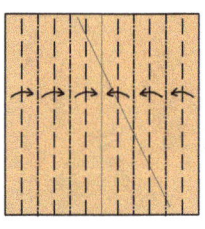

9. Pleat each side, by inserting valley folds.

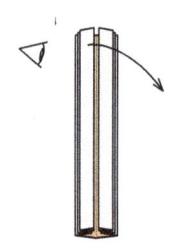

10. Open out one set of pleats.

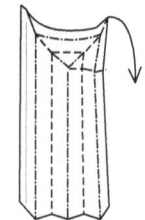

11. Stretch the corner while pleating the top edge down.

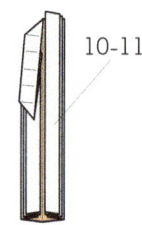

12. Repeat steps 10-11 on the other side.

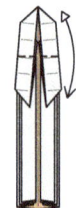

13. Precrease through all layers.

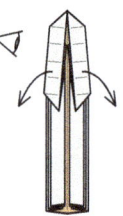

14. Pull the flaps forward, allowing the back pleats to come undone.

15. Stretch apart the indicated area, forming a ridge. Repeat behind.

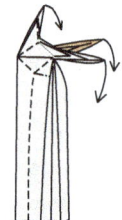

16. Swing the three flaps down, allowing the pleats to collapse flat.

reindeer

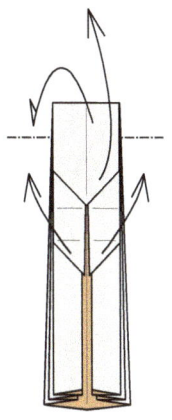
17. Flip the three flaps up.

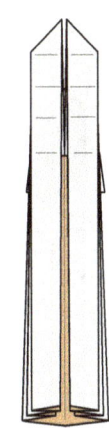
18. Turn over.

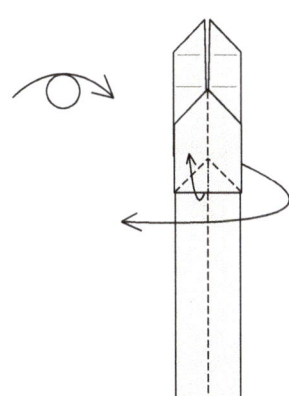
19. Valley fold in half while incorporating a reverse fold.

20. Valley fold.

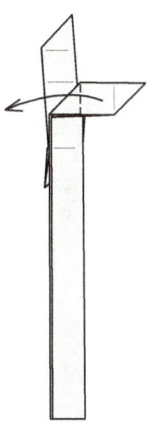
21. Valley fold again.

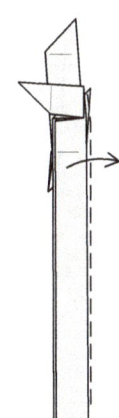
22. Swing one layer over, pulling out trapped paper.

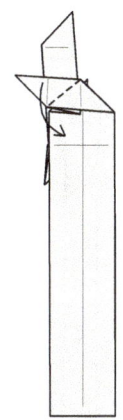
23. Valley fold down.

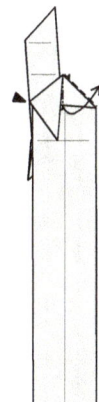
24. Squash fold upwards.

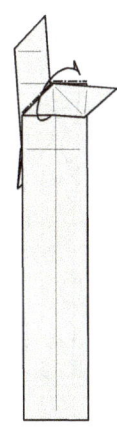
25. Wrap a single layer around.

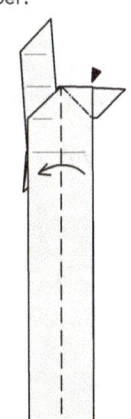
26. Squash fold.

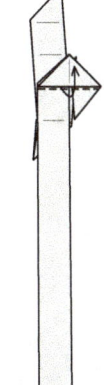
27. Wrap a single layer around from the interior.

28. Swing down.

reindeer

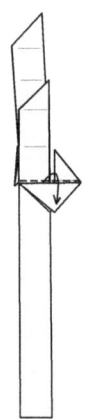 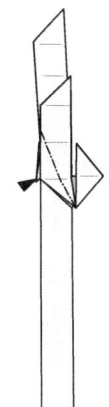 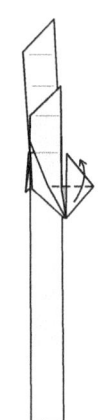 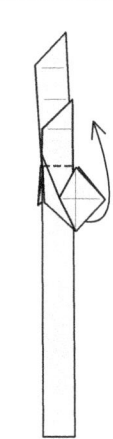

29. Wrap a single layer around from the interior.
30. Open sink.
31. Valley fold one flap up.
32. Swing up the cluster of flaps.

  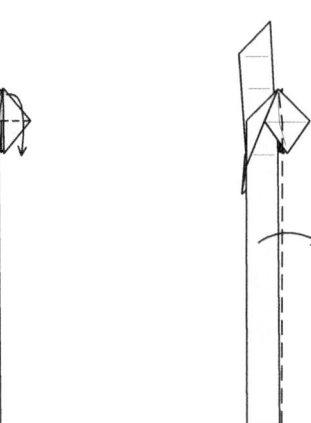 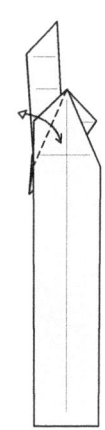

33. Open sink.
34. Valley fold one flap down.
35. Swing over one flap.
36. Precrease along the angle bisector.

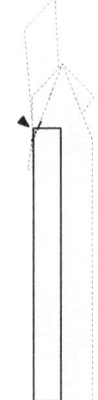 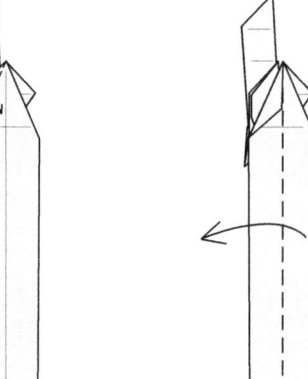 

37. Reverse fold the hidden corner.
38. Valley fold.
39. Swing the flap back.
40. Precrease along the angle bisectors.

reindeer

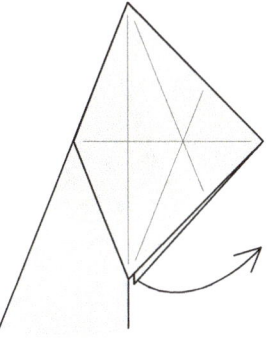
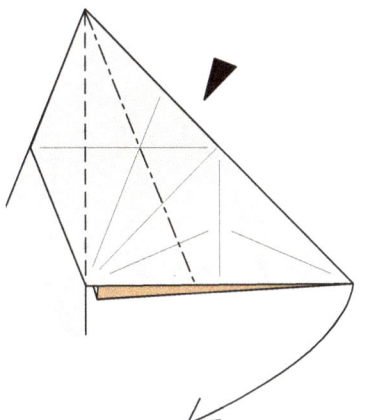
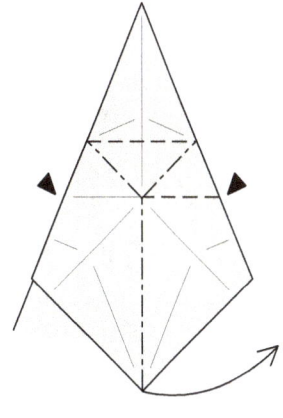

41. Pull out the center flap.

42. Squash fold.

43. Collapse upwards.

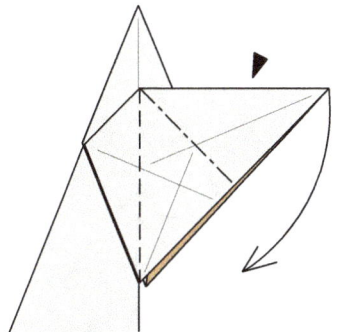
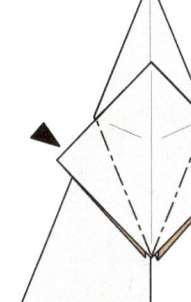
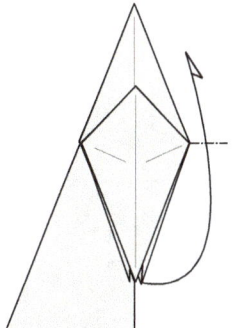

44. Squash fold.

45. Reverse fold the sides.

46. Swing the back flap up.

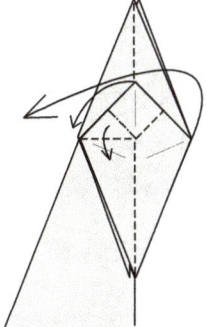
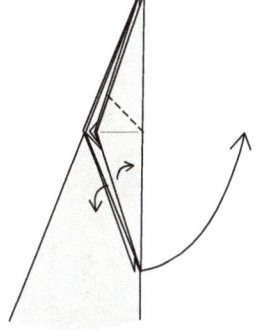
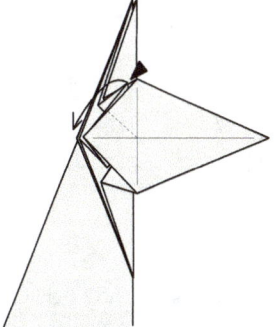

47. Valley fold in half, while twisting the center flap.

48. Bring the flap over, while spreading apart the sides.

49. Reverse fold the tiny trapped point through.

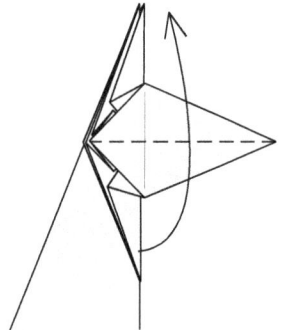
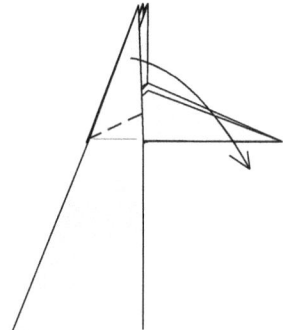
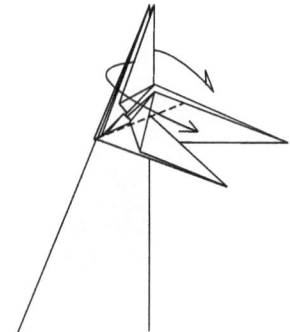

50. Swing up.

51. Valley fold down, allowing a squash fold to form.

52. Outside reverse fold.

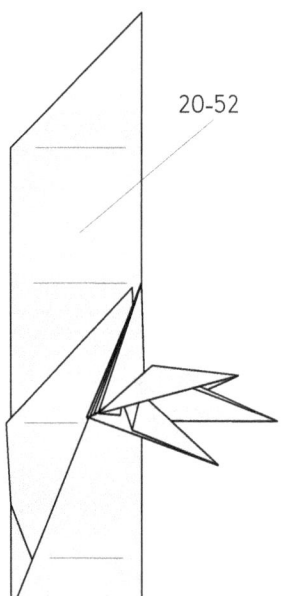
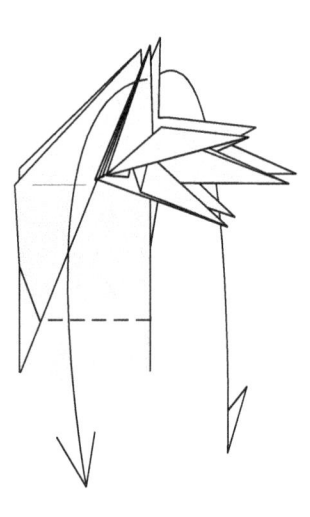
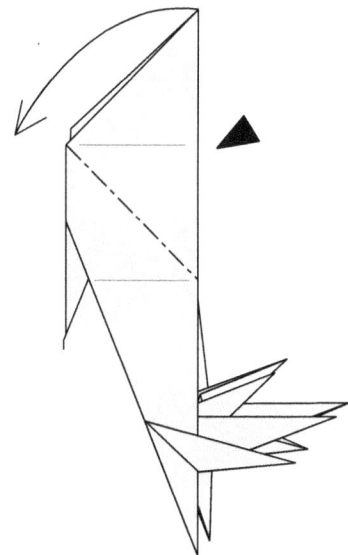

53. Repeat steps 20-52 behind (and in mirror image).

54. Swing the cluster of flaps down at each side.

55. Reverse fold.

reindeer

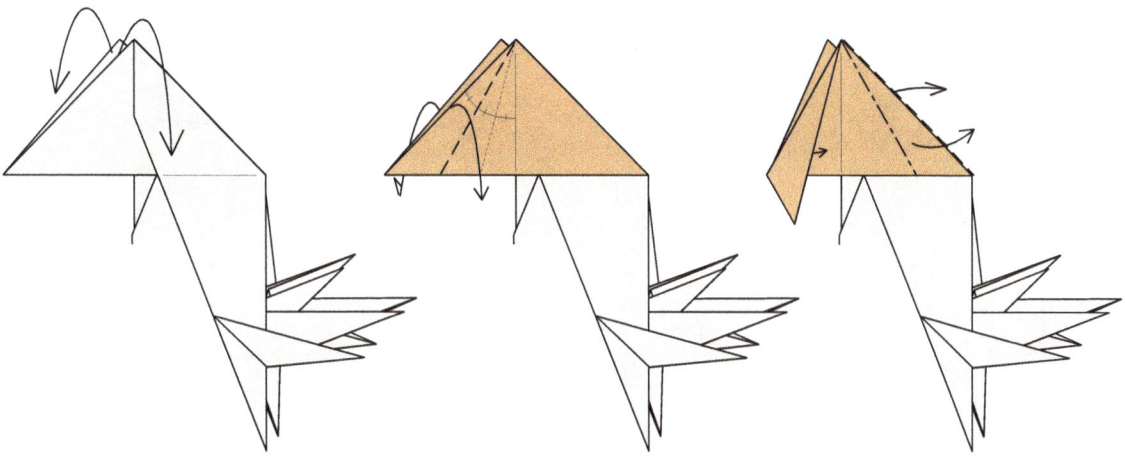

56. Wrap a layer around at each side.

57. Outside reverse fold along the angle trisector.

58. Slide a single layer out at each side.

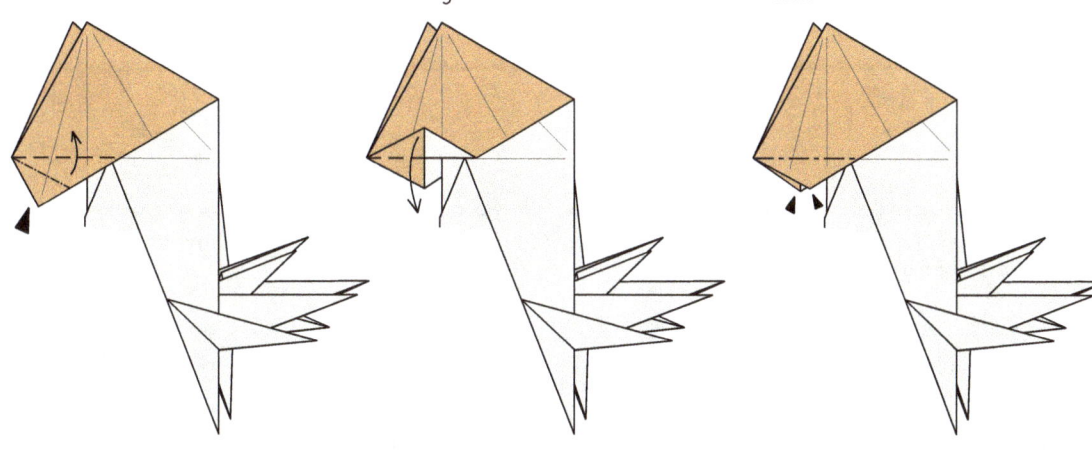

59. Squash fold.

60. Valley fold down.

61. Reverse fold the two corners up.

62. Pleat upwards, while incorporating a rabbit-ear though all of the layers.

63. Swivel fold a single layer through. Repeat behind.

64. Valley fold the corners down at a slight angle.

101

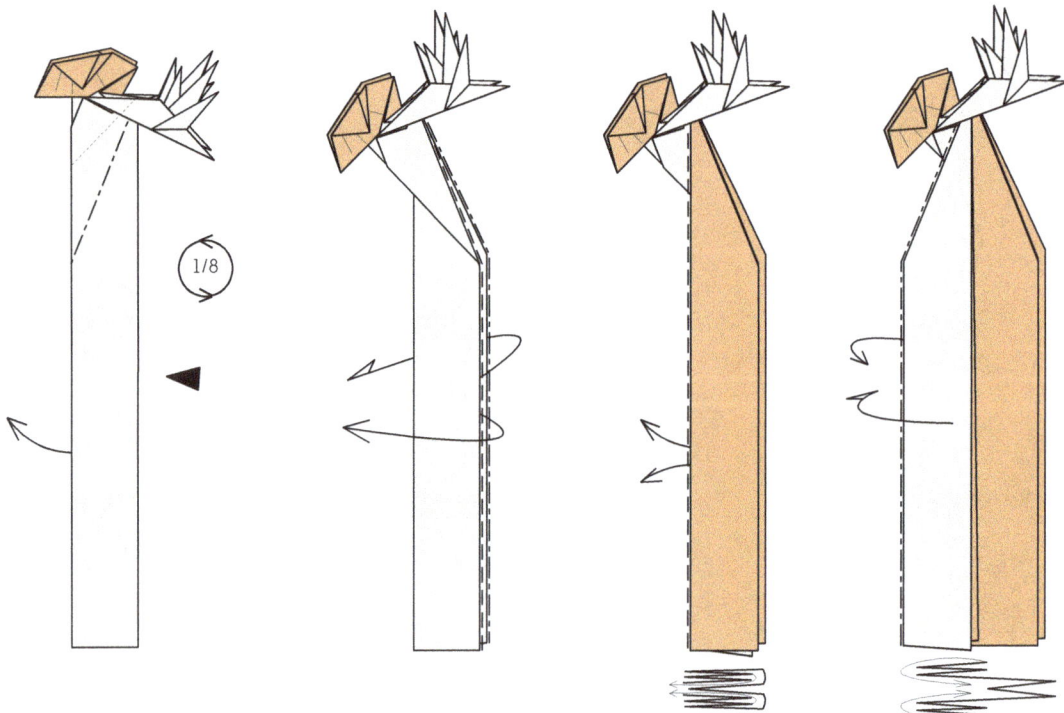

65. Reverse fold to lie along the hidden cluster of edges. Rotate the model.

66. Wrap around all of the layers at each side.

67. Pull out the interior pleats at each side and flatten.

68. Wrap around a single layer at each side.

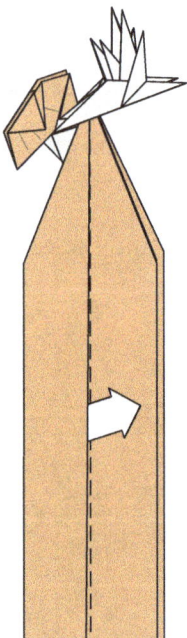 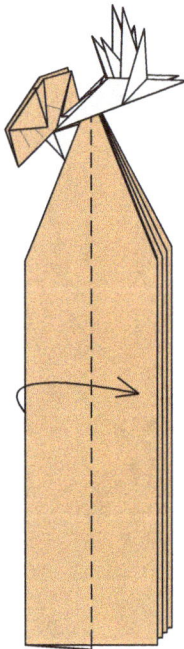 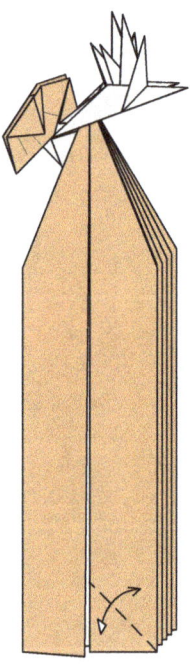 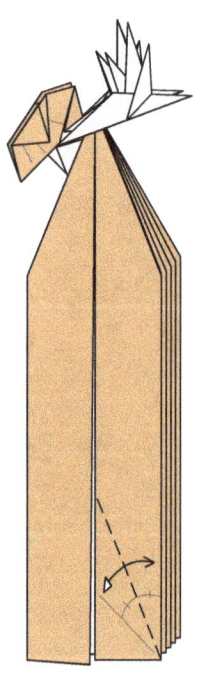

69. Unsink at each side.

70. Swing over one flap.

71. Precrease lightly.

72. Precrease along the angle bisector.

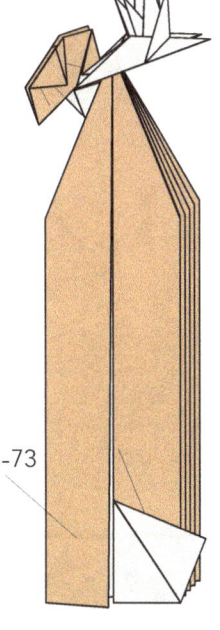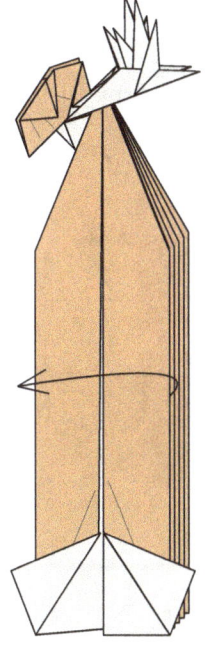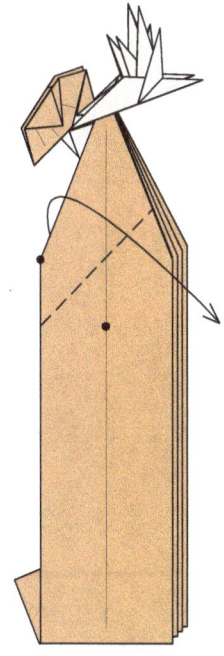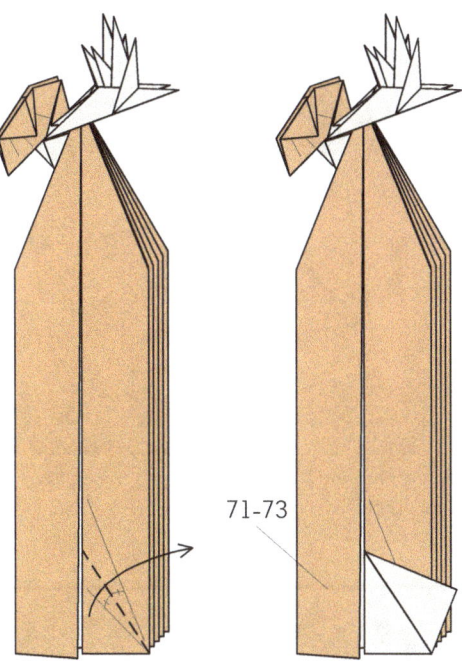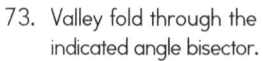

73. Valley fold through the indicated angle bisector.

74. Repeat steps 71-73 in mirror image.

75. Swing over one flap.

76. Valley fold, such that the corner hits the center crease.

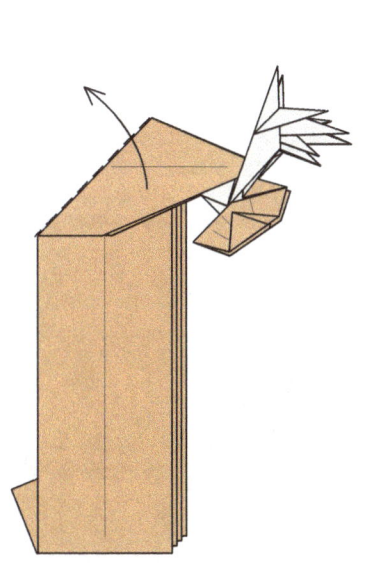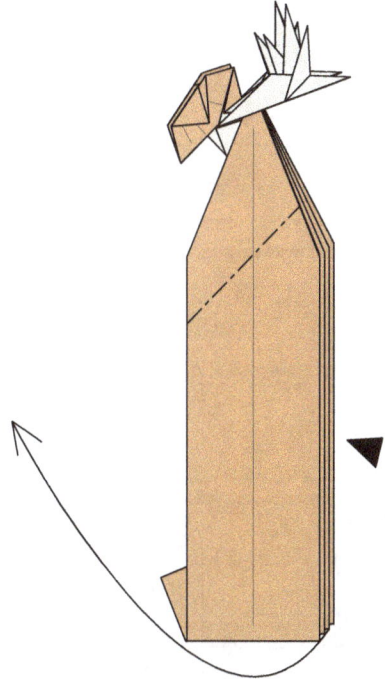

77. Unfold.

78. Reverse fold, noting the center pleats cannot be distributed evenly. Leave the extra pleat towards the bottom.

reindeer

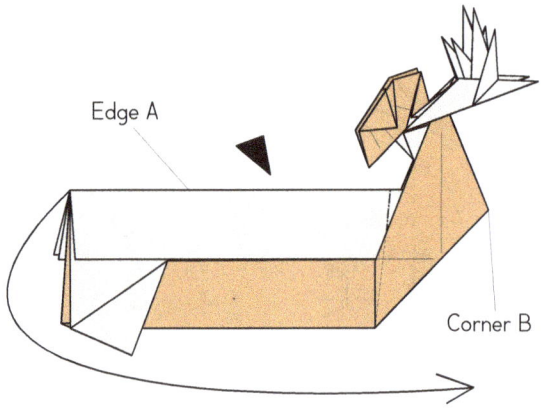

79. Reverse fold, such that edge A hits corner B.

80. Crimp fold, such that interior edge B and edge A are perpendicular. The next step shows the model rotated slightly.

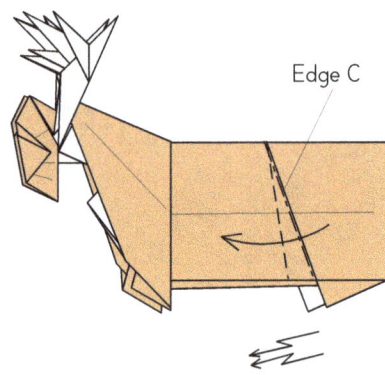

81. Crimp fold, such that interior edge C lies straight.

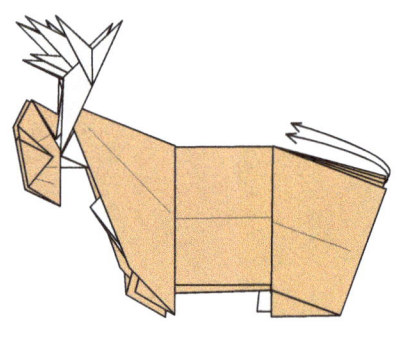

82. Pull up the two middle trapped corners, and flatten.

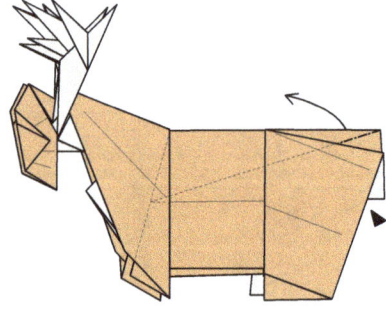

83. Reverse fold the center flap up as far as possible.

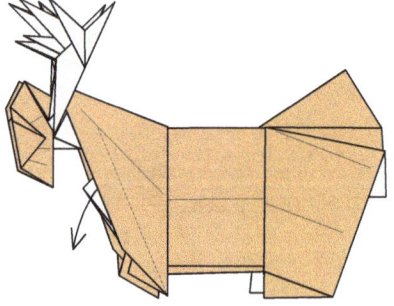

84. Pull out a hidden single layer, such that the leading raw edge lies straight.

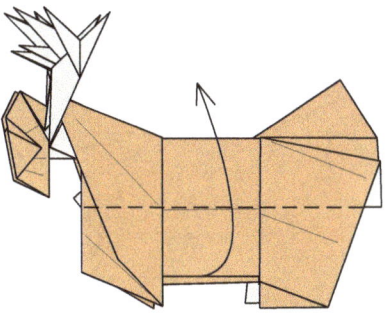

85. Lightly swing the body section up.

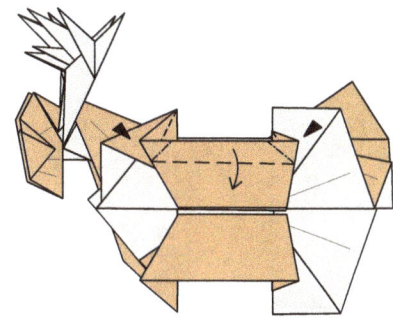

86. Valley fold the edge down as far as possible, allowing swivel folds to form at the sides.

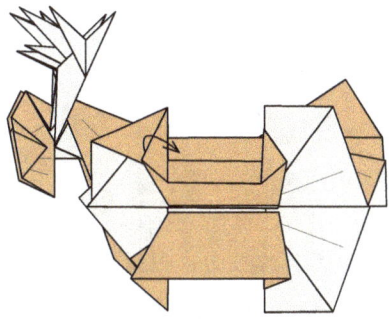

87. Wrap a single layer around to the surface.

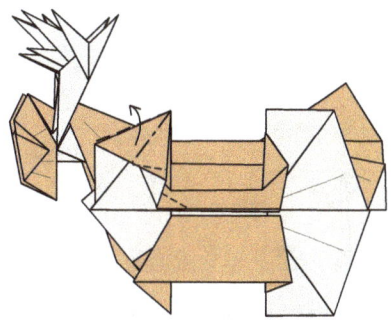

88. Stretch the single layer upwards, such that the top edge lies straight. A squash fold will form, running along the leg.

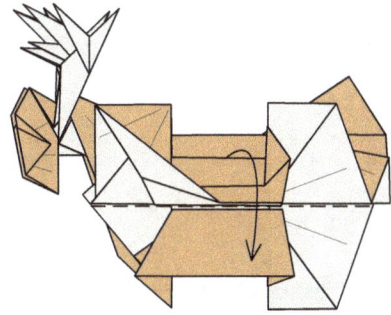

89. Swing the body section back down.

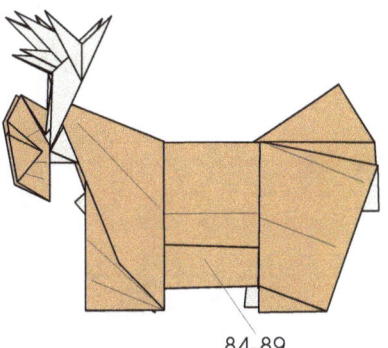

84-89

90. Repeat steps 84-89 behind.

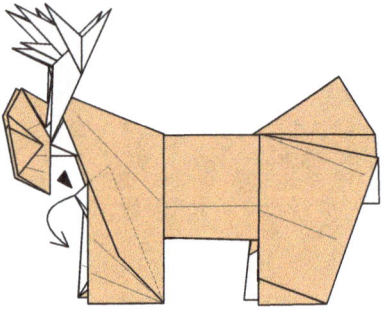

91. Reverse fold the protruding corner.

92. Mountain fold the back edges.

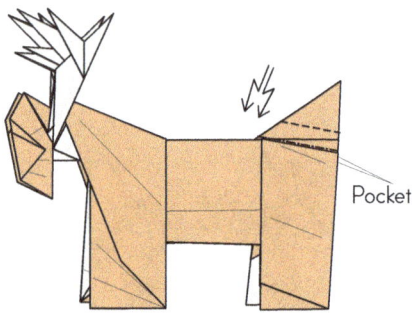

93. Crimp the tail, tucking the resulting corners into the pockets at the top of the legs.

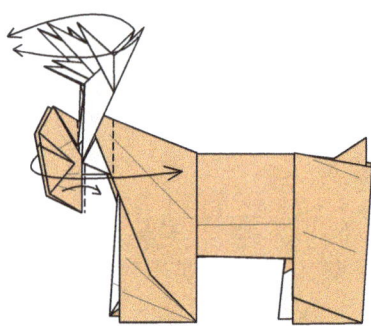

94. Open out the head and spread apart the antlers. Position the head section to taste.

95. Completed *Reindeer*.

Skunk

The standard approach to devising an origami skunk typically involves having opposite edges of the paper not quite meeting at the center. This will form a single stripe along the length, and the remaining features can then be formed. As it turns out in nature, there is a set of stripes that run along the body. So, this *Skunk* solves this stripe complication by using discrete flaps to form the color pattern. There is even a flap to form the patch of white on the head. The tip of the tail gets inverted to complete the distinctive markings.

skunk

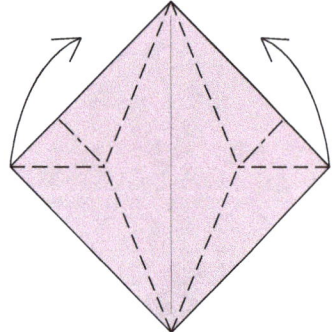

1. Rabbit ear both sides upwards.

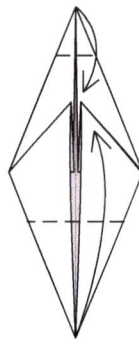

2. Valley fold towards the center flaps.

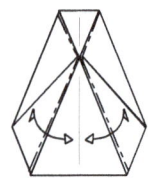

3. Precrease using mountain folds.

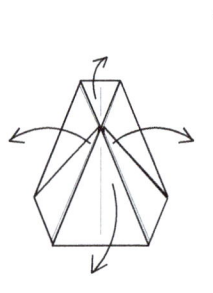

4. Unfold completely. Turn over

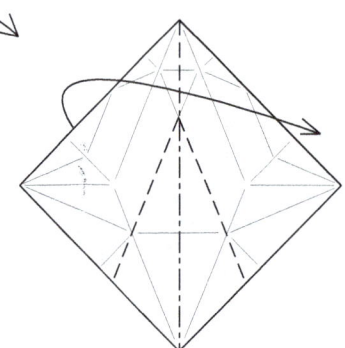

5. Collapse, using the existing creases as a guide.

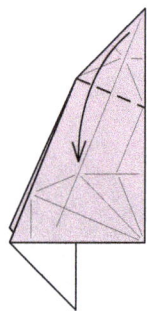

6. Valley fold to the intersection of creases.

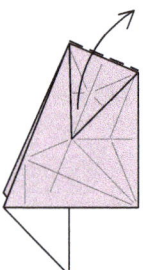

7. Unfold.

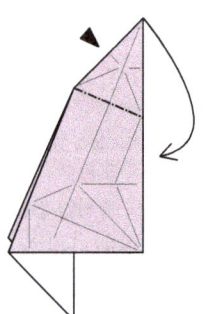

8. Reverse fold along the existing crease.

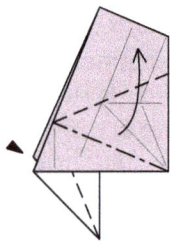

9. Swivel fold upwards.

skunk

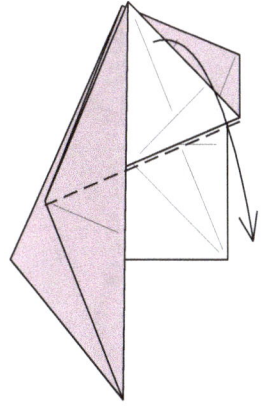

10. Swing the flap down.

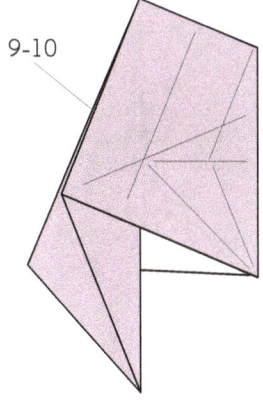

11. Repeat steps 9-10 behind.

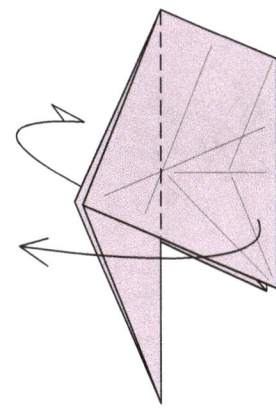

12. Swing over a flap at each side.

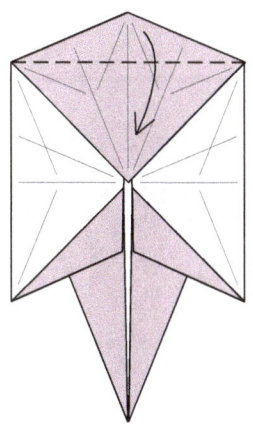

13. Valley fold down.

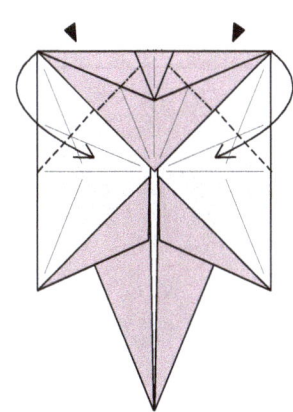

14. Reverse fold the sides.

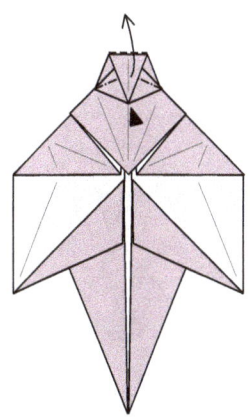

15. Spread squash the top.

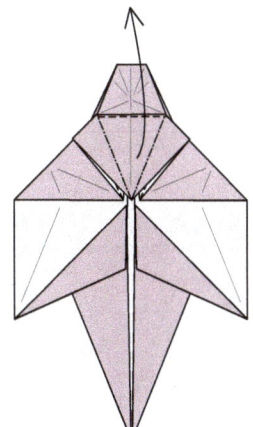

16. Petal fold upwards.

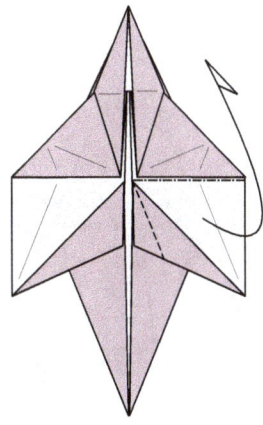

17. Swivel fold the flap behind.

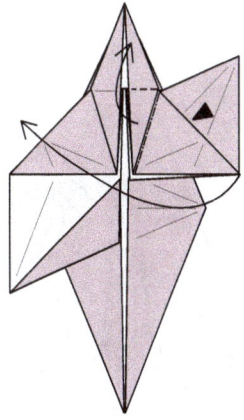

18. Squash fold.

109

skunk

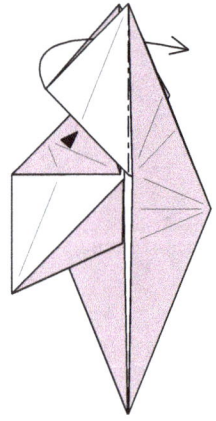
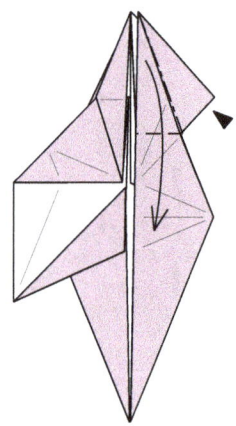
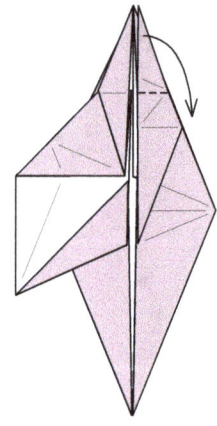

19. Reverse fold.

20. Squash fold the flap down.

21. Swing the top flap down.

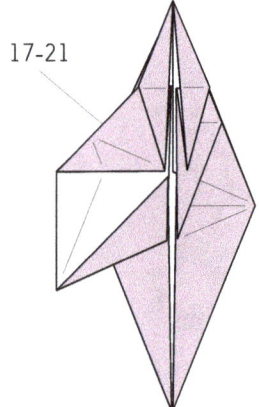
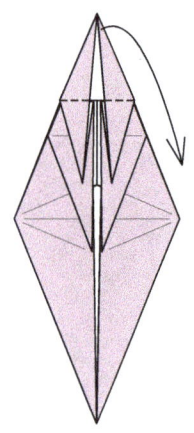
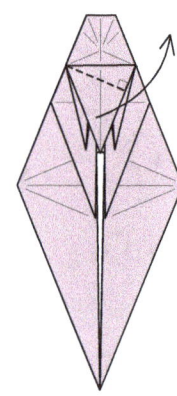

22. Repeat steps 17-21 in mirror image.

23. Swing the top flap down.

24. Valley fold up.

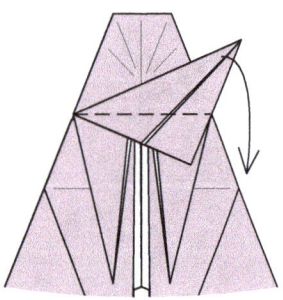
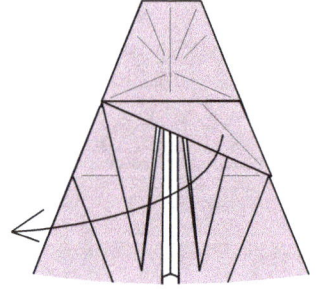
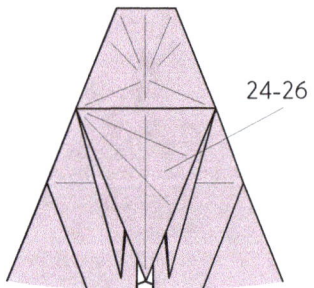

25. Valley fold down.

26. Unfold the pleat.

27. Repeat steps 24-26 in mirror image.

skunk

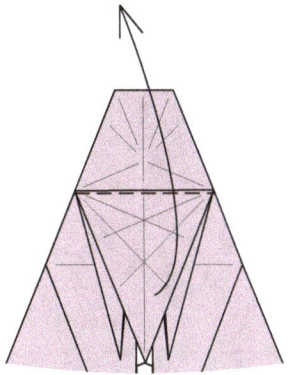

28. Swing the flap up.

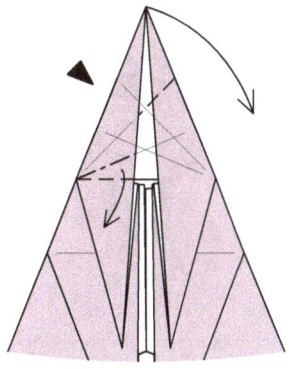

29. Squash fold.

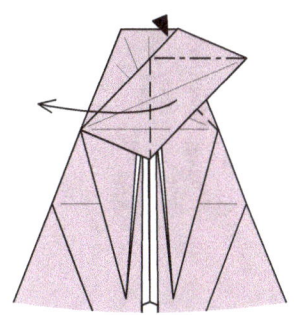

30. Squash fold over.

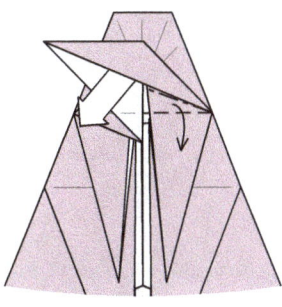

31. Pull out the single layer to match the other side.

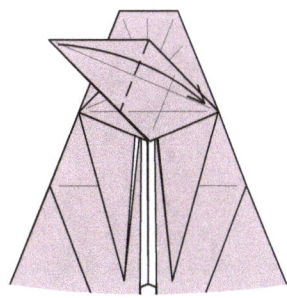

32. Valley fold over to the corner.

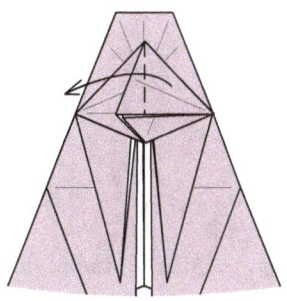

33. Valley fold over.

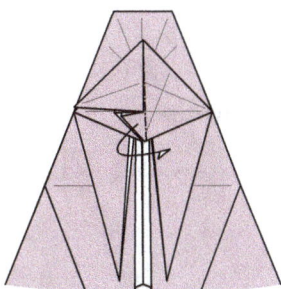

34. Mountain fold the small flap into the pocket.

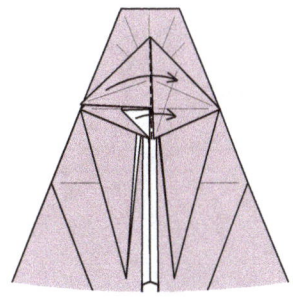

35. Swing over two flaps.

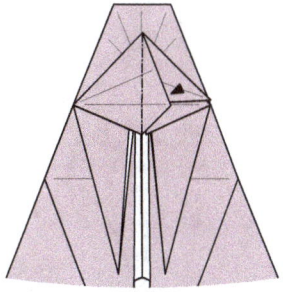

36. Reverse fold the flap through to match the other side.

skunk

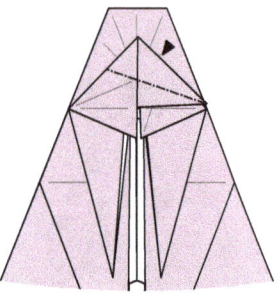

37. Sink the center flap, being careful not to let the layers shift.

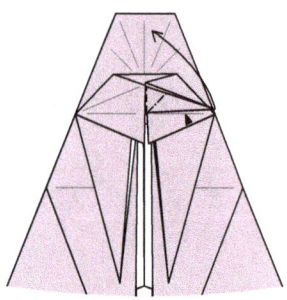

38. Spread squash the center flap.

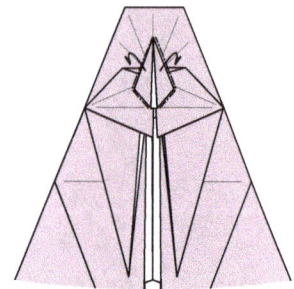

39. Wrap around a single layer at each side.

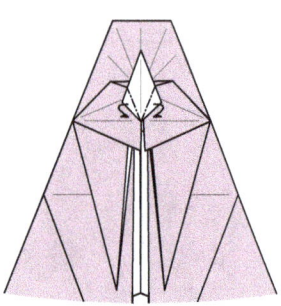

40. Mountain fold the lower edges.

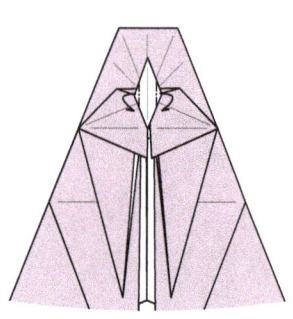

41. Mountain fold the sides.

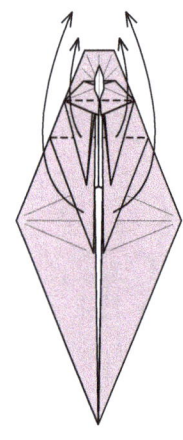

42. Swing the indicated sets of flaps upwards.

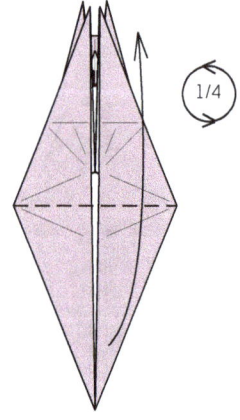

43. Valley fold the flap upwards. Rotate the model 1/4 turn.

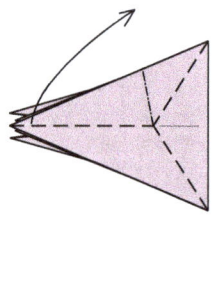

44. Rabbit ear the flap upwards.

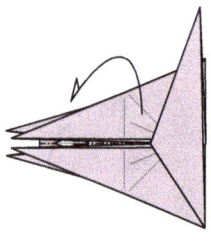

45. Mountain fold the model in half.

skunk

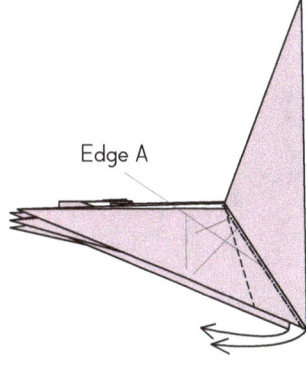

46. Crimp the back section, allowing edge A to lie straight.

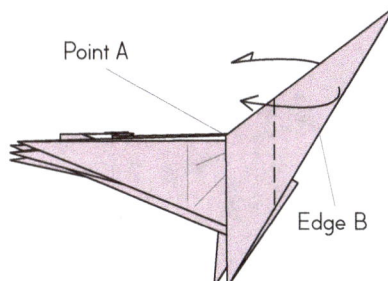

47. Outside reverse fold the flap, such that edge B hits point A.

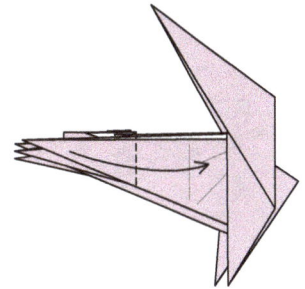

48. Valley fold the top flap over, starting at the point where the head flap begins.

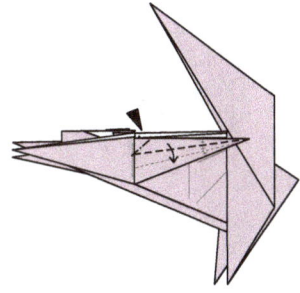

49. Squash fold the edge of the flap down along the angle trisector.

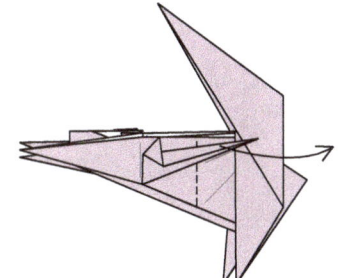

50. Pull the flap open.

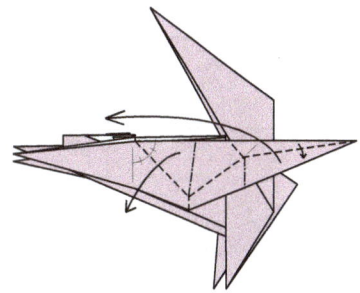

51. Replace the pleat, while reverse folding the top layer.

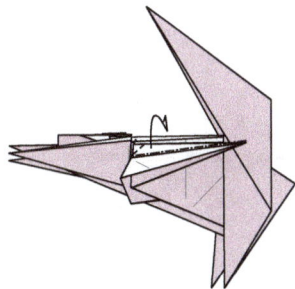

52. Swivel fold the top edge of the flap behind.

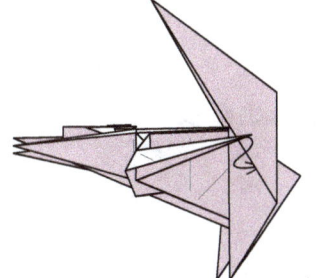

53. Tuck the tip of the flap underneath the tail flap.

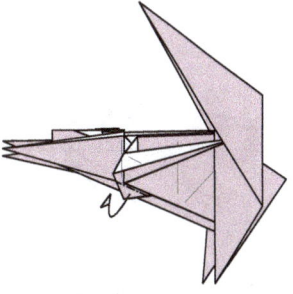

54. Mountain fold the protruding section into the model.

skunk

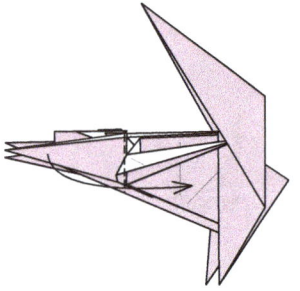

55. Swing over one flap.

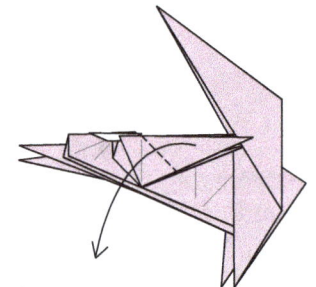

56. Valley fold the flap down.

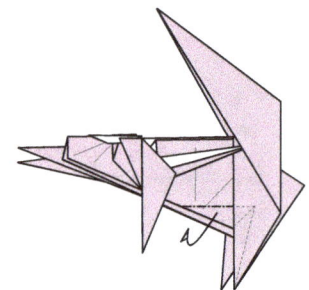

57. Swivel fold the double layered side under.

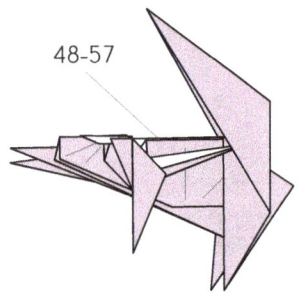

58. Repeat steps 48-57 behind.

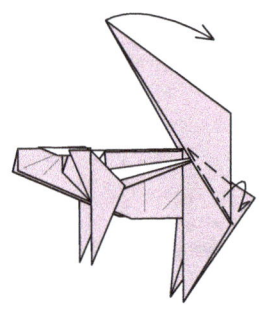

59. Crimp the tail into an upright position.

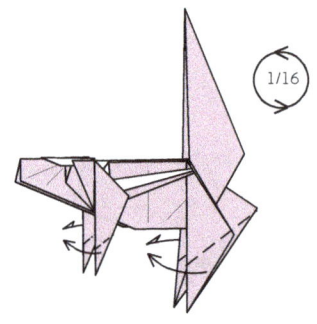

60. Rotate the model slightly, and valley fold the bottom flaps forward, ensuring the model stands evenly.

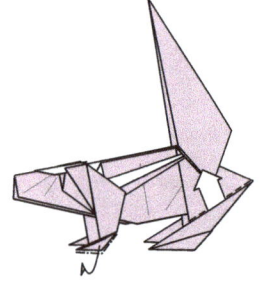

61. Wrap around a layer at the front foot flap and pull out paper at the rear foot flap.

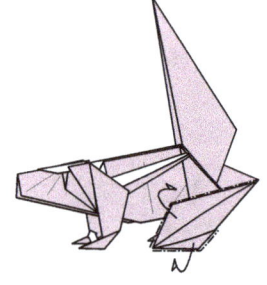

62. Pull out all the layers from the front flap and wrap around two layers at the rear flap.

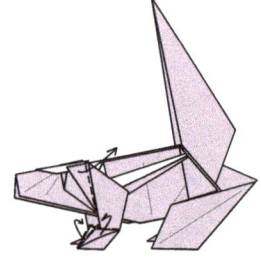

63. Wrap around a layer at each side of the foot flap and swing over the ear flap.

skunk

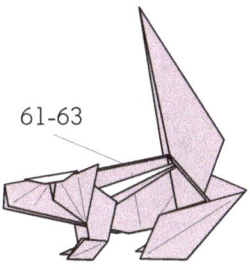

64. Repeat steps 61-63 behind.

65. Reverse fold the center flap.

66. Softly reverse fold the tip of the tail flap.

67. Softly wrap around the tip of the flap.

68. Crimp the head down and shape the body and tail to taste.

69. Completed *Skunk*.

Spectacled Bear

An origami folding challenge was created to raise awareness on how The Spectacled Bear species existence was being threatened. Admittedly this *Spectacled Bear* entry missed the mark, as it more closely resembles the polar bear moniker used for a famous cola brand. Adding to its cartoonish quality are stylized feet sporting colored triangles. As expected, this bear did not win any prizes for this competition, but it did win over some hearts with its unabashed cuteness.

spectacled bear

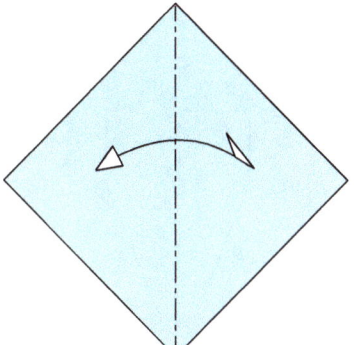

1. Precrease with a mountain fold.

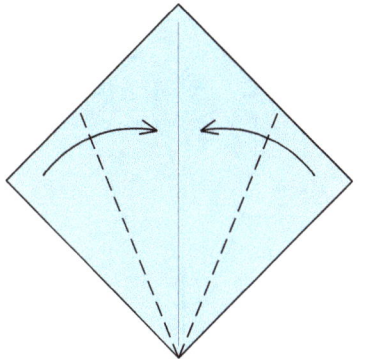

2. Valley fold the sides to the center.

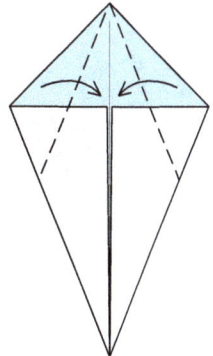

3. Valley fold the upper edges to the center.

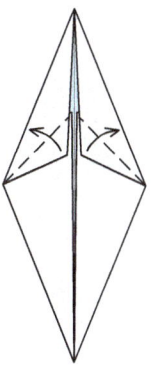

4. Valley fold towards the outer edges.

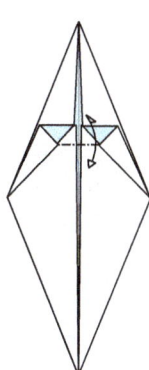

5. Precrease.

6. Swing the sides outwards.

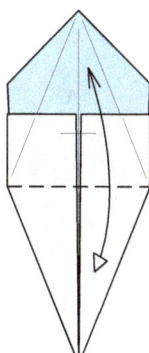

7. Precrease in half.

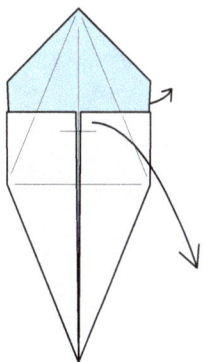

8. Unfold one side completely.

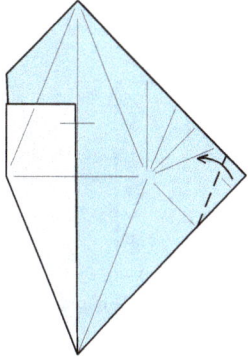

9. Valley fold the corner to meet the crease.

117

spectacled bear

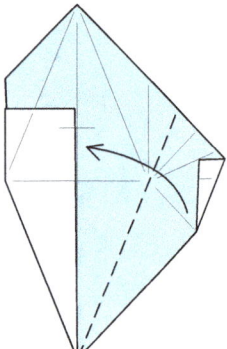
10. Valley fold.

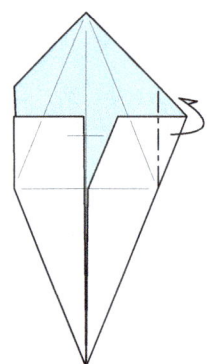
11. Mountain fold.

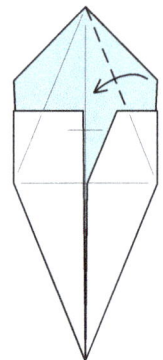
12. Valley fold. Part of the fold is hidden.

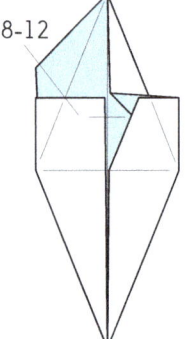
13. Repeat steps 8-12 in mirror image.

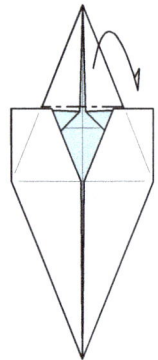
14. Mountain fold.

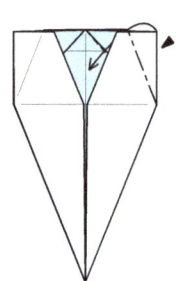
15. Reverse fold the corner.

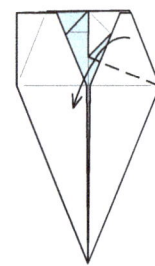
16. Swing the flap down.

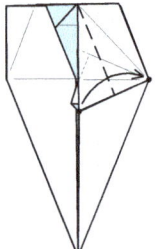
17. Valley fold over, allowing a squash fold to form.

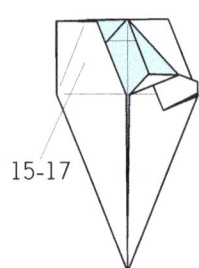
18. Repeat steps 15-17 in mirror image.

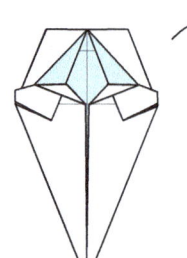
19. Turn over.

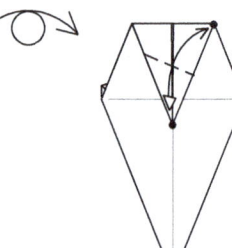
20. Precrease.

spectacled bear

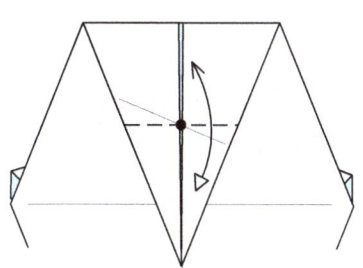

21. Precrease through the indicated intersection.

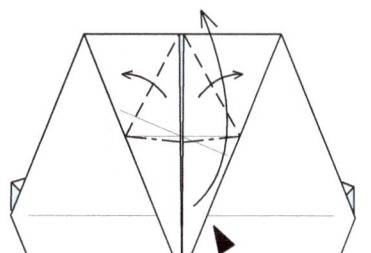

22. Squash fold.

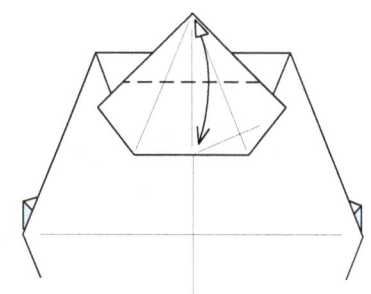

23. Precrease in half.

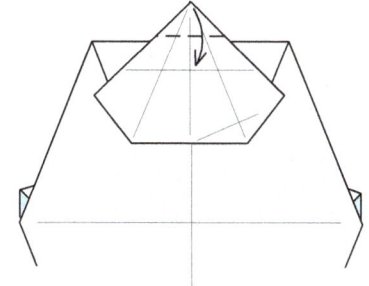

24. Valley fold to the crease.

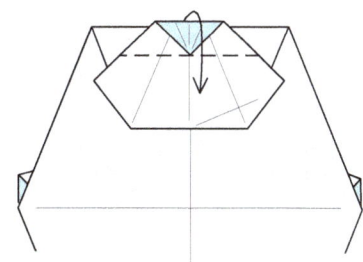

25. Valley fold along the existing crease.

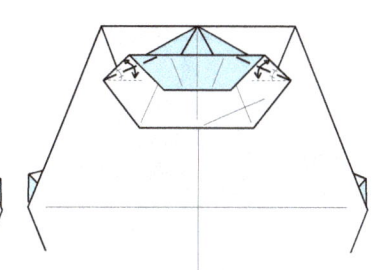

26. Precrease along the indicated bisectors.

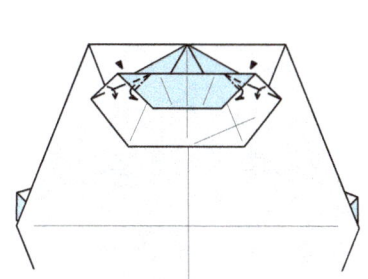

27. Swivel fold the sides inwards.

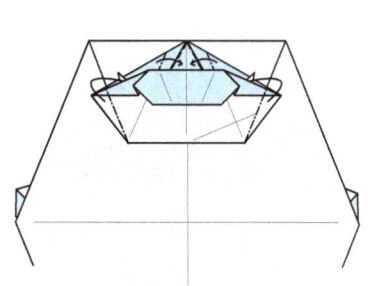

28. Swivel fold the sides inwards.

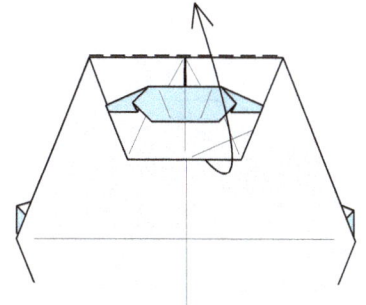

29. Swing the flap up.

119

spectacled bear

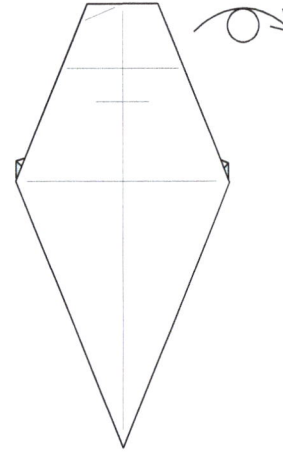

30. Turn over.

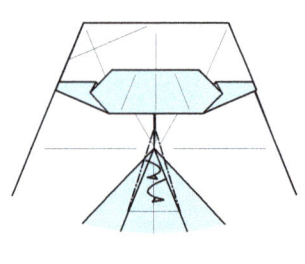

31. Mountain fold a tiny amount of the sides inwards.

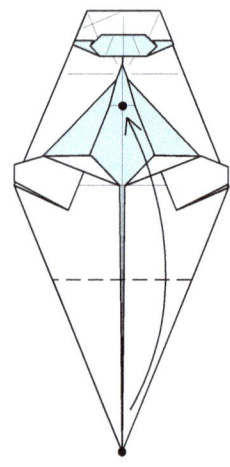

32. Valley fold to the crease.

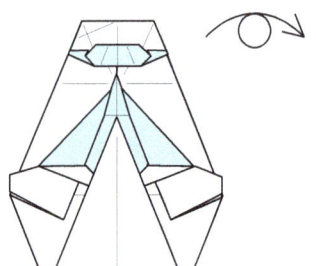

33. Turn over.

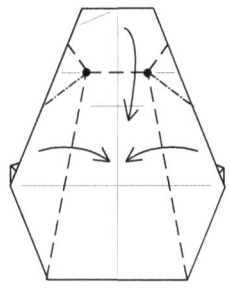

34. Valley fold the sides to the center, while swiveling in at the top.

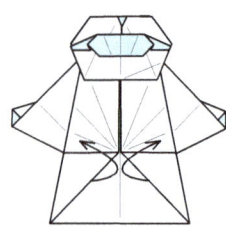

35. Pull the single layer around to the surface (closed sink).

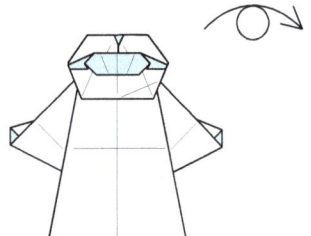

36. Turn over.

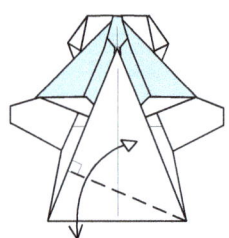

37. Precrease.

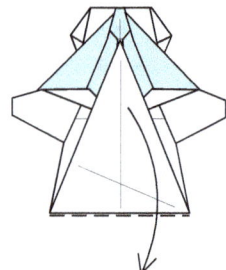

38. Swing the flap down.

spectacled bear

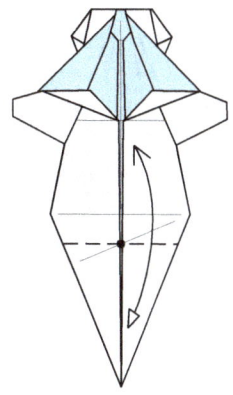

39. Valley fold through the indicated intersection.

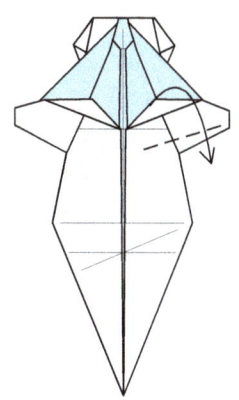

40. Lightly swing the flap down, releasing the trapped flap.

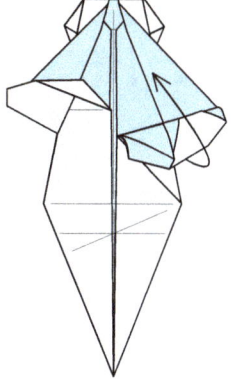

41. Swing the flap back up.

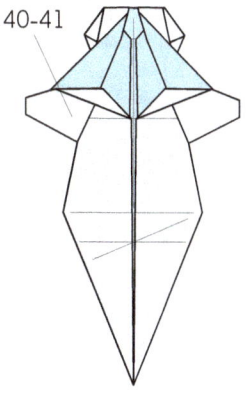

42. Repeat steps 40-41 on the other side.

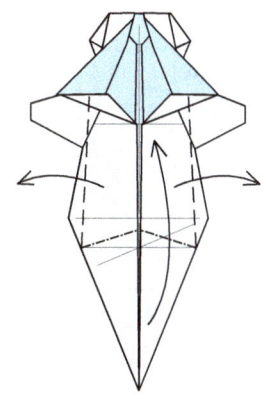

43. Valley fold the flap up along the existing crease while swiveling out the sides as far as possible.

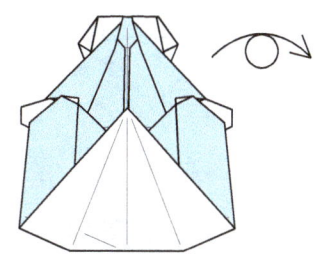

44. Turn over.

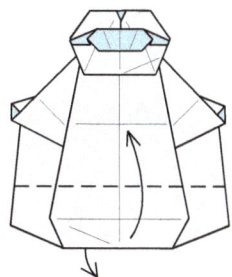

45. Valley fold towards the crease, allowing the flap from behind to flip forward.

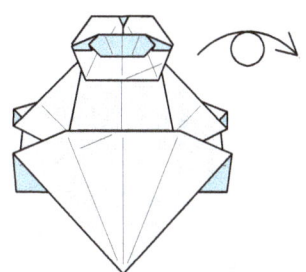

46. Turn over.

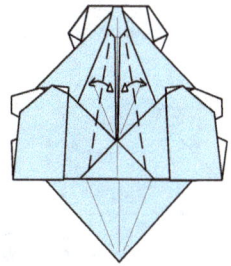

47. Valley fold towards the edges.

spectacled bear

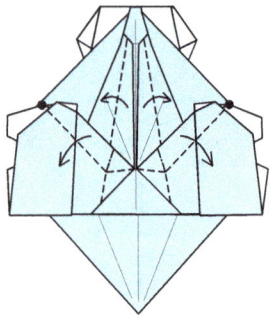
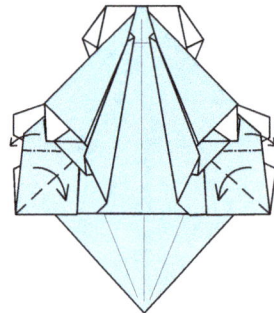
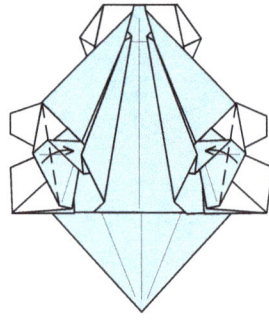

48. Replace the previous valley folds while swivelling down. Note the dotted references.

49. Valley fold the single layers down while pulling through the excess paper and flattening.

50. Valley fold the sides inwards.

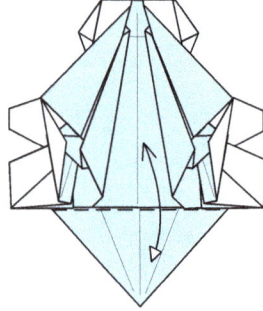
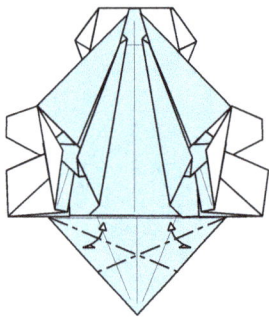
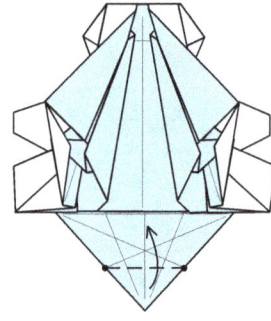

51. Precrease.

52. Precrease with mountain folds.

53. Valley fold up.

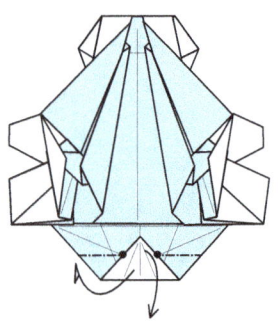
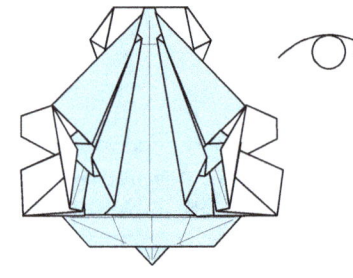
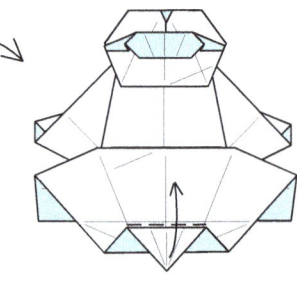

54. Mountain fold at the indicated intersections, flipping the flap behind.

55. Turn over.

56. Flip the flap up.

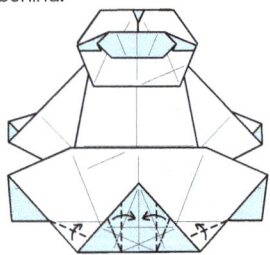
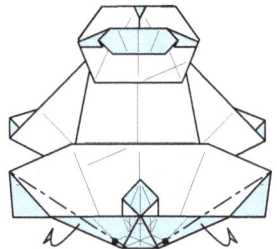
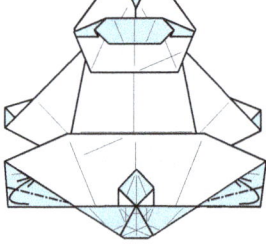

57. Swivel the sides inwards.

58. Mountain fold, noting the indicated intersections.

59. Valley fold the sides up, tucking a small part of the edges under.

spectacled bear

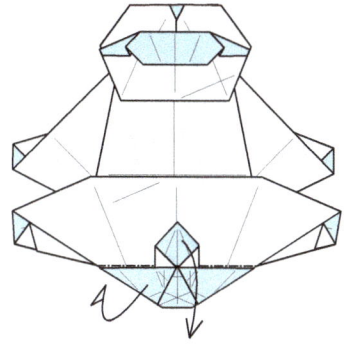
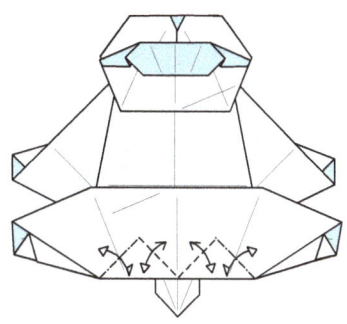
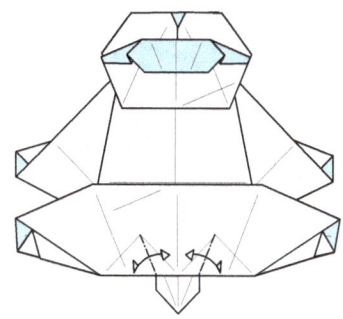

60. Mountain fold, flipping the flap down.

61. Precrease with mountain and valley folds.

62. Precrease with mountain folds.

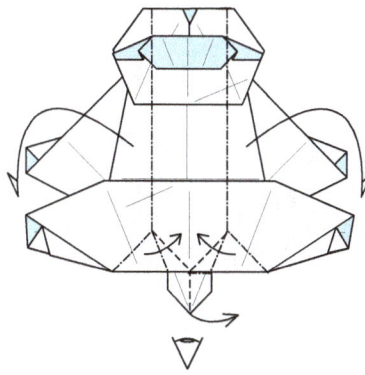

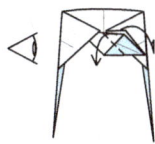

63. Rabbit ear the small flap while folding the sides down at ninety degrees.

64. View from previous step. Wrap around a single layer at each side.

65. Outside reverse fold.

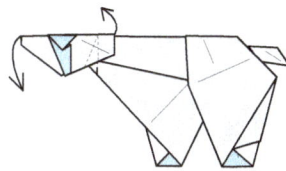
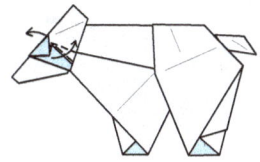
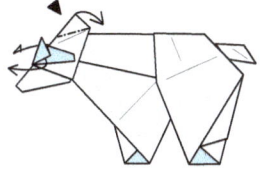

66. View from previous step. Crimp the flap down.

67. Pleat the sides up.

68. Reverse fold the top and open out and shape the glasses to taste.

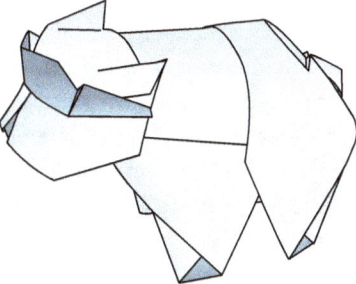

69. Completed *Spectacled Bear*.

123

Swan

The classic Bird Base is utilized to create this origami *Swan*. This base has many more available flaps than the classic Kite Base that is used to make the traditional model. This allows for more articulated appendages for a slightly more realistic look. There is an unusual sink and stretch sequence that allows the neck to tilt far back, giving it a regal look. At under twenty steps, this model is one of the simpler ones in this collection.

swan

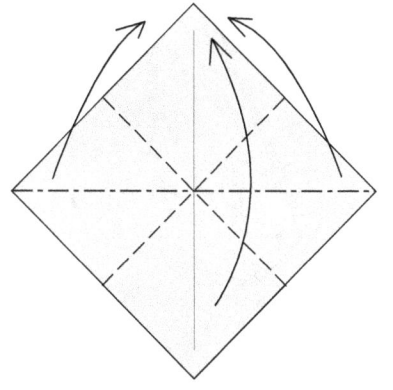

1. Collapse upwards (form a colored preliminary base).

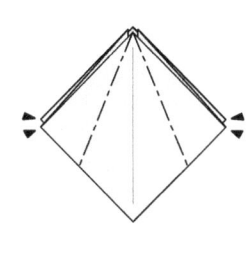

2. Reverse fold four times.

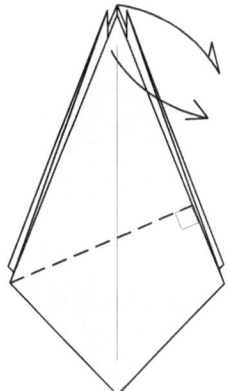

3. Valley fold the outer flaps.

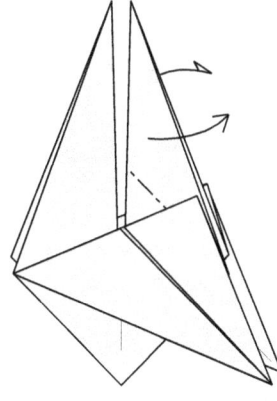

4. Pull out a single layer at each side.

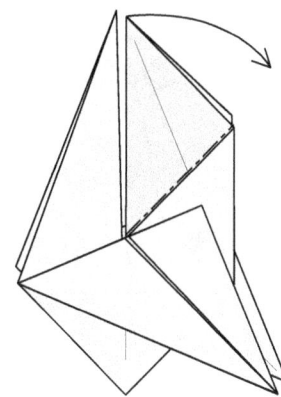

5. Reverse fold through.

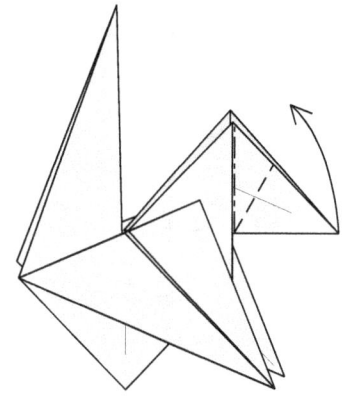

6. Crimp the flap upwards.

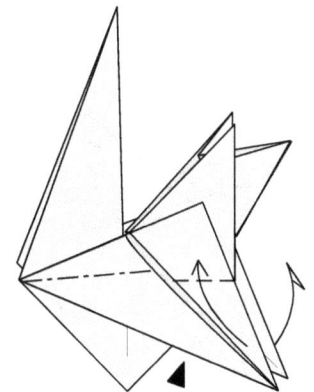

7. Squash fold the wings.

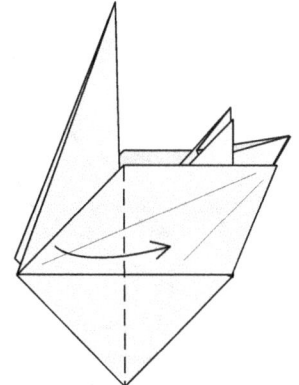

8. Open out the front.

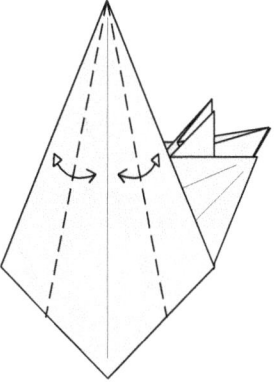

9. Precrease along the angle bisectors.

125

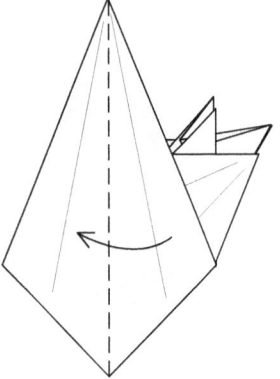

10. Close back up.

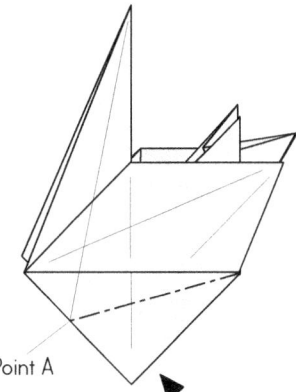

Point A

11. Sink triangularly, noting reference point A.

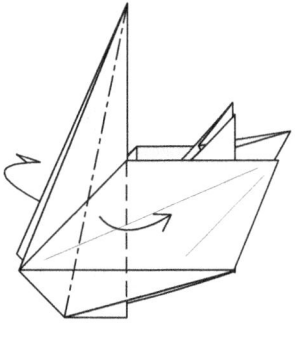

12. Pleat the sides along the existing creases.

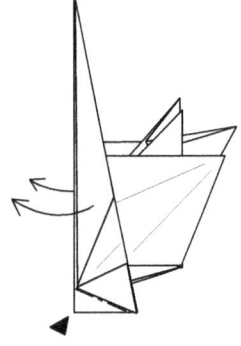

13. Keeping the neck layers intact, undo the pleat at the body. Allow a sink to form at the bottom.

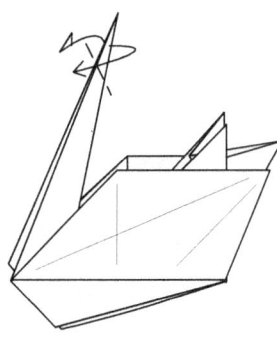

14. Outside reverse fold.

15. Pull out layers from inside.

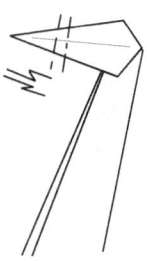

16. Crimp and shape the head to taste. Rotate the model slightly.

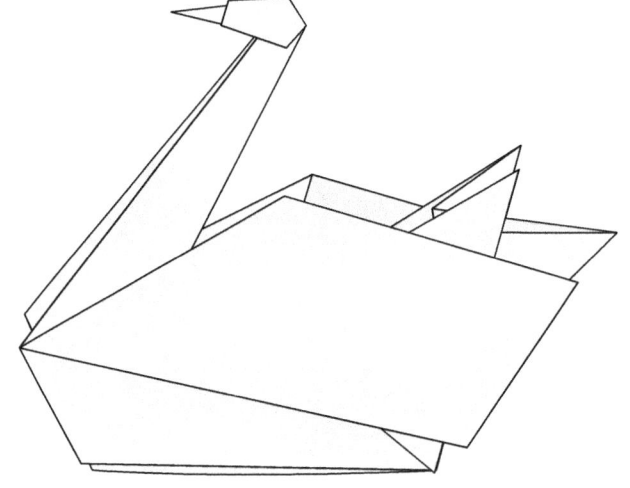

17. Completed *Swan*.

Toucan

The toucan is distinctive with its colorful bill that can be bigger than its body. Making a model from paper would typically have balance issues, even when using lightweight materials. This *Toucan* solves that problem by forming the legs from the middle portion of the paper. Most of the model's mass centers around its limbs, allowing it to sit stably. Small flaps are used for the wings and tail to further emphasize the magnitude of the beak.

toucan

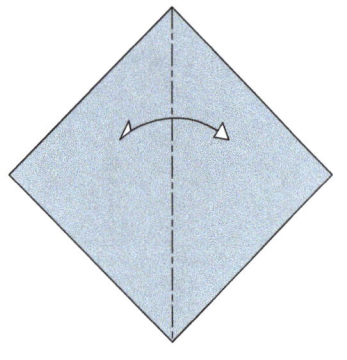

1. Precrease the diagonal with a mountain fold.

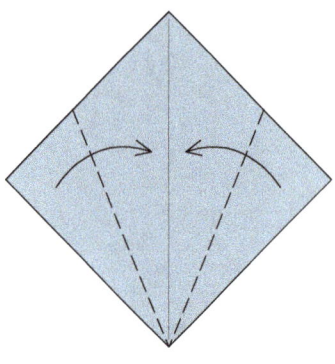

2. Valley fold the sides to the center.

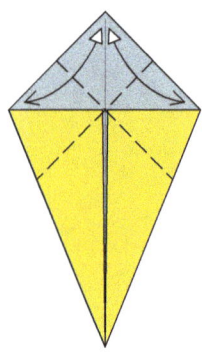

3. Precrease the top edges in half.

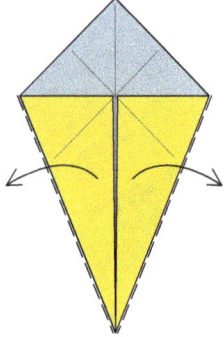

4. Open out the sides.

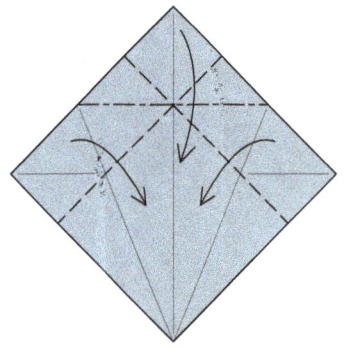

5. Extend the existing creases and collapse the top corner down.

6. Turn over.

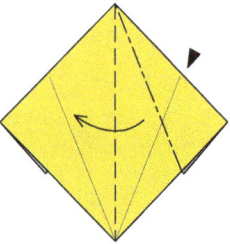

7. Squash fold.

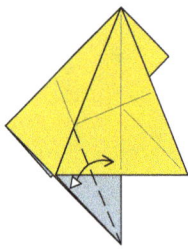

8. Precrease along the angle bisector.

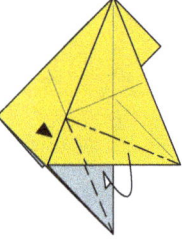

9. Reverse fold the edge inside.

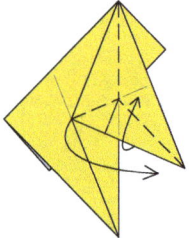

10. Valley fold over while forming a rabbit ear.

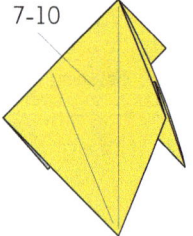

11. Repeat steps 7-10 in mirror image.

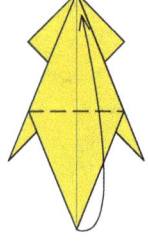

12. Valley fold the flap up.

toucan

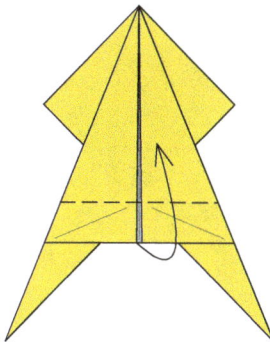

13. Valley fold the edge up as far as possible.

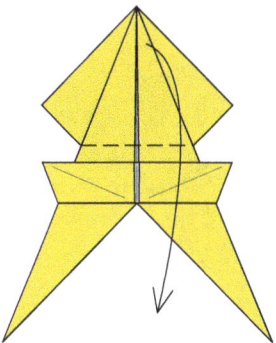

14. Valley fold the top flap down, starting from where it intersects the top edges.

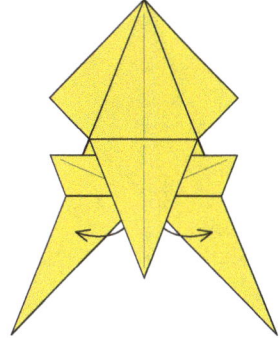

15. Slide out a single layer at each side.

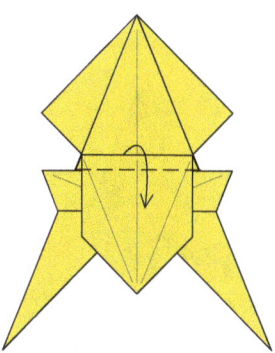

16. Valley fold the edge down.

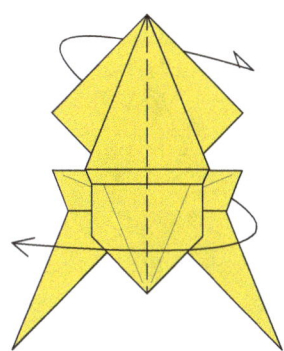

17. Valley fold in half while swinging the rear flap over.

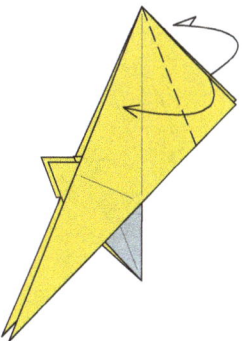

18. Valley fold an edge over at each side.

19. Precrease towards the dotted corner.

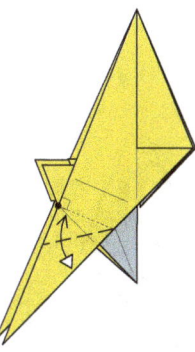

20. Precrease towards the dotted intersection.

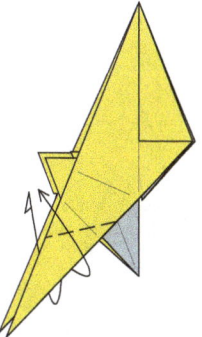

21. Outside reverse fold the flap, leaving only a single layer at the surface.

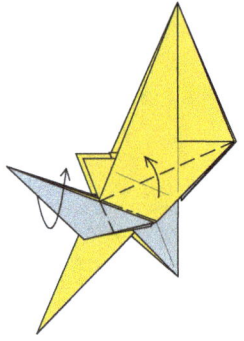

22. Valley fold the colored flap over while swiveling up a single layer.

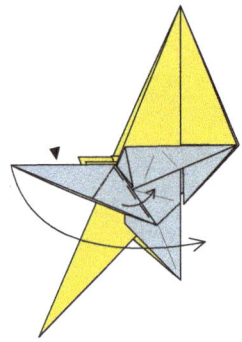

23. Squash fold the flap over.

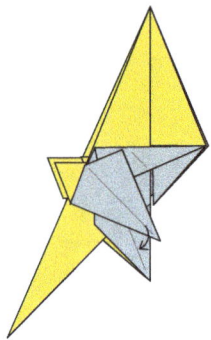

24. Slide the flap over to align with the crease below.

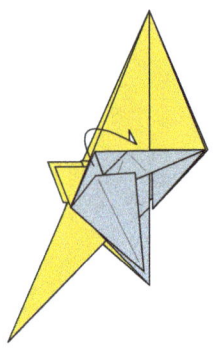

25. Mountain fold along the angle bisector.

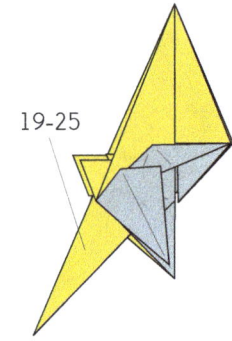

26. Repeat steps 19–25 behind.

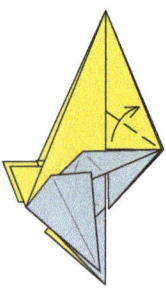

27. Valley fold along the angle bisector.

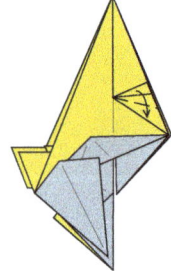

28. Pleat the flap along the angle trisectors.

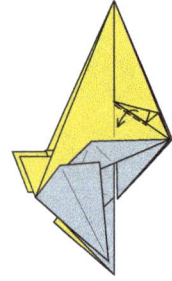

29. Open out the top edge.

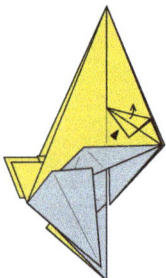

30. Squash fold the flap.

toucan

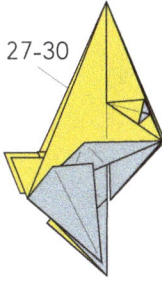

31. Repeat steps 27-30 behind.

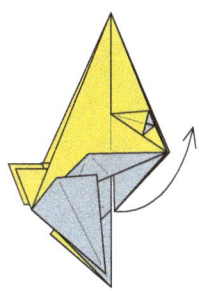

32. Pull out the center flap.

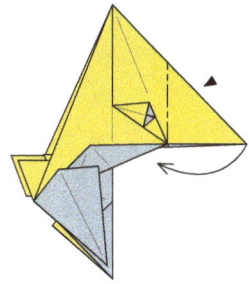

33. Reverse fold the flap inside.

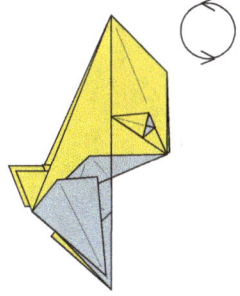

34. Rotate the model slightly.

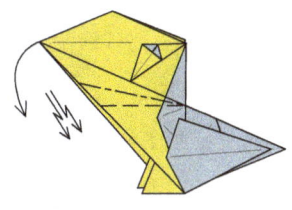

35. Crimp the head down.

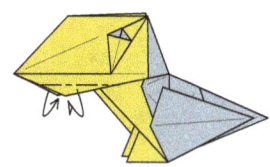

36. Mountain fold the lower corners inside.

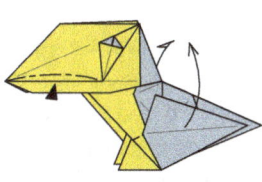

37. Curve the edge at each side. Pull the wings up and out, so they are apart from the body.

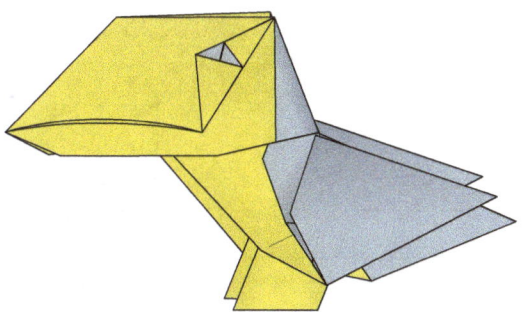

38. Completed *Toucan*.

131

Turtle

This origami *Turtle* sports a shell that is from an articulated flap. This gives a bit more freedom to adjust the shaping of the carapace. A neat consequence is that there is a fully formed belly which is a rarity amongst paper folded renderings. The toes are formed by inserting pleats along the basic folded form which also gives the head section more volume. After much investigation, it turns out in nature that turtles do not have a consistent number of toes, sometimes with variation from the hindlegs and the forelegs. To reduce the complexity slightly, this model settles on four digits per limb.

turtle

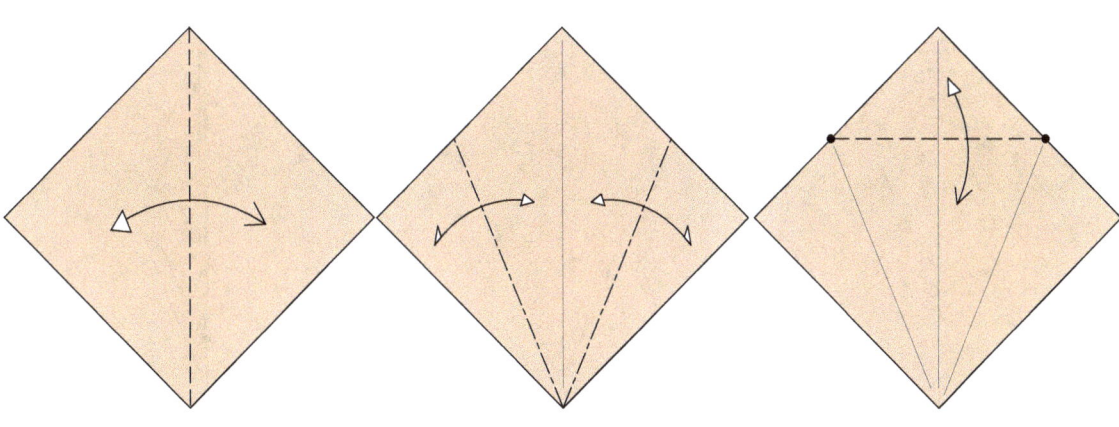

1. Precrease in half.

2. Precrease with mountain folds.

3. Precrease, noting the indicated intersections.

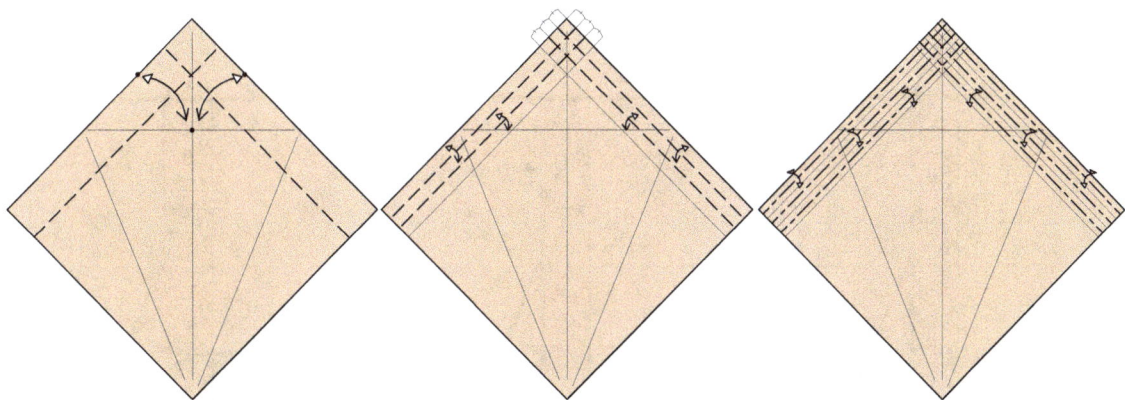

4. Precrease, noting the indicated intersection.

5. Precrease the side sections into thirds.

6. Precrease each section in half with mountain folds.

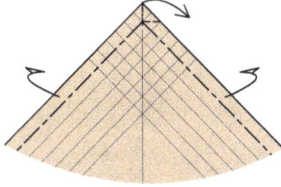

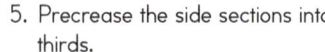

7. View of the top corner. Rabbit ear behind.

8. Rabbit ear along the next set of creases.

9. Rabbit ear again.

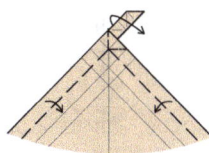

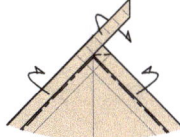

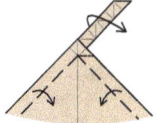

10. Rabbit ear again.

11. Rabbit ear again.

12. Rabbit ear along the last set of creases.

133

turtle

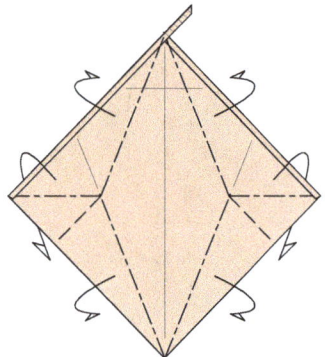
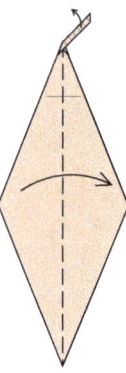
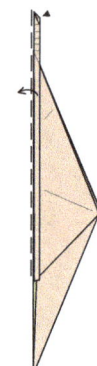

13. Rabbit ear the sides behind.

14. Valley fold in half while pulling up the top point.

15. Swing over one flap, while spread squashing the top point.

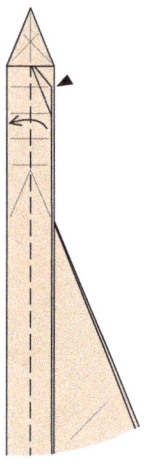
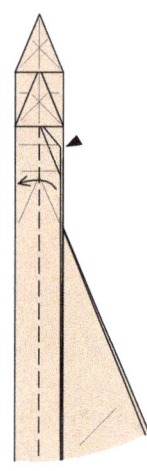
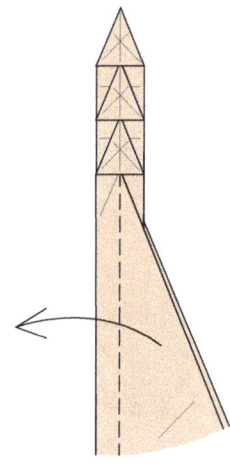

16. Detail of the top flap. Swing over the next flap, allowing a spread squash to form.

17. Swing over the next flap, so as to spread squash the remaining corner.

18. Swing over the large flap.

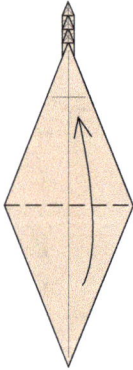
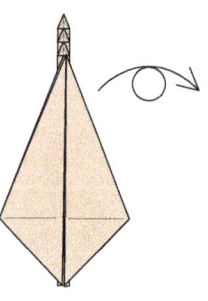
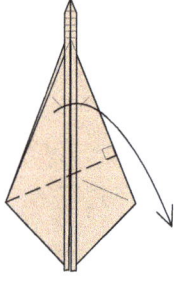

19. Valley fold the flap up.

20. Turn over.

21. Valley fold the flap down.

134

turtle

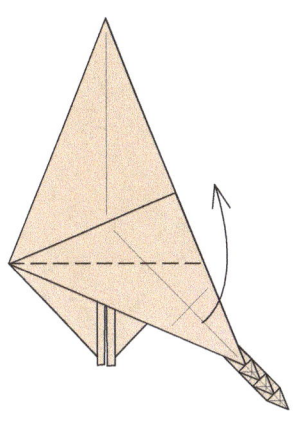

22. Valley fold up.

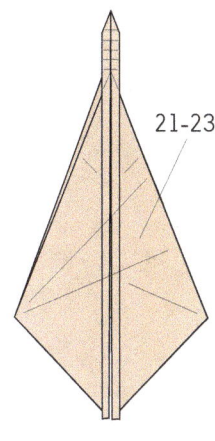

23. Unfold the pleat.

24. Repeat steps 21-23 in mirror image.

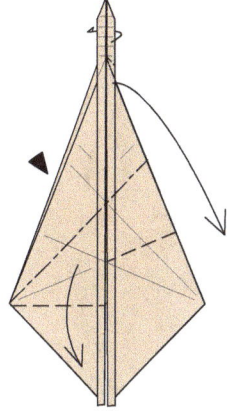

25. Form an asymmetrical squash, allowing the top point to fold in half.

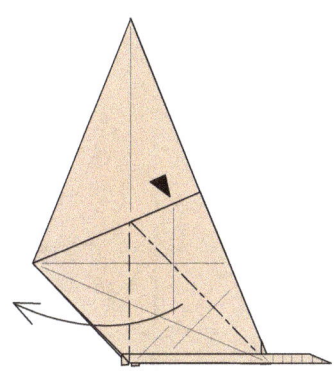

26. Squash the flap over.

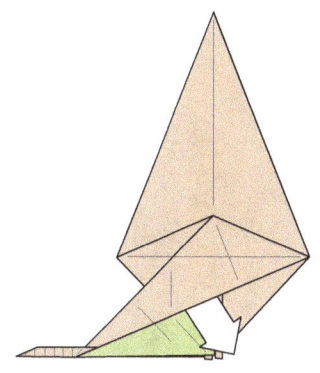

27. Pull out a single layer.

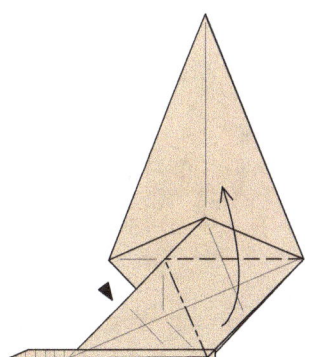

28. Squash the flap upwards.

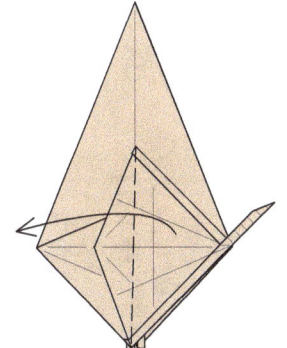

29. Valley fold the flap over.

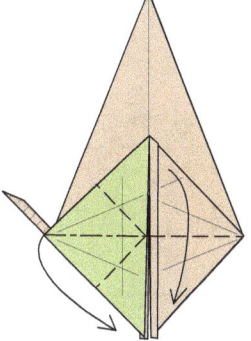

30. Valley fold down, while reverse folding.

135

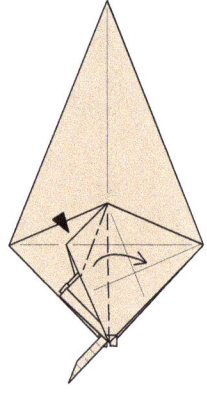

31. Swing over, allowing a spread squash to form.

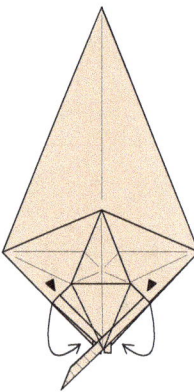

32. Reverse fold the side flaps.

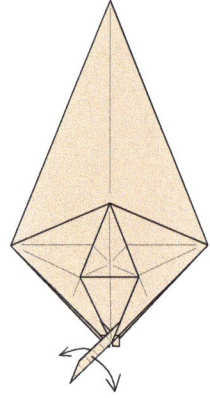

33. Pull down the bottom flap, allowing it to spread apart.

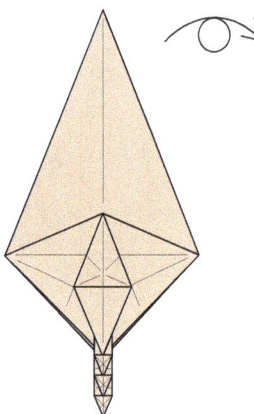

34. Turn over.

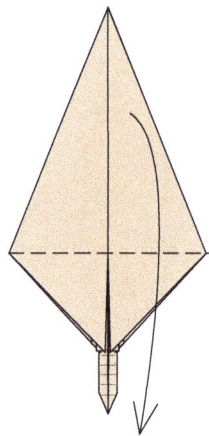

35. Valley fold the flap down as far as possible.

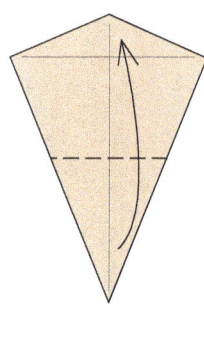

36. Valley fold the flap up.

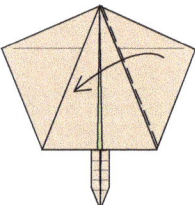

37. Valley fold the side flap over.

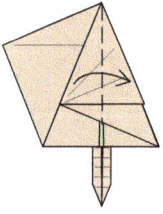

38. Valley fold to meet the outer edge.

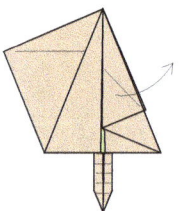

39. Unfold the pleat.

turtle

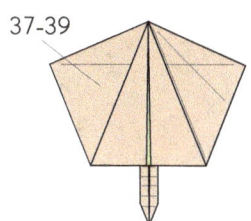
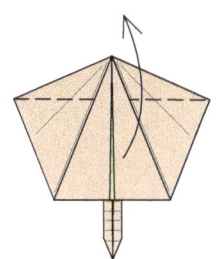
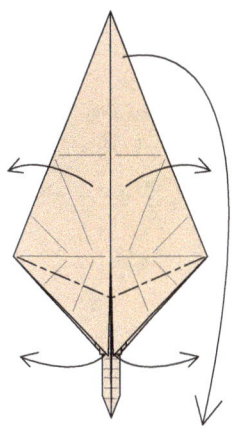

40. Repeat steps 37-39 in mirror image.

41. Pull the flap straight up.

42. Swing the top flap down while pulling out the sides.

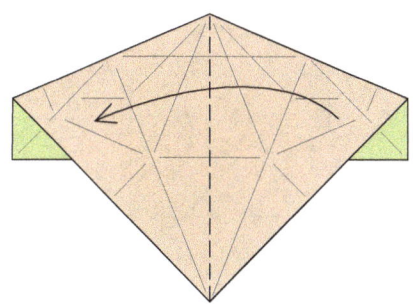
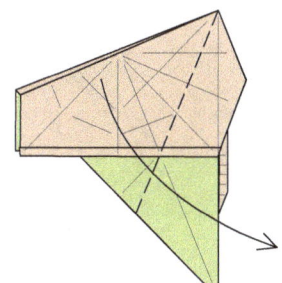
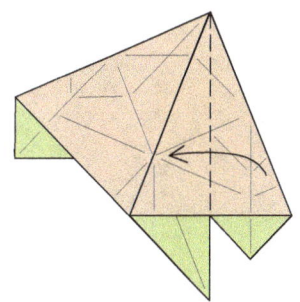

43. Valley fold the large flap over.

44. Valley fold, noting the next step to see how the bottom colored triangles meet.

45. Valley fold the flap in half.

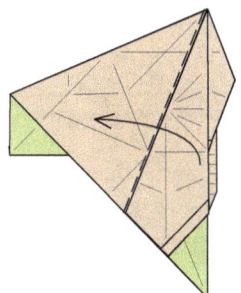
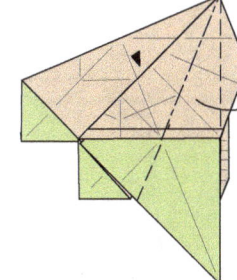
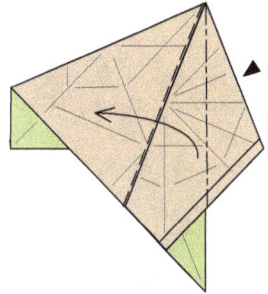

46. Swing the flap over.

47. Squash fold.

48. Squash fold the top layer over.

137

turtle

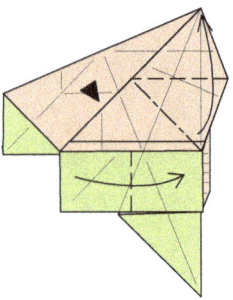

49. Swivel the flap up.

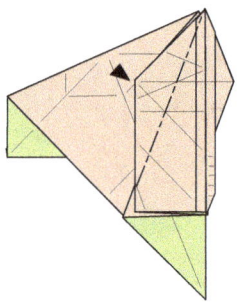

50. Open sink along the angle bisector.

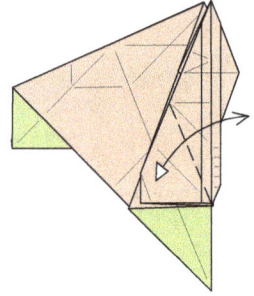

51. Precrease the top flap.

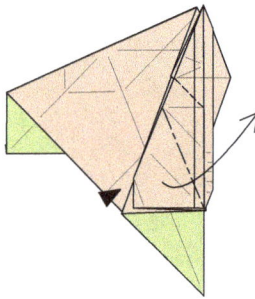

52. Spread squash the top flap.

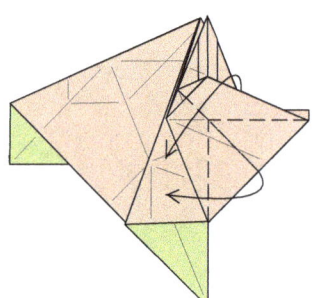

53. Valley fold in half while incorporating a reverse fold.

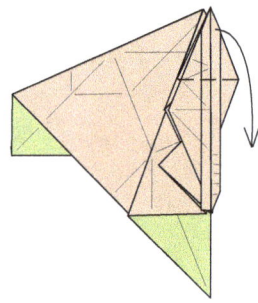

54. Swing the top flap down.

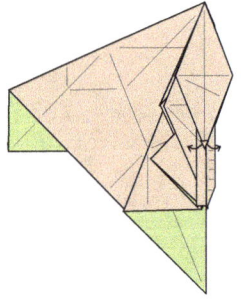

55. Pull out the trapped layers.

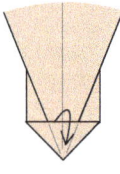

56. Pull around the trapped flap to the surface.

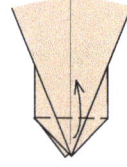

57. Swing upwards.

turtle

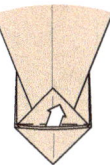

58. Unsink the flap.

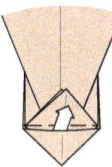

59. Unsink the next flap.

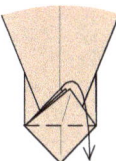

60. Swing all of the flaps down.

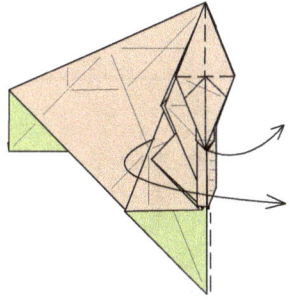

61. Swing over while incorporating a reverse fold.

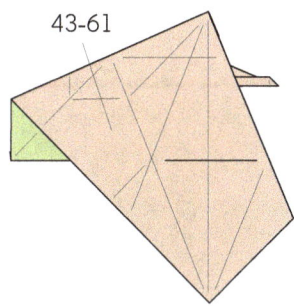

62. Repeat steps 43-61 in mirror image.

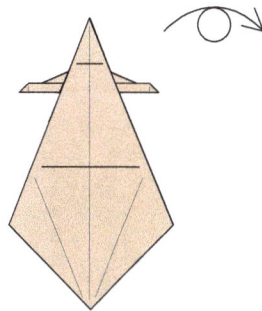

63. Turn over.

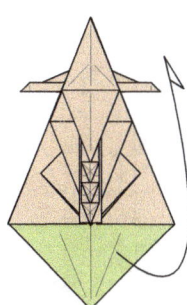

64. Mountain fold.

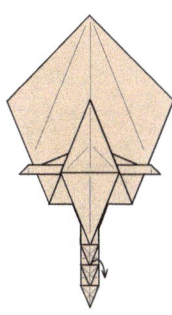

65. Unsink the tiny flap.

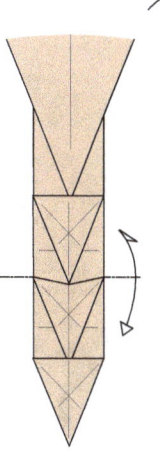

66. Precrease with a mountain fold and turn over.

139

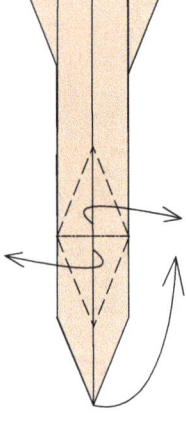
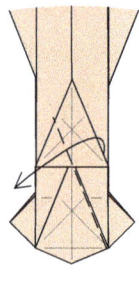
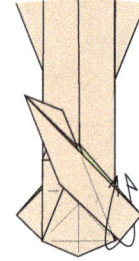

67. Fold the flap up while reverse folding all the layers outwards.

68. Valley fold over.

69. Unwrap a single layer. The model will not lie flat.

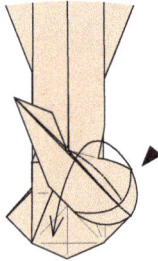
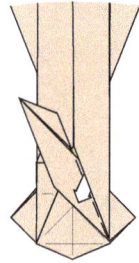
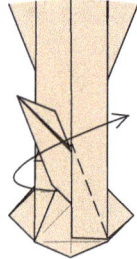

70. Squash the flap down flat.

71. Pull out the trapped single layer.

72. Swing all of the layers back up.

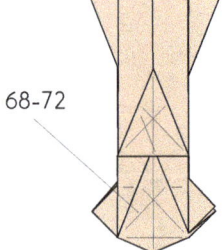
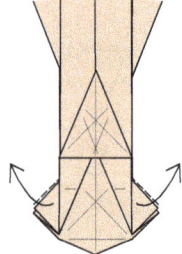
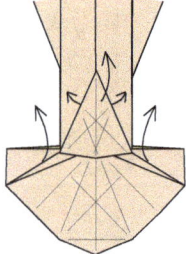

73. Repeat steps 68-72 in mirror image.

74. Open out the side pleats. The top will not lie flat.

75. Pull out a single layer along the top edges, allowing the flap to flatten.

turtle

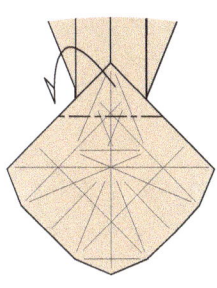

76. Mountain fold the corner.

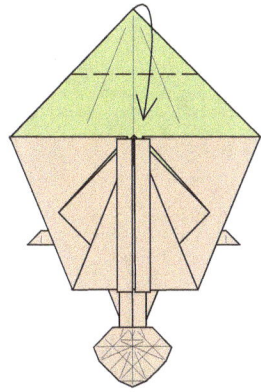

77. Lightly valley fold the corner.

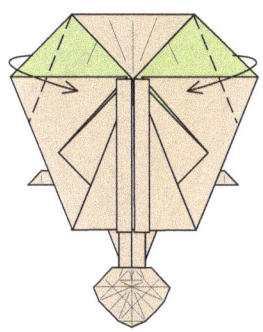

78. Valley fold the sides in.

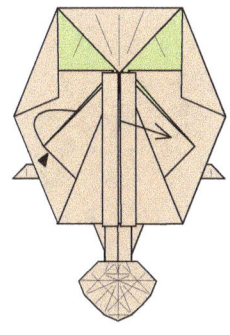

79. Reverse fold a flap through.

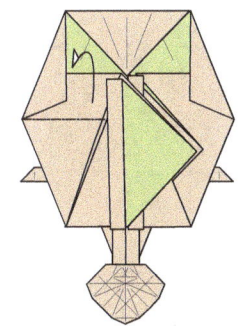

80. Mountain fold, swiveling the excess paper behind.

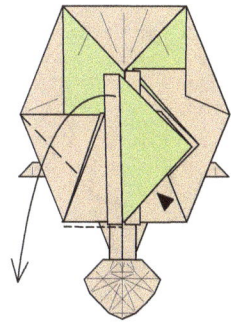

81. Squash fold the flap down.

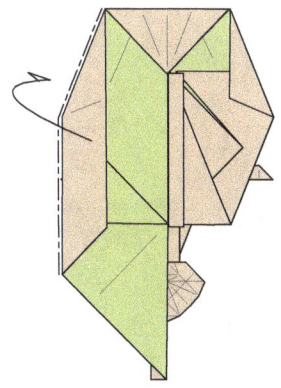

82. Wrap a single layer around.

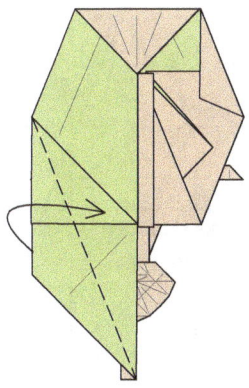

83. Valley fold to the center.

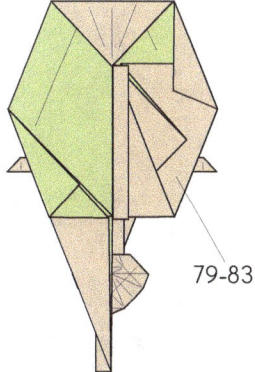

84. Repeat steps 79-83 in mirror image.

141

turtle

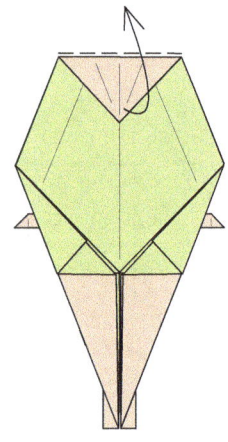

85. Open out the top flap.

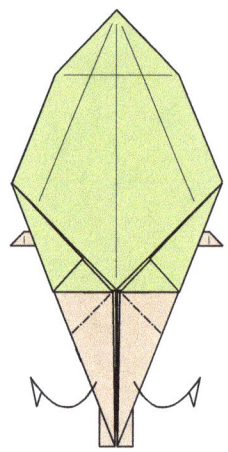

86. Mountain fold the bottom flaps.

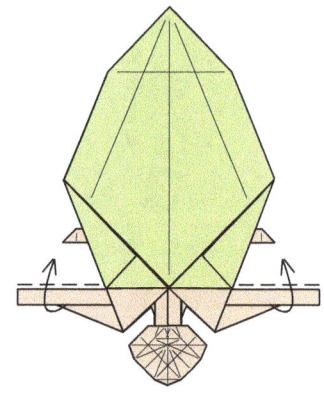

87. Swivel fold the clusters of pleats up at each side.

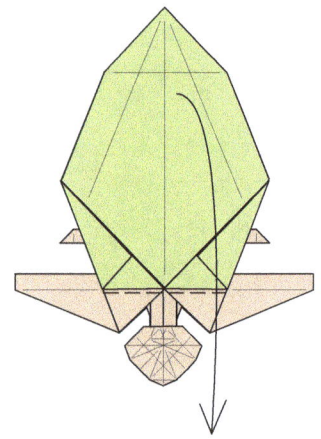

88. Swing the large flap down.

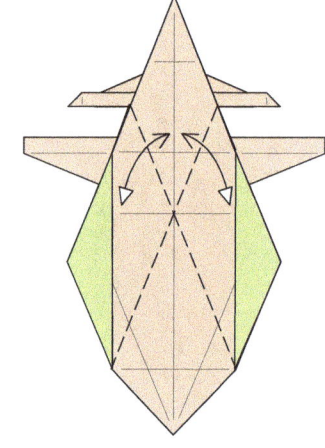

89. Precrease from corner to inside corner.

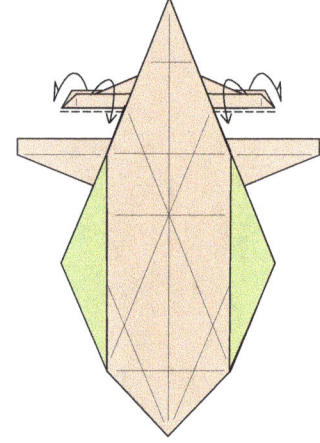

90. Wrap around the clusters of pleats at each side.

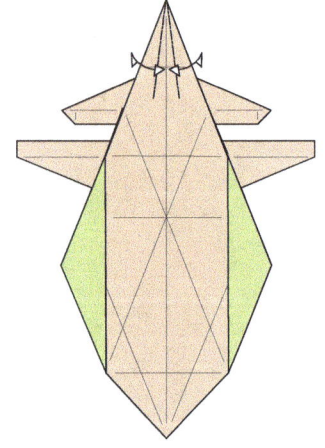

91. Precrease along the angle trisectors.

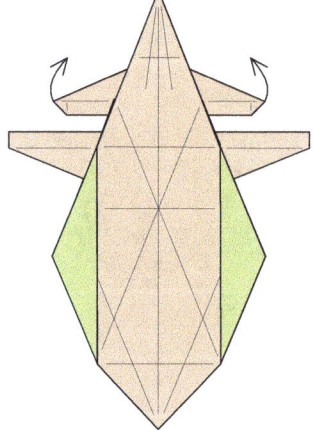

92. Slide the flaps up, until the top edges lie straight.

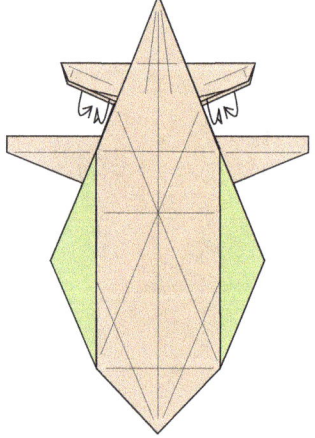

93. Swivel fold in part of the lower edges.

turtle

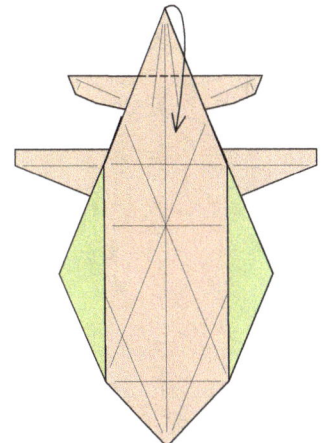

94. Valley fold the flap down.

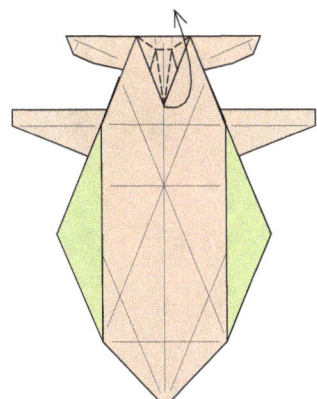

95. Valley fold up while swiveling in the sides.

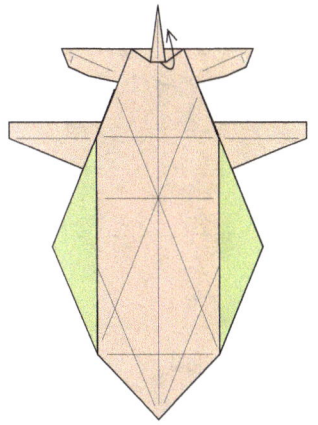

96. Pull around a single layer to the surface (closed sink).

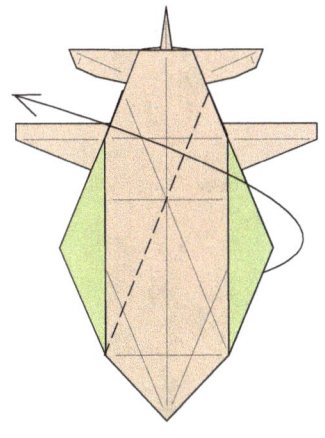

97. Valley fold over.

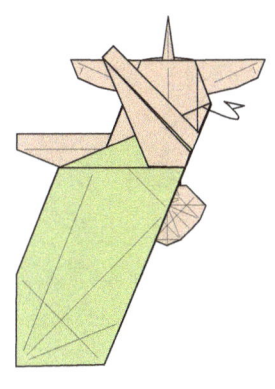

98. Mountain fold inside.

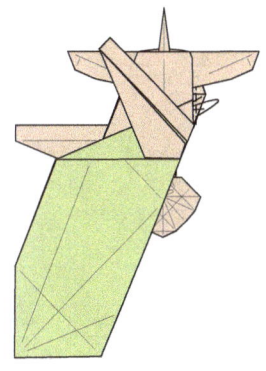

99. Valley fold inside.

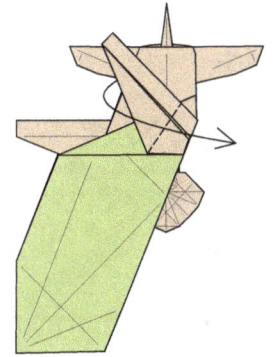

100. Valley fold the flap over.

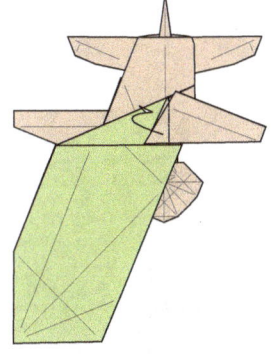

101. Mountain fold the corner behind.

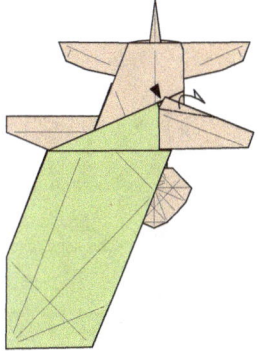

102. Reverse fold part of the edge behind.

143

turtle

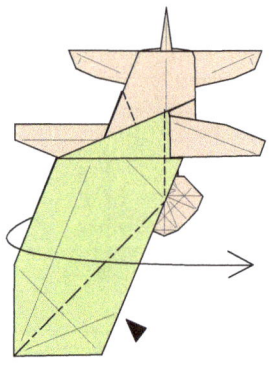

103. Squash fold the flap over.

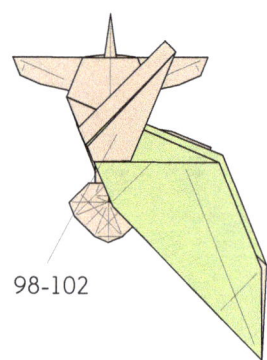

104. Repeat steps 98-102 in mirror image.

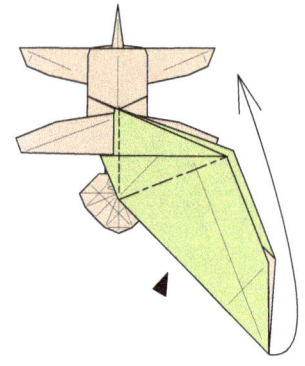

105. Spread squash the large flap.

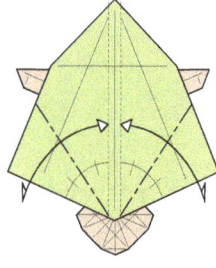

106. Precrease along the indicated angle bisectors, leaving a small gap at the center.

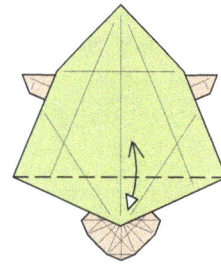

107. Precrease the top flap.

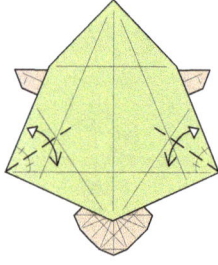

108. Precrease along the angle bisectors.

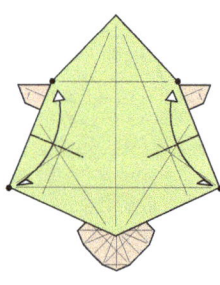

109. Precrease using the dotted corners as guides.

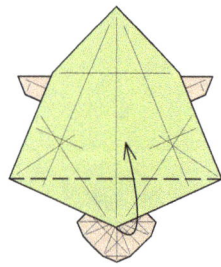

110. Valley fold up.

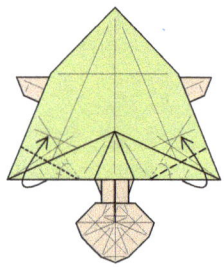

111. Valley fold towards the creases.

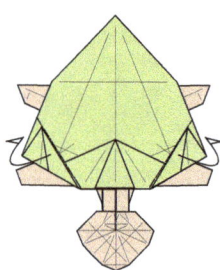

112. Mountain fold the sides behind.

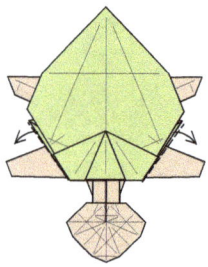

113. Slide out the trapped center layer at each side.

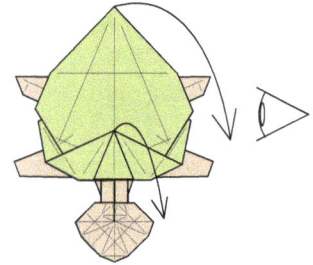

114. Raise the flap up, undoing the side pleats.

144

turtle

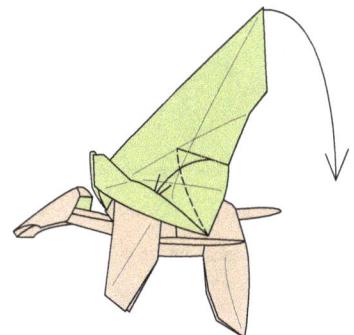

115. View from the previous step. Pull the flap back down, crimping the sides into the shallow pockets.

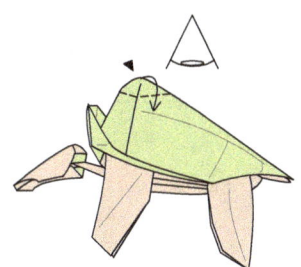

116. Press the corners down.

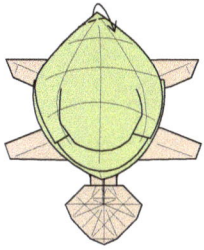

117. View from the previous step. Make a small valley fold.

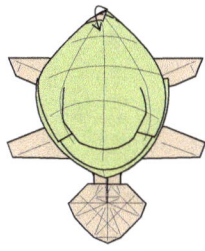

118. Valley fold in the opposite direction.

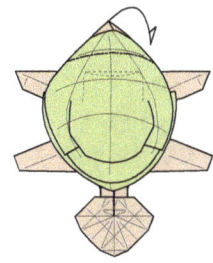

119. Tuck the corner into the hidden pocket.

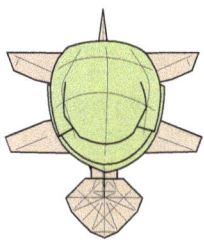

120. Completed shell. The next steps focus on the leg flaps.

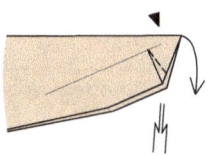

121. Crimp the corner down evenly. The top edge will be slightly rounded.

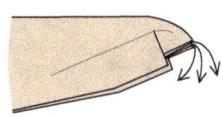

122. Spread apart the cluster of flaps evenly.

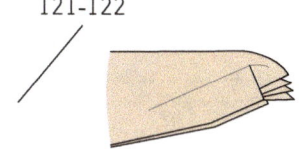

123. Repeat steps 121-122 on the opposite flap.

turtle

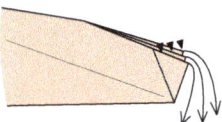

124. Reverse fold the three corners.

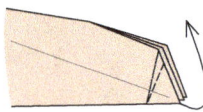

125. Crimp the layers up evenly.

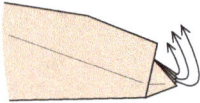

126. Spread apart the cluster of flaps evenly.

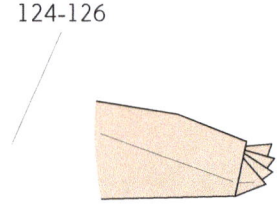

127. Repeat steps 124-126 on the opposite flap.

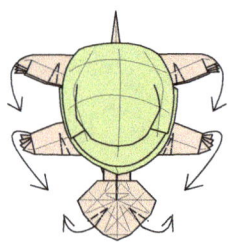

128. Crimp the legs forward. Crimp the front of the head to make it round.

129. Completed *Turtle*.

www.ingramcontent.com/pod-product-compliance
Lightning Source LLC
Chambersburg PA
CBHW081723100526
44591CB00016B/2473